W9-BLV-127

The *New* Daily Study Bible

The Letters of
James and Peter

The *New* Daily Study Bible

The Letters of
James and Peter

William Barclay

Westminster John Knox Press
LOUISVILLE • LONDON

© The William Barclay Estate, 1975, 2003

First edition published in 1958 as *The Daily Study Bible: The Letters of James* and in 1958 as *The Daily Study Bible: I and II Peter*
Revised edition published in 1975
This third edition fully revised and updated by Saint Andrew Press and published as *The New Daily Study Bible: The Letters of James and Peter* in 2003

Published in the United States by
Westminster John Knox Press
Louisville, Kentucky

All rights reserved. No part of this book may be reproduced or transmitted in any form or by any means, electronic or mechanical, including photocopying, recording, or by any information storage or retrieval system, without permission in writing from the publisher. For information, address Westminster John Knox Press, 100 Witherspoon Street, Louisville, KY 40202–1396.

The Scripture quotations contained herein are from the New Revised Standard Version of the Bible, Anglicized Edition, copyright 1989, 1995 by the Division of Christian Education of the National Council of the Churches of Christ in the United States of America, and are used by permission. All rights reserved.

PRINTED IN THE UNITED STATES OF AMERICA

12 – 10 9

Library of Congress Cataloging-in-Publication Data is on file at the Library of Congress, Washington, D.C.

ISBN 0–664–22678–7

To

J.M.

ON WHOSE STAFF

IT WAS MY PRIVILEGE TO SERVE

IN GRATITUDE FOR HELP AND GUIDANCE

SO OFTEN AND SO GRACIOUSLY GIVEN

CONTENTS

JAMES

I PETER

SERIES FOREWORD
(by Ronnie Barclay)

My father always had a great love for the English language and its literature. As a student at the University of Glasgow, he won a prize in the English class – and I have no doubt that he could have become a Professor of English instead of Divinity and Biblical Criticism. In a pre-computer age, he had a mind like a computer that could store vast numbers of quotations, illustrations, anecdotes and allusions; and, more remarkably still, he could retrieve them at will. The editor of this revision has, where necessary, corrected and attributed the vast majority of these quotations with considerable skill and has enhanced our pleasure as we read quotations from Plato to T. S. Eliot.

There is another very welcome improvement in the new text. My mother was one of five sisters, and my grandmother was a commanding figure as the Presbyterian minister's wife in a small village in Ayrshire in Scotland. She ran that small community very efficiently, and I always felt that my father, surrounded by so many women, was more than somewhat overawed by it all! I am sure that this is the reason why his use of English tended to be dominated by the words 'man', 'men' and so on, with the result that it sounded very male-orientated. Once again, the editor has very skilfully improved my father's English and made the text much more readable for all of us by amending the often one-sided language.

It is a well-known fact that William Barclay wrote at breakneck speed and never corrected anything once it was on paper – he took great pride in mentioning this at every possible opportunity! This revision, in removing repetition and correcting the inevitable errors that had slipped through, has produced a text free from all the tell-tale signs of very rapid writing. It is with great pleasure that I commend this revision to readers old and new in the certainty that William Barclay speaks even more clearly to us all with his wonderful appeal in this new version of his much-loved *Daily Study Bible*.

Ronnie Barclay
Bedfordshire
2001

GENERAL INTRODUCTION

(by William Barclay, from the 1975 edition)

The Daily Study Bible series has always had one aim – to convey the results of scholarship to the ordinary reader. A. S. Peake delighted in the saying that he was a 'theological middle-man', and I would be happy if the same could be said of me in regard to these volumes. And yet the primary aim of the series has never been academic. It could be summed up in the famous words of Richard of Chichester's prayer – to enable men and women 'to know Jesus Christ more clearly, to love him more dearly, and to follow him more nearly'.

It is all of twenty years since the first volume of *The Daily Study Bible* was published. The series was the brain-child of the late Rev. Andrew McCosh, MA, STM, the then Secretary and Manager of the Committee on Publications of the Church of Scotland, and of the late Rev. R. G. Macdonald, OBE, MA, DD, its Convener.

It is a great joy to me to know that all through the years *The Daily Study Bible* has been used at home and abroad, by minister, by missionary, by student and by layman, and that it has been translated into many different languages. Now, after so many printings, it has become necessary to renew the printer's type and the opportunity has been taken to restyle the books, to correct some errors in the text and to remove some references which have become outdated. At the same time, the Biblical quotations within the text have been changed to use the Revised Standard Version, but my own original translation of the New Testament passages has been retained at the beginning of each daily section.

There is one debt which I would be sadly lacking in courtesy if I did not acknowledge. The work of revision and correction has been done entirely by the Rev. James Martin, MA, BD, Minister of High Carntyne Church, Glasgow. Had it not been for him this task would never have been undertaken, and it is impossible for me to thank him enough for the selfless toil he has put into the revision of these books.

It is my prayer that God may continue to use *The Daily Study Bible* to enable men better to understand His word.

William Barclay
Glasgow
1975
(Published in the 1975 edition)

GENERAL FOREWORD

(by John Drane)

I only met William Barclay once, not long after his retirement from the chair of Biblical Criticism at the University
of Glasgow. Of course I had known about him long before
that, not least because his theological passion – the Bible –
was also a significant formative influence in my own life
and ministry. One of my most vivid memories of his influence goes back to when I was working on my own doctoral
research in the New Testament. It was summer 1971, and I
was a leader on a mission team working in the north-east of
Scotland at the same time as Barclay's Baird Lectures were
being broadcast on national television. One night, a young
Ph.D. scientist who was interested in Christianity, but still
unsure about some things, came to me and announced: 'I've
just been watching William Barclay on TV. He's convinced
me that I need to be a Christian; when can I be baptized?'
That kind of thing did not happen every day. So how could it
be that Barclay's message was so accessible to people with
no previous knowledge or experience of the Christian faith?

I soon realised that there was no magic ingredient that
enabled this apparently ordinary professor to be a brilliant
communicator. His secret lay in who he was, his own sense
of identity and purpose, and above all his integrity in being
true to himself and his faith. Born in the far north of Scotland,
he was brought up in Motherwell, a steel-producing town
south of Glasgow where his family settled when he was only
five, and this was the kind of place where he felt most at

home. Though his association with the University of Glasgow provided a focus for his life over almost fifty years, from his first day as a student in 1925 to his retirement from the faculty in 1974, he never became an ivory-tower academic, divorced from the realities of life in the real world. On the contrary, it was his commitment to the working-class culture of industrial Clydeside that enabled him to make such a lasting contribution not only to the world of the university but also to the life of the Church.

He was ordained to the ministry of the Church of Scotland at the age of twenty-six, but was often misunderstood even by other Christians. I doubt that William Barclay would ever have chosen words such as 'missionary' or 'evangelist' to describe his own ministry, but he accomplished what few others have done, as he took the traditional Presbyterian emphasis on spirituality-through-learning and transformed it into a most effective vehicle for evangelism. His own primary interest was in the history and language of the New Testament, but William Barclay was never only a historian or literary critic. His constant concern was to explore how these ancient books, and the faith of which they spoke, could continue to be relevant to people of his own time. If the Scottish churches had known how to capitalize on his enormous popularity in the media during the 1960s and 1970s, they might easily have avoided much of the decline of subsequent years.

Connecting the Bible to life has never been the way to win friends in the world of academic theology, and Barclay could undoubtedly have made things easier for himself had he been prepared to be a more conventional academic. But he was too deeply rooted in his own culture – and too seriously committed to the gospel – for that. He could see little purpose in a belief system that was so wrapped up in arcane and complicated terminology that it was accessible only to experts. Not only did he demystify Christian theology, but he also did it for working people, addressing the kind of things that mattered to ordinary folks in their everyday lives. In doing so, he also challenged the elitism that has often been deeply ingrained in the twin worlds of academic theology and the Church, with their shared assumption that popular culture is an inappropriate vehicle for serious thinking. Professor Barclay can hardly have been surprised when his predilection for writing books for the masses – not to mention talking to them on television – was questioned by his peers and even occasionally dismissed as being 'unscholarly' or insufficiently 'academic'. That was all untrue, of course, for his work was soundly based in reliable scholarship and his own extensive knowledge of the original languages of the Bible. But like One many centuries before him (and unlike most of his peers, in both Church and academy), 'the common people heard him gladly' (Mark 12:37), which no doubt explains why his writings are still inspirational – and why it is a particular pleasure for me personally to commend them to a new readership in a new century.

John Drane
University of Aberdeen
2001

EDITOR'S PREFACE

(by Linda Foster)

When the first volume of the original *Daily Bible Readings*, which later became *The Daily Study Bible* (the commentary on Acts), was published in 1953, no one could have anticipated or envisaged the revolution in the use of language which was to take place in the last quarter of the twentieth century. Indeed, when the first revised edition, to which William Barclay refers in his General Introduction, was completed in 1975, such a revolution was still waiting in the wings. But at the beginning of the twenty-first century, inclusive language and the concept of political correctness are well-established facts of life. It has therefore been with some trepidation that the editing of this unique and much-loved text has been undertaken in producing *The New Daily Study Bible*. Inevitably, the demands of the new language have resulted in the loss of some of Barclay's most sonorous phrases, perhaps best remembered in the often-repeated words 'many a man'. Nonetheless, this revision is made in the conviction that William Barclay, the great communicator, would have welcomed it. In the discussion of Matthew 9:16–17 ('The Problem of the New Idea'), he affirmed the value of language that has stood the test of time and in which people have 'found comfort and put their trust', but he also spoke of 'living in a changing and expanding world' and questioned the wisdom of reading God's word to twentieth-century men and women in Elizabethan English. It is the intention of this new edition to heed that warning and to bring

William Barclay's message of God's word to readers of the twenty-first century in the language of their own time.

In the editorial process, certain decisions have been made in order to keep a balance between that new language and the familiar Barclay style. Quotations from the Bible are now taken from the New Revised Standard Version, but William Barclay's own translation of individual passages has been retained throughout. Where the new version differs from the text on which Barclay originally commented, because of the existence of an alternative reading, the variant text is indicated by square brackets. I have made no attempt to guess what Barclay would have said about the NRSV text; his commentary still refers to the Authorized (King James) and Revised Standard Versions of the Bible, but I believe that the inclusive language of the NRSV considerably assists the flow of the discussion.

For similar reasons, the dating conventions of BC and AD – rather than the more recent and increasingly used BCE (before the common era) and CE (common era) – have been retained. William Barclay took great care to explain the meanings of words and phrases and scholarly points, but it has not seemed appropriate to select new terms and make such explanations on his behalf.

One of the most difficult problems to solve has concerned monetary values. Barclay had his own system for translating the coinage of New Testament times into British currency. Over the years, these equivalent values have become increasingly out of date, and often the force of the point being made has been lost or diminished. There is no easy way to bring these equivalents up to date in a way that will continue to make sense, particularly when readers come from both sides of the Atlantic. I have therefore followed the only known yardstick that gives any feel for the values concerned, namely that a *denarius* was a day's wage for a working man, and I have made alterations to the text accordingly.

One of the striking features of *The Daily Study Bible* is the range of quotations from literature and hymnody that are used by way of illustration. Many of these passages appeared without identification or attribution, and for the new edition I have attempted wherever possible to provide sources and authors. In the same way, details have been included about scholars and other individuals cited, by way of context and explanation, and I am most grateful to Professor John Drane for his assistance in discovering information about some of the more obscure or unfamiliar characters. It is clear that readers use *The Daily Study Bible* in different ways. Some look up particular passages while others work through the daily readings in a more systematic way. The descriptions and explanations are therefore not offered every time an individual is mentioned (in order to avoid repetition that some may find tedious), but I trust that the information can be discovered without too much difficulty.

Finally, the 'Further Reading' lists at the end of each volume have been removed. Many new commentaries and individual studies have been added to those that were the basis of William Barclay's work, and making a selection from that ever-increasing catalogue is an impossible task. It is nonetheless my hope that the exploration that begins with these volumes of *The New Daily Study Bible* will go on in the discovery of new writers and new books.

Throughout the editorial process, many conversations have taken place – conversations with the British and American publishers, and with those who love the books and find in them both information and inspiration. Ronnie Barclay's contribution to this revision of his father's work has been invaluable. But one conversation has dominated the work, and that has been a conversation with William Barclay himself through the text. There has been a real sense of listening to his voice in all the questioning and in the searching for new words to convey the meaning of that text. The aim of *The New Daily Study Bible* is to make clear his message, so that the distinctive voice, which has spoken to so many in past years, may continue to be heard for generations to come.

Linda Foster
London
2001

The Letter of James

INTRODUCTION TO
THE LETTER OF JAMES

James is one of the books which had a very hard fight to get into the New Testament. Even when it did come to be regarded as Scripture, it was spoken of with a certain reserve and suspicion, and even as late as the sixteenth century the reformer Martin Luther would gladly have banished it from the New Testament altogether.

The Doubts of the Early Christian Fathers

In the Latin-speaking part of the Church, it is not until the middle of the fourth century that James emerges in the writings of the fathers. The first list of New Testament books ever to be compiled is the Muratorian Canon, which dates to about AD 170 – and James is absent from it. Tertullian, writing in the middle of the third century, is an immense quoter of Scripture; he has 7,258 quotations from the New Testament, but never one from James. The first appearance of James in Latin is in a Latin manuscript called the Codex Corbeiensis, which dates to about AD 350. This manuscript attributes the authorship of the book to James the son of Zebedee, and includes it, not with the universally acknowledged New Testament books, but with a collection of religious tracts written by the early fathers. James has now emerged, but it is accepted with a certain reservation. The first Latin writer to quote James verbatim is Hilary of Poitiers in a work *On the Trinity*, written about AD 357.

If, then, James was so late in emerging in the Latin church, and if, when it did emerge, it was still regarded with some uncertainty, how did it become integrated into the New Testament? The moving influence was that of the biblical scholar Jerome, for he unhesitatingly included James in his Latin version of the New Testament, the Vulgate, completed early in the fifth century. But even then there is an accent of doubt. In his book *On Famous Men*, Jerome writes: 'James, who is called the brother of the Lord . . . wrote only one epistle, which is one of the seven catholic epistles, and which, some people say, was issued by someone else under James' name.' Jerome fully accepted the letter as Scripture, but he felt that there was some doubt as to who the writer was. The doubt was finally set at rest by the fact that Augustine fully accepted James and was not in doubt that the James in question was the brother of our Lord.

James was late in emerging in the Latin church; for a long time there was a kind of question mark against it, but in the end, and only after a struggle, Jerome's inclusion of it in the Vulgate and Augustine's full acceptance of it brought it full recognition.

The Syrian Church

One would have thought that the Syrian church would have been the first to accept James, if it was really written in Palestine and was really the work of the brother of our Lord; but in the Syrian church there was the same wavering and swinging of opinion. The official New Testament of the Syrian church is called the Peshitto. This was to the Syrian church what the Vulgate was to the Latin church. It was made by Rabbula, the Bishop of Edessa, about AD 412, and in it for the first time James was translated into Syriac. Up to that time there was no Syriac version of the book, and up to AD 451 there is no trace of James in Syriac religious literature. After that, James was widely enough accepted, but as late as AD 545 Paul of Nisibis was still questioning its right to be in the New Testament. It was not, in fact, until mid-way through the eighth century that the great authority of the Greek theologian John of Damascus did for James in the Syrian church what Augustine had done for it in the Latin.

The Greek Church

Although James emerged sooner in the Greek-speaking church than it did in the Latin and Syrian, it was nonetheless late in making a definite appearance. The first writer to quote it by name is Origen, head of the school of Alexandria. Writing almost mid-way through the third century, he says: 'If faith is called faith, but exists apart from works, such a faith is dead, as we read in the letter which is currently reported to be by James.' It is true that in other works he quotes it as being without doubt by James and shows that he believes James to be the brother of our Lord, but once again there is the accent of doubt. Eusebius, the great scholar of Caesarea, investigated the position of the various books in the New Testament or on its fringe mid-way through the fourth century. He classes James among the books which are 'disputed', and he writes of it: 'The first of the epistles called Catholic is said to be his [James']; but it must be noted that some regard it as spurious; and it is certainly true that very few of the ancient writers mention it.' Here again, there is evidence of doubt. Eusebius himself accepted James, but he was well aware that there were those who did not. The turning point in the Greek-speaking church came in AD 367. In that year, Athanasius, the theologian and Bishop of Alexandria, issued his famous Easter Letter in Egypt. Its purpose was to inform his people what books were Scripture and what were not, because apparently their reading had become too wide, or, at least, too many books were being regarded as holy writ. In that Letter, James was included without qualification, and its position from that point onwards was safe.

So, in the early Church, no one really questioned the value of James, but in every branch of it the letter was late in emerging and had to go through a period when its right to be considered a New Testament book was under dispute.

In fact, the history of James is still to be seen in its position in the Roman Catholic Church. In 1546, the Council of Trent once and for all laid down the Roman Catholic Bible. A list of books was given to which none could be added and from which none could be subtracted, and which had to be read in the Vulgate version and in no other. The books were divided into two classes: those which were *proto-canonical*, that is to say, those which had been unquestioningly accepted from the beginning; and those which were *deutero-canonical*, that is to say, those which only gradually won their way into the New Testament. Although the Roman Catholic Church never had any doubts about James, it is nonetheless in the second class that it is included.

Luther and James

In our own day, it is true to say that James, at least for most people, does not occupy a position in the forefront of the New Testament. Few would mention it in the same breath as John or Romans, or Luke or Galatians. There is still for many a kind of reservation about it. Why should that be? It cannot have to do with the doubt about James in the early Church, for the history of the New Testament books in those distant days is not known to many people in the

6

modern Church. The reason lies in this. In the Roman Catholic Church, the position of James was finally settled by the Edict of the Council of Trent; but in the Protestant Church its history continued to be troubled, and indeed became even more troubled, because Luther attacked it and would have removed it from the New Testament altogether. In his printing of the German New Testament, Luther had a contents page with the books set out and numbered. At the end of the list, there was a little group, separate from the others and with no numbers assigned to them. That group consisted of James, Jude, Hebrews and Revelation. These were books which Luther held to be secondary.

Luther was especially severe on James – and the adverse judgment of a great scholar on any book can be a millstone round its neck forever. It is in the concluding paragraph of his *Preface to the New Testament* that Luther's famous verdict on James can be found:

> In sum: the gospel and the first epistle of St John, St Paul's epistles, especially those to the Romans, Galatians and Ephesians; and St Peter's first epistle, are the books which show Christ to you. They teach everything you need to know for your salvation, even if you were never to see or hear any other book or hear any other teaching. In comparison with these, the epistle of James is an *epistle full of straw*, because it contains nothing evangelical. But more about this in other prefaces.

As he promised, Luther developed this verdict in the *Preface to the Epistles of St James and St Jude*. He begins: 'I think highly of the epistle of James, and regard it as valuable although it was rejected in early days. It does not expound human doctrines, but lays much emphasis on God's law. Yet to give my own opinion, without prejudice to that of anyone else, I do not hold it to be of apostolic authorship.' He then goes on to give his reasons for this rejection.

First, in direct opposition to Paul, and the rest of the Bible, it ascribes justification to works, quoting Abraham wrongly as one who was justified by his works. This in itself proves that the epistle cannot be of apostolic origin.

Second, not once does it give to Christians any instruction or reminder of the passion, resurrection or Spirit of Christ. It mentions Christ only twice. Then Luther goes on to state his own principle for testing any book: 'The true touchstone for testing any book is to discover whether it emphasises the prominence of Christ or not . . . What does not teach Christ is not apostolic, not even if taught by Peter or Paul. On the other hand, what does preach Christ is apostolic, even if Judas, Annas, Pilate, or Herod does it.' On that test, James fails. So Luther goes on: 'The epistle of James however only drives you to the law and its works. He mixes one thing to another to such an extent that I suspect some good and pious man assembled a few things said by disciples of the apostles, and put them down in black and white; or perhaps the epistle was written by someone else who made notes of a sermon of his. He calls the law a law of freedom (James 1:25, 2:12), although St Paul calls it a law of slavery, wrath, death, and sin' (Galatians 3:23–4; Romans 4:15, 7:10–11).

So Luther comes to his conclusion: 'In sum: he wishes to guard against those who depended on faith without going on to works, but he had neither the spirit, nor the thought, nor the eloquence equal to the task. He does violence to Scripture and so contradicts Paul and all Scripture. He tries to accomplish by emphasizing law what the apostles bring about by attracting man to love. I therefore refuse him a place among the writers of the true canon of my Bible; but I would not prevent anyone else placing him or raising him where he likes, for the epistle contains many excellent passages. One man does not count as a man even in the eyes of the world; how then shall this single and isolated writer count against Paul and all the rest of the Bible?'

Luther does not spare James, and it may be that once we have studied the book we may think that for once he allowed personal prejudice to injure sound judgment.

Such, then, is the troubled history of James. Now we must try to answer the questions it poses regarding authorship and date.

The Identity of James

The author of this letter gives us practically no information about himself. He calls himself simply: 'James, a servant of God and of the Lord Jesus Christ' (James 1:1). So who is he? In the New Testament, there are apparently at least five people who bear that name.

(1) There is the James who was the father of the member of the Twelve called Judas, not Iscariot (Luke 6:16). He is no more than a name and cannot have had any connection with this letter.

(2) There is James, the son of Alphaeus, who was a member of the Twelve (Matthew 10:3; Mark 3:18; Luke 6:15; Acts 1:13). A comparison of Matthew 9:9 with Mark 2:14 makes it certain that Matthew and Levi were one and the same person. Levi was also a son of Alphaeus, and therefore Matthew and this James must have been brothers. But of James, the son of Alphaeus, nothing else is known; and he also can have had no connection with this letter.

(3) There is the James who is called James the younger and is mentioned in Mark 15:40 (cf. Matthew 27:56; John 19:25). Again nothing is known of him, and he cannot have had any connection with this letter.

9

(4) There is James, the brother of John, and the son of Zebedee, a member of the Twelve (Matthew 10:2; Mark 3:17; Luke 6:14; Acts 1:13). In the gospel story, James never appears independently of his brother John (Matthew 4:21, 17:1; Mark 1:19, 1:29, 5:37, 9:2, 10:35, 10:41, 13:3, 14:33; Luke 5:10, 8:51, 9:28, 9:54). He was the first of the apostolic band to be martyred, for he was beheaded on the orders of Herod Agrippa I in the year AD 44. He has been connected with the letter. The fourth-century Latin Codex Corbeiensis, at the end of the epistle, has a note quite definitely attributing it to James the son of Zebedee. The only place where this view on the authorship was taken seriously was in the Spanish church, in which, down to the end of the seventeenth century, he was often held to be the author. This was due to the fact that St James of Compostella, the patron saint of Spain, is identified with James the son of Zebedee; and it was natural that the Spanish church should be predisposed to wish that their country's patron saint should be the author of a New Testament letter. But the martyrdom of James came too early for him to have written the letter, and in any case there is nothing beyond the Codex Corbeiensis to connect him with it.

(5) Finally, there is James, who is called the brother of Jesus. Although the first definite connection of him with this letter does not emerge until Origen in the first half of the third century, it is to him that it has always been traditionally attributed. The Roman Catholic Church agrees with this view, for in 1546 the Council of Trent laid it down that James is canonical and is written by an apostle.

Let us then collect the evidence about this James. From the New Testament, we learn that he was one of the brothers of Jesus (Mark 6:3; Matthew 13:55). We shall later discuss in what sense the word 'brother' is to be taken. During Jesus' ministry, it is clear that his family did not understand or sympathize with him and would have wished to restrain him (Matthew 12:46–50; Mark 3:21, 3:31–5; John 7:3–9). John says bluntly: 'For not even his brothers believed in him' (John 7:5). So, during Jesus' earthly ministry, James was numbered among his opponents.

With the Acts of the Apostles, there comes a sudden and unexplained change. When Acts opens, Jesus' mother and his brothers are there with the little group of Christians (Acts 1:14). From there onwards, it becomes clear that James has become the leader of the Jerusalem church, although how that came about is never explained. It is to James that Peter sends the news of his escape from prison (Acts 12:17). James presides over the Council of Jerusalem, which agreed to the entry of the Gentiles into the Christian Church (Acts 15). It is James and Peter whom Paul meets when he first goes to Jerusalem, and it is with Peter, James and John, the pillars of the Church, that he discusses and settles his sphere of work (Galatians 1:19, 2:9). It is to James that Paul comes with his collection from the Gentile churches on the visit to Jerusalem which is destined to be his last and which leads to his imprisonment (Acts 21:18–25). This last episode is important, for it shows James very sympathetic to the Jews who still observe the Jewish law, and so eager that their scruples should not be offended that he actually persuades Paul to demonstrate his loyalty to the law by assuming responsibility for the expenses of certain Jews who are fulfilling a Nazirite vow, a vow taken in gratitude for some special blessing from God.

Plainly, then, James was the leader of the Jerusalem church. As might be expected, this was something which tradition greatly developed. Hegesippus, the second-century Church historian, says that James was the first bishop of the church at Jerusalem. The early Christian theologian Clement of

Alexandria goes further and says that he was chosen for that office by Peter and John. Jerome, in his book *On Famous Men*, says: 'After the passion of the Lord, James was immediately ordained bishop of Jerusalem by the apostles . . . He ruled the church of Jerusalem for thirty years, that is, until the seventh year of the reign of Nero.' *The Clementine Recognitions* take the final step in the development of the legend, for they say that James was ordained Bishop of Jerusalem by none other than Jesus himself. Clement of Alexandria relates a strange tradition: 'To James the Just, and John and Peter, after the resurrection, the Lord committed knowledge; they committed it to the other apostles; and the other apostles to the seventy.' The later developments are not to be accepted, but the basic fact remains that James was the undisputed head of the church at Jerusalem.

James and Jesus

Such a change must have some explanation. It may well be that we have it in a brief sentence in the New Testament itself. In 1 Corinthians 15, Paul gives us a list of the resurrection appearances of Jesus and includes the words: 'Then he appeared to James' (1 Corinthians 15:7). It so happens that there is a strange reference to James in the Gospel according to the Hebrews, which was one of the early gospels which did not gain admittance to the New Testament but which, to judge from its surviving fragments, had much of value in it. The following passage from it is handed down by Jerome:

> Now the Lord, when he had given the linen cloth unto the servant of the high priest, went unto James and appeared to him (for James had sworn that he would not eat bread from that hour, wherein he had drunk the Lord's cup, until he should see him risen again from among them that sleep). And again after a little, 'Bring

ye', saith the Lord, 'a table and bread', and immediately
it is added: 'He took bread and blessed and brake it and
gave it unto James the Just and said unto him: "My
brother, eat thy bread, for the Son of Man is risen from
among them that sleep."'

That passage is not without its difficulties. The beginning
seems to mean that Jesus, when he rose from the dead and
emerged from the tomb, handed the linen shroud, which he
had been wearing in death, to the servant of the high priest
and went to meet his brother James. It also seems to imply
that James was present at the Last Supper. But although the
passage has its obscurities, one thing is clear. Something about
Jesus in the last days and hours had fastened on James' heart,
and he had vowed that he would not eat until Jesus had risen
again; and so Jesus came to him and gave him the assurance
for which he waited. That there was a meeting of James and
the risen Christ is certain. What happened at that moment we
shall never know. But we do know this, that after it the James
who had been hostile and unsympathetic to Jesus became his
servant for life and his martyr in death.

James the Martyr of Christ

That James died a martyr's death is the consistent statement
of early tradition. The accounts of the circumstances vary,
but the fact that he was martyred remains constant. The Jewish
historian Josephus' account is very brief (*Antiquities*, 20:9:1):

So Ananus, being that kind of man, and thinking that
he had got a good opportunity because Festus was dead
and Albinus not yet arrived, holds a judicial council;
and he brought before it the brother of Jesus, who was
called Christ – James was his name – and some others,
and on the charge of violating the law he gave them
over to be stoned.

Ananus was a Jewish high priest; Festus and Albinus were procurators of Palestine, holding the same position as Pilate had held. The point of the story is that Ananus took advantage of the interregnum, the period between the death of one procurator and the arrival of his successor, to eliminate James and other leaders of the Christian Church. This, in fact, fits well with the character of Ananus as it is known to us, and would mean that James was martyred in AD 62.

A much longer account is given in the history of Hegesippus. Hegesippus' history is itself lost, but his account of the death of James has been preserved in full by the Church historian Eusebius, who wrote early in the fourth century (*Ecclesiastical History*, 2:23). It is lengthy, but it is of such interest that it must be quoted in its entirety.

> To the government of the Church in conjunction with the apostles succeeded the Lord's brother, James, he whom all from the time of the Lord to our own day call the Just, as there were many named James. And he was holy from his mother's womb; wine and strong drink he drank not, nor did he eat flesh; no razor touched his head, he anointed himself not with oil, and used not the bath. To him alone was it permitted to enter the Holy Place, for neither did he wear wool, but linen clothes. And alone he would enter the Temple, and be found prostrate on his knees beseeching pardon for the people, so that his knees were callous like a camel's in consequence of his continual kneeling in prayer to God and beseeching pardon for the people. Because of his exceeding righteousness he was called the Just, and Oblias, which is in Greek Bulwark of the People, and Righteousness, as the prophets declare concerning him.
>
> Therefore, certain of the seven sects among the people, already mentioned by me in the *Memoirs*, asked him: 'What is the door of Jesus?' and he said that He

was the Saviour – of whom some accepted the faith that Jesus is the Christ. Now the aforesaid sects were not believers either in a Resurrection or in One who should come to render to every man according to his deeds; but as many as believed did so because of James. So, since many of the rulers, too, were believers, there was a tumult of the Jews and scribes and Pharisees, for they said there was danger that all the people would expect Jesus the Christ. Accordingly they said, when they had met together with James: 'We entreat thee restrain the people since it has gone astray unto Jesus, holding him to be the Christ. We entreat thee to persuade concerning Jesus all those who come to the day of the Passover, for we all listen to thee. For we and all the people testify to thee that thou art just and that thou respectest not persons. So thou, therefore, persuade the people concerning Jesus not to go astray, for all the people and all of us listen to thee. Take thy stand, therefore, on the pinnacle of the Temple, that up there thou mayest be well seen, and thy words audible to all the people. For because of the Passover all the tribes have come together and the gentiles also.'

So the aforesaid scribes and Pharisees set James on the pinnacle of the Temple and called to him: 'O thou, the Just, to whom we all ought to listen, since the people is going astray after Jesus the crucified, tell us what is the door of Jesus?' And with a loud voice he answered: 'Why do you ask me concerning the Son of Man? He sitteth himself in heaven on the right hand of the great Power, and shall come on the clouds of heaven.' And when many were convinced and gave glory for the witness of James, and said: 'Hosanna to the Son of David', then again the same scribes and Pharisees said to one another: 'We were wrong to permit such a testimony to Jesus; but let us go up and cast him [James] down, that through fear they may not believe him.' And they cried out saying: 'Ho, Ho! even the Just has gone astray', and they fulfilled the Scriptures written in Isaiah: 'Let us away with the Just, because he is troublesome to us; therefore they shall eat the fruits of their doings.'

Accordingly they went up and cast the Just down. And they said to one another: 'Let us stone James the Just', and they began to stone him, since he was not killed by the fall, but he turned and knelt down saying: 'I beseech thee, Lord God Father, forgive them, for they know not what they do.' And so, as they were stoning him, one of the Priests of the sons of Rechab, the son of Rechabim, mentioned by Jeremiah the prophet, cried out saying: 'Stop! what are ye doing? The Just prays for you.' And a certain one of them, one of the fullers, taking the club with which he pounds clothes, brought it down on the head of the Just; and so he suffered martyrdom.

And they buried him there on the spot, near the Temple. A true witness has he become both to Jews and Greeks that Jesus is Christ. And immediately Vespasian besieges them.

The last sentence shows that Hegesippus had a different date for the death of James. Josephus makes it AD 62; but, if this happened just before the siege of Vespasian, the date is perhaps about AD 66.

Much in the story of Hegesippus may well be legendary; but, from it, two things emerge. First, it is again evidence that James died a martyr's death. Second, it is evidence that, even after James became a Christian, he remained in complete loyalty to the orthodox Jewish law, so loyal that the Jews regarded him as one of themselves. This would fit well with what we have already noted of James' attitude to Paul when he came to Jerusalem with the collection for the Jerusalem church (Acts 21:18–25).

The Brother of our Lord

There is one other question about the person of James which we must try to solve. In Galatians 1:19, Paul speaks of him as *the Lord's brother*. In Matthew 13:55 and in Mark 6:3, he is named among the brothers of Jesus; and in Acts 1:14, although no names are given, the brothers of Jesus are said to be among his followers in the earliest Church. The question of the meaning of *brother* is one which must be faced, for the Roman Catholic Church in particular attaches a great deal of importance to the answer. Ever since the time of Jerome, there has been continuous argument in the Church on this question. There are three theories of the relationship of these 'brothers' to Jesus, and we shall consider them one by one.

The Hieronymian Theory

The Hieronymian Theory takes its name from Jerome, whose name in Greek is Hieronymos. It was he who worked out the theory which declares that the 'brothers' of Jesus were in fact his *cousins*; and this is the belief of the Roman Catholic Church, for which it is an article of faith. It was put forward by Jerome in AD 383, and the best way to grasp his complicated argument is by setting it out in a series of steps.

(1) James the brother of our Lord is included among the apostles. Paul writes: 'But I did not see any other apostle except James the Lord's brother' (Galatians 1:19).

(2) Jerome insists that the word *apostle* can be used only of the Twelve. If that is so, we must look for James among them. He cannot be identified with James, brother of John and son of Zebedee, who, apart from anything else, was martyred by the time of Galatians 1:19, as Acts 12:2 plainly tells us. Therefore, he must be identified with the only other James among the Twelve, James the son of Alphaeus.

(3) Jerome proceeds to make another identification. In Mark 6:3, we read: 'Is not this the carpenter, the son of Mary and brother of James and Joses?'; and in Mark 15:40 we find beside the cross Mary the mother of James the younger and of Joses. Since James the younger is the brother of Joses and the son of Mary, he must therefore be the same person as the James of Mark 6:3, who is the brother of our Lord. Therefore, according to Jerome, James the brother of the Lord, James the son of Alphaeus and James the younger are all the same person described in different ways.

(4) Jerome bases the next and final step of his argument on a deduction made from the lists of the women who were there when Jesus was crucified. Let us set down that list as given by the three gospel writers.

In Mark 15:40, it is:

> Mary Magdalene, Mary the mother of James the younger and Joses, and Salome.

In Matthew 27:56, it is:

> Mary Magdalene, Mary the mother of James and of Joseph, and the mother of the sons of Zebedee.

In John 19:25, it is:

> Jesus' mother, his mother's sister, Mary the wife of Clopas, and Mary Magdalene.

Now let us analyse these lists. In each of them, Mary Magdalene appears by name. It is safe to identify Salome and the mother of the sons of Zebedee. But the real problem is: *how many women are there in John's list?* Is the list to be read like this:

> (1) Jesus' mother;
> (2) Jesus' mother's sister;

(3) Mary the wife of Clopas;

(4) Mary Magdalene?

Or is the list to be read like this:

(1) Jesus' mother;

(2) Jesus' mother's sister, Mary the wife of Clopas;

(3) Mary Magdalene?

Jerome insists that the second way is correct and that Jesus' mother's sister and Mary, the wife of Clopas, are one and the same person. If that is so, she must also be the Mary who in the other lists is the mother of James and Joses. This James who is her son is the man who is variously known as James the younger and as James the son of Alphaeus and as James the apostle who is known as the brother of our Lord. This means that James is the son of Mary's sister and therefore is Jesus' cousin.

There, then, is Jerome's argument. Against it, at least four criticisms can be levelled.

(1) Again and again, James is called the *brother* of Jesus or is numbered among the *brothers* of Jesus. The word used in each case is *adelphos*, the normal word for *brother*. True, it can describe people who belong to a common fellowship, just as the Christians called each other *brother* and *sister*. True, it can be used as a term of endearment, and we may call someone to whom we are very close a *brother*. But when it is used of those who are kin, it is, to say the least of it, very doubtful that it can mean *cousin*. If James was the *cousin* of Jesus, it is extremely unlikely – perhaps impossible – that he would be called the *adelphos* of Jesus.

(2) Jerome was quite wrong in assuming that the term *apostle* could be used only of the Twelve. Paul was an apostle (Romans 1:1; 1 Corinthians 1:1; 2 Corinthians 1:1; Galatians 1:1). Barnabas was an apostle (Acts 14:14; 1 Corinthians 9:6).

Silas was an apostle (Acts 15:22). Andronicus and Junia were apostles (Romans 16:7). It is impossible to limit the word *apostle* to the Twelve. Since, therefore, it is not necessary to look for James the Lord's brother among the Twelve, Jerome's whole argument collapses.

(3) It is, on the face of it, much more likely that John 19:25 is a list of four women, not three, for, if Mary the wife of Clopas were the sister of Mary, Jesus' mother, it would mean that there were two sisters in the same family both called Mary, which is extremely unlikely.

(4) It must be remembered that the Church knew nothing of this theory until AD 383, when Jerome produced it; and it is quite certain that it was produced for no other reason than to preserve the doctrine of the perpetual virginity of Mary.

The theory that those called Jesus' brothers were, in fact, his cousins must be dismissed. The facts of the case do not support it.

The Epiphanian Theory

The second of the great theories concerning the relationship of Jesus and his 'brothers' holds that these 'brothers' were, in fact, his half-brothers, sons of Joseph by a previous marriage. This is called the Epiphanian Theory after Epiphanius, who argued strongly for it in about AD 370. He did not construct it. It existed long before this and may indeed be said to be the most usual opinion in the early Church.

The substance of it already appears in an apocryphal book called the Book of James or the Protevangelium, which dates back to the middle of the second century. That book tells how there was a devout husband and wife called Joachim and Anna. Their great grief was that they did not have children. To their great joy, in their old age a child was born to them, and this too, apparently, was regarded as a virgin birth. The child, a girl, was called Mary and was to be the mother of Jesus. Joachim and Anna dedicated their child to the Lord, and when she reached the age of three they took her to the Temple and left her there in the charge of the priests. She grew up in the Temple, and when she reached the age of twelve the priests began to consider her marriage. They called together the widowers of the people, telling each man to bring his rod with him. Among those who came was Joseph the carpenter. The high priest took the rods, and Joseph's was last. To the other rods nothing happened, but from the rod of Joseph there flew a dove which came and settled on Joseph's head. In this way, it was revealed that Joseph was to take Mary as his wife. Joseph at first was very unwilling. 'I have sons,' he said, 'and I am an old man, but she is a girl: lest I become a laughing-stock to the children of Israel' (Protevangelium 9:1). But in the end he took her in obedience to the will of God, and in due course Jesus was born. The material of the Protevangelium is, of course, simply legend, but it shows that by the middle of the second century the theory which was one day to bear the name of Epiphanius was widely held.

There is no direct evidence for this theory whatsoever, and all the support produced in its favour is of an indirect character.

(1) It is asked: would Jesus have handed the care of his mother to John, if she had other sons besides himself (John 19.26–7)? The answer is that, as far as we know, Jesus' family were quite out of sympathy with him, and it would hardly have been possible to hand the care of his mother to them.

(2) It is argued that the behaviour of Jesus' 'brothers' towards him is that of elder brothers towards a younger brother. They questioned his sanity and wanted to take him home (Mark 3:21, 3:31–5); they were actively hostile to him (John 7:1–5). But it could just as well be argued that their

behaviour was due to the simple fact that they found him an embarrassment to the family in a way that had nothing to do with age.

(3) It is argued that Joseph must have been older than Mary because he vanishes completely from the gospel story and, therefore, probably had died before Jesus' public ministry began. The mother of Jesus was at the wedding feast at Cana of Galilee, but there is no mention of Joseph (John 2:1). Jesus is called, at least sometimes, the son of Mary, and the implication is that Joseph was dead and Mary was a widow (Mark 6:3; but cf. Matthew 13:55). Further, Jesus' long stay in Nazareth until he was thirty years old (Luke 3:23) is most easily explained by the assumption that Joseph had died and that Jesus had become responsible for the support of the household. But the fact that Joseph was older than Mary does not by any means prove that he had no other children by her, and the fact that Jesus stayed in Nazareth as the village carpenter in order to support the family would much more naturally indicate that he was the eldest, and not the youngest, son.

But basically this theory springs from the same origin as the Hieronymian theory. Its aim is to preserve the perpetual virginity of Mary. There is no direct evidence whatsoever for it, and no one would ever have thought of it had it not been for the desire to think that Mary never ceased to be a virgin.

The Helvidian Theory

The third theory is called the Helvidian Theory. It states quite simply that the brothers and sisters of Jesus were in the full sense of the term his brothers and sisters – that, to use the technical term, they were his uterine brothers and sisters. Nothing whatever is known of the Helvidius with whose name this theory is connected except that he wrote a treatise to support it, which Jerome strongly opposed. What may be said in favour of it?

(1) No one reading the New Testament story without theological presuppositions would ever think of anything else. On the face of it, that story does not think of Jesus' brothers and sisters as anything other than his brothers and sisters in the full sense of the term.

(2) The birth narratives in both Matthew and Luke presuppose that Mary had other children. Matthew writes: 'When Joseph awoke from sleep, he did as the angel of the Lord commanded him; he took her as his wife, but had no marital relations with her until she had borne a son' (Matthew 1:24-5). The clear implication is that Joseph entered into a normal married relationship with Mary after the birth of Jesus. Tertullian, in fact, uses this passage to prove that both virginity and the married state are consecrated in Christ by the fact that Mary was first a virgin and then a wife in the full sense of the term. Luke, in writing of the birth of Jesus, says: 'She gave birth to her *firstborn* son' (Luke 2:7). To call Jesus a first-born son is plainly to indicate that other children followed.

(3) As we have already said, the fact that Jesus remained in Nazareth as the village carpenter until the age of thirty is at least an indication that he was the eldest son and had to take upon himself the responsibility of the support of the family after the death of Joseph.

We believe that the brothers and sisters of Jesus really were his brothers and sisters. Any other theory ultimately springs from the glorification of self-denial and from a wish to regard Mary as forever a virgin. It is surely a far more lovely thing to believe in the sanctity of the home than to insist that celibacy is to be valued more than married love.

So, we believe that James, called the Lord's brother, was in every sense the brother of Jesus.

James as the Author

Can we then say that this James was also the author of this letter? Let us collect the evidence in favour of that view.

(1) If James wrote a letter at all, it would most naturally be a general letter, as this is. James was not, like Paul, a traveller and a man of many congregations. He was the leader of the Jewish section of the Church, and the kind of letter we would expect him to write would be a general letter directed to all Jewish Christians.

(2) There is scarcely anything in the letter that a good Jew could not accept – so much so that there are those who think that it is actually a Jewish ethical tract which has found its way into the New Testament. The New Testament scholar A. H. McNeile has pointed out that in instance after instance there are phrases in James which can be read equally well in a Christian or a Jewish sense. The twelve tribes of the Dispersion (1:1) could be taken to refer either to the exiled Jews scattered all over the world or to the Christian Church, the new Israel of God. 'The Lord' can again and again in this letter be understood equally well of Jesus or of God (1:7; 4:10, 15; 5:7, 8, 10, 11, 14, 15). Our bringing forth by God by the word of his truth to be the first fruits of his creation (1:18) can equally well be understood of God's first act of creation or of his re-creation of men and women in Jesus Christ. The perfect law and the royal law (1:25, 2:8) can equally well be understood of the ethical law of the Ten Commandments or of the new law of Christ. The elders of the church, the *ekklēsia* (5:14), can equally well be understood as meaning the elders of the Christian Church or the Jewish elders – for in the Septuagint, the Greek edition of the

traditional Hebrew Scriptures that was most widely used in
the synagogues in New Testament times, *ekklēsia* is the title
of the chosen nation of God. In 2:2, 'your *assembly*' is spoken
of. The word there used for assembly is *sunagōgē*, which can
mean the synagogue even more readily than it can mean the
Christian congregation. The habit of addressing its readers
as brothers is thoroughly Christian, but it is equally thoroughly
Jewish. The coming of the Lord and the picture of the Judge
standing at the door (5:7, 5:9) are just as common in Jewish
thought as in Christian thought. The accusation that they have
murdered the righteous one (5:6) is a phrase which occurs
again and again in the prophets; but a Christian could read it
as a statement of the crucifixion of Christ. There is nothing
in this letter which orthodox Jews could not heartily accept,
if they read it in their own terms.

It could be argued that all this perfectly suits James. He
was the leader of what might be called Jewish Christianity;
he was the head of that part of the Church which remained
centred in Jerusalem. There must have been a time when the
Church was very close to Judaism and it was more a reformed
Judaism than anything else. There was a kind of Christianity
which did not have the width or the universality which the
mind of Paul put into it. Paul himself said that the task of
preaching to the Gentiles had been allocated to him and the
task of taking the good news to the Jews was given to Peter,
James and John (Galatians 2:9). The letter of James may well
represent a kind of Christianity that had remained in its earliest
form. This would explain two things.

First, it would explain the frequency with which James
repeats the teaching of the Sermon on the Mount. We may,
out of many instances, compare James 2:12–13 and Matthew
6:14–15; James 3:11–13 and Matthew 7:16–20; James 5:12
and Matthew 5:34–7. Any Jewish Christian would be

supremely interested in the ethical teaching of the Christian faith.

Second, it would help to explain the relationship of this letter to the teaching of Paul. At a first reading, James 2:14–26 reads like a direct attack on Paulinism. 'A person is justified by works and not by faith alone' (James 2:24) seems a flat contradiction of the Pauline teaching of justification by faith. But what James is attacking is a so-called faith which has no ethical results, and one thing is quite clear – anyone who charges Paul with preaching such a faith cannot possibly have read his letters. They are full of ethical demands, as, for instance, a chapter like Romans 12 illustrates. Now James died in AD 62 and, therefore, could not have read Paul's letters, which did not become the common property of the Church until at least AD 90. Therefore, what James is attacking is either a misunderstanding of what Paul said or a distortion of it, and nowhere was such a misunderstanding or distortion more likely to arise than in Jerusalem, where Paul's stress on faith and grace and his attack on the law were likely to be regarded with more suspicion than anywhere else.

(3) It has been pointed out that James and the letter of the Council of Jerusalem to the Gentile churches have at least two rather curious similarities. Both begin with the word *Greeting* (James 1:1; Acts 15:23). The Greek is *chairein*. This was the normal Greek beginning to a letter, but nowhere else in all the New Testament is it found other than in the letter of Claudius Lysias, the military officer, to the governor of the province quoted in Acts 23:26–30. Second, Acts 15:17 has a phrase in the letter of the Council of Jerusalem in which, as the Revised Standard Version has it, it speaks of the Gentiles *who are called by my name*. This phrase occurs nowhere else in the New Testament other than in James 2:7, where it is translated as *the name by which you are called*. Although

these translations differ slightly, the Greek is exactly the same. It is curious that the letter of the Council of Jerusalem presents us with two unusual phrases which recur only in James, when we remember that the letter of the Council of Jerusalem must have been drafted by James.

There is, then, evidence which supports the belief that the Letter of James was the work of James, the Lord's brother and head of the Jerusalem church.

On the other hand, there are facts which make us a little doubtful whether he was, after all, the author.

(1) If the writer was the brother of our Lord, we would have expected him to make some reference to that fact. All he calls himself is 'a servant of God and of the Lord Jesus Christ' (1:1). Such a reference would not have been in any sense for his own personal glory, but simply to lend authority to his letter. And such authority would have been especially useful outside Palestine, in countries where James could hardly have been known. If the author was indeed the Lord's brother, it is surprising that he makes no reference, direct or indirect, to that fact.

(2) Failing a reference to his relationship to Jesus, we would have expected a reference to the fact that he was an apostle. It was Paul's regular custom to begin his letters with a reference to his apostleship. Again, it is not a question of personal prestige but simply a guarantee of the authority by which he writes. If this James was indeed the Lord's brother and the head of the Jerusalem church, we should have expected some reference at the beginning of the letter to his apostolic status.

(3) The most surprising fact of all is that which made Luther question the right of this letter to a place in the New Testament – the almost complete absence of any references to Jesus Christ. Only twice in the whole letter is his name

mentioned, and these mentions are almost incidental (1:1, 2:1).

There is no reference at all to his resurrection. We know well that the early Church was built on faith in the risen Christ. If this letter is the work of James, it is contemporary with the events of Acts in which the resurrection is mentioned no fewer than twenty-five times. What makes it still more surprising is that James had a personal reason for writing about the appearance of Jesus which may well have been what changed the direction of his life. It is surprising that anyone writing at such a time in the Church's history should write without reference to the resurrection of Jesus, and it is doubly surprising if the writer should be James, the brother of our Lord.

Further, there is no reference to Jesus as Messiah. If James, the leader of the Jewish church, was writing to Jewish Christians in these very early days, one would have thought his main aim would have been to present Jesus as Messiah, or that at least he would have made his belief in that fact plain; but the letter does not mention it.

(4) It is plain that the writer of this letter is steeped in the Old Testament. It is also plain that he is intimately acquainted with the Wisdom Literature; and that in James is only to be expected. There are in his letter twenty-three apparent quotations from the Sermon on the Mount; that too is easy to understand, because from the very beginning, long before the gospels were written, compendiums of Jesus' teaching must have circulated. It is argued by some that he must have known Paul's letters to the Romans and to the Galatians in order to write as he does about faith and works, and it is argued rightly that a Jew who had never been outside Palestine and who died in AD 62 could not have known these letters. As we have seen, this argument will not stand, because the criticism of

Paul's teaching in James is criticism which could have been offered only by someone who had not read the letters of Paul at first hand and who is dealing with a misunderstanding or a distortion of Pauline doctrine. But the phrase in 1:17, 'Every generous act of giving, with every perfect gift', is a hexameter line (a line with six accented beats) and clearly a quotation from some Greek poet; and the phrase in 3:6: 'the cycle of nature', may be an Orphic phrase from the mystery religions. How could James of Palestine pick up quotations like these?

There are things which are difficult to account for on the assumption that James, the brother of our Lord, was the author of this letter.

The evidence for and against James' authorship of this letter is extraordinarily evenly balanced. For the moment, we must leave the matter unresolved and turn to certain other questions.

The Date of the Letter

When we turn to the evidence for the date of the letter, we find this same even balance. It is possible to argue that it is very early, and equally possible to argue that it is rather late.

(1) When James was writing, it is clear that the hope of the second coming of Jesus Christ was still very real (5:7–9). Now the expectation of the second coming never left the Christian Church, but it did to some extent fade from the foreground of its thought as it was unexpectedly delayed for longer and longer. This would suggest an early date.

(2) In the early chapters of Acts and in the letters of Paul, there is a continuous background of Jewish controversy against acceptance of the Gentiles into the Church on the basis of faith alone. Wherever Paul went, the Judaizers followed him, and the acceptance of the Gentiles was not a battle which was easily won. In James, there is not even a

hint of this Jewish–Gentile controversy, a fact which is doubly surprising when we remember that James, the Lord's brother, took a leading part in settling the matter at the Council of Jerusalem. That being so, this letter could be either very early and written before that controversy emerged, or it could be late and written after the last echo of the controversy had died away. The fact that there is no mention of the Jewish–Gentile controversy can be used as an argument either way.

(3) The evidence from the church order reflected in the letter is equally conflicting. The meeting place of the Church is still called the *sunagōgē* (2:2). That points to an early date; later, an assembly of Christians would definitely be called the *ekklēsia*, for the Jewish term was soon dropped. The elders of the Church are mentioned (5:14), but there is no mention of either deacons or bishops. This again indicates an early date, and possibly a Jewish connection, for the eldership was a Jewish institution before it was a Christian one. James is worried about the existence of *many teachers* (3:1). This could well indicate a very early situation, before the Church had systematized its ministry and introduced some kind of order; or it could indicate a late date, when many false teachers had arisen to plague the Church.

There are two general facts which seem on the whole to indicate that James is late. First, as we have seen, there is hardly any mention of Jesus at all. The subject of the letter is, in fact, the inadequacies and the imperfections, the sins and the mistakes of the members of the church. This seems to point to a fairly late date. The early preaching was ablaze with the grace and the glory of the risen Christ; later preaching became, as it so often is today, a tirade against the imperfections of the members of the church. The second general fact is the condemnation of the rich (2:1–3, 5:1–6). The flattery of the rich and the arrogance of the rich seem to have been real problems when this letter was written. Now in the very early Church there were few, if any, rich people (1 Corinthians 1:26–7). James seems to indicate a later time when the once poor Church was being threatened with a spirit of worldliness in its members.

The Preachers of the Ancient World

It will help us to date this so-called letter of James, and may also help us to identify its author, if we place it in its context in the ancient world.

The sermon is identified with the Christian Church, but it was by no means its invention. It had roots in both the Hellenistic and the Jewish world, and when we set James beside the Hellenistic and the Jewish sermons we cannot fail to be struck by the resemblances.

1. Let us look first at the Greek preachers and their sermons. The wandering philosopher was a common figure in the ancient world. Sometimes he was a Stoic; far more often he was a Cynic. Wherever people were gathered together, you would find him there calling them to virtue. You would find him at the street corner and in the city squares; you would find him at the vast concourses which gathered for the games; you would even find him at the gladiatorial games, sometimes even directly addressing the emperor, rebuking him for luxury and tyranny, and calling him to virtue and justice. The ancient preacher, the philosopher-missionary, was a regular figure in the ancient world. There was a time when philosophy had been chiefly the concern of the schools; but now its voice and its ethical demands were to be heard daily in the public places.

These ancient sermons had certain characteristics. The method was always the same; and that method had deeply influenced Paul's presentation of the gospel, and James followed the same tradition. We will list some of the tricks of the trade of these ancient preachers, noting how they occur in James and bearing in mind the way in which Paul writes to his churches. The main aim of these ancient preachers, it must be remembered, was not to investigate new truth; it was to awaken sinners to the error of their ways and compel them to look at truths, which they knew but were deliberately neglecting or had forgotten. Their aim was to confront people with the good life in the midst of the looseness of their living and their forgetfulness of the gods.

(1) They frequently carried on imaginary conversations with imaginary opponents, speaking in what has been called a kind of 'truncated dialogue'. James also uses that method in 2:18–19 and 5:13–14.

(2) They habitually made the transition from one part of the sermon to another by way of a question which introduced the new subject. Again, James does that in 2:14 and 4:1.

(3) They were very fond of imperatives, direct orders, in which they commanded their hearers to right action and to the abandoning of their errors. In James' 108 verses, there are almost sixty imperatives.

(4) They were very fond of the rhetorical question flung out at their audience. James frequently employs such questions (cf. James 2:4–5, 2:14–16, 3:11–12, 4:4).

(5) They frequently used vivid direct addresses, known by the term 'apostrophes', to particular sections of the audience. So James speaks pointedly to the merchants out for gain and to the arrogant rich (4:13, 5:6).

(6) They were fond of personifying virtues and vices, sins and graces. So James personifies sin (1:15), mercy (2:13) and rust (5:3).

(7) They sought to awaken the interest of their audience by pictures and figures from everyday life. The figures of the

bridle, the rudder and the forest fire are standard figures in the ancient sermons (cf. James 3:3–6). Among many other illustrations, James vividly uses the picture of the farmer and his patience (5:7).

(8) They frequently used the example of famous men and women as illustrations for their moral. So James uses the examples of Abraham (2:21 3), Rahab (2:25), Job (5:11) and Elijah (5:17).

(9) It was the custom of the ancient preachers to begin their sermons with a paradox which would hold the attention of their hearers. James does that by telling his readers to consider it nothing but joy when they are involved in trials (1:2). In the same way, the ancient preachers often pointed out how true goodness meant the reversal of all popular verdicts on life. So James insists that the happiness of the rich lies in their being 'brought low' (1:10). They used the weapon of irony as James does (2:14–19, 5:1–6).

(10) The ancient preachers could speak with harshness and with sternness. So James addresses his reader as a 'senseless person' and calls those who listen to him adulterers (2:20, 4:4). The ancient preachers had sharp tongues, and so has James.

(11) The ancient preachers had certain standard ways of constructing their sermons.

(a) They often concluded a section with a vivid antithesis, a pairing of stark opposites, setting the right beside the wrong way. James follows the same custom (cf. 2:13, 2:26).

(b) They often made their point by means of a searching question fired at the hearer, and so does James (4:12).

(c) They often used quotations in their preaching. James also does this (5:20, 1:11, 1:17, 4:6, 5:11).

It is true that we do not find in James the bitterness, the scolding, the frivolous and often broad humour that the Greek preachers used; but it is plain to see that he uses all the other methods which the wandering Hellenistic preachers used in order to win their way into the minds and hearts of men and women.

2. The Jewish world also had its tradition of preaching. That preaching was done mainly by the Rabbis at the services of the synagogue. It had many of the characteristics of the preaching of the Greek wandering philosophers. It had its rhetorical questions and its imperatives and its pictures taken from life, and its quotations and its citations of the heroes of the faith. But Jewish preaching had one curious characteristic. It was deliberately disconnected. The Jewish masters instructed their pupils never to linger for any length of time on any one subject, but to move quickly from one subject to another in order to maintain the interest of listeners. Hence one of the names for preaching was *charaz*, which literally means *stringing beads*. The Jewish sermon was frequently a string of moral truths and exhortations coming one after another. This is exactly what the Letter of James is. It is difficult, if not impossible, to extract from it a continuous and coherent plan. Its sections follow each other with a certain disconnectedness. The American scholar E. J. Goodspeed writes: 'The work has been compared to a chain, each link related to the one before and the one after it. Others have compared its contents to beads on a string . . . And, perhaps, James is not so much a chain of thoughts or beads as it is a handful of pearls dropped one by one into the hearer's mind.'

James, whether looked at from the Hellenistic or from the Jewish point of view, is a good example of an ancient sermon. And here is, perhaps, the clue we need to its authorship. With all this in mind, let us now turn to ask who the author is.

The Author of James

There are five possibilities.

(1) We begin with a theory worked out in detail by the German New Testament scholar Heinrich Meyer in the early years of the twentieth century and revived by B. S. Easton in the *Interpreter's Bible*. One of the most common things in the ancient world was for books to be published in the name of some great figure of the past. Jewish literature between the Testaments is full of writings like that, ascribed to Moses, the Twelve Patriarchs, Baruch, Enoch, Isaiah and people of similar standing in order that the added authority might give greater encouragement to their readers. This was an accepted practice. One of the best-known books in the Apocrypha is the Wisdom of Solomon, in which the later sage attributes new wisdom to the wisest of the kings.

Let us remember three things about James. (a) There is nothing in it which an orthodox Jew could not accept if the two references to Jesus in 1:1 and 2:1 are removed, as they easily may be. (b) The Greek for James is in fact *Iakōbos*, which of course is the Old Testament *Jacob*. (c) The book is addressed to 'the twelve tribes in the Dispersion'. This theory holds that James is nothing other than a Jewish writing, written under the name of Jacob and meant for the Jews who were scattered throughout the world to encourage them in faith and belief amid the trials through which they might be passing in Gentile lands.

This theory is further elaborated in this way. In Genesis 49, we have Jacob's last address to his sons. The address consists of a series of short descriptions in which each son is in turn characterized. Meyer professed to be able to find in James allusions to the descriptions of each of the patriarchs and, therefore, of each of the twelve tribes, in Jacob's address. Here are some of his identifications.

Asher is the worldly rich man; James 1:9–11; Genesis 49:20.

Issachar is the doer of good deeds; James 1:12; Genesis 49:14–15.

Reuben is the first fruits; James 1:18; Genesis 49:3.

Simeon stands for anger; James 1:19–20; Genesis 49:5–7.

Levi is the tribe which is specially connected with religion and is alluded to in James 1:26–7.

Naphtali is characterized by peace; James 3:18; Genesis 49:21.

Gad stands for wars and fightings; James 4:1–2; Genesis 49:19.

Dan represents waiting for salvation; James 5:7; Genesis 49:18.

Joseph represents prayer; James 5:13–18; Genesis 49:22–6.

Benjamin stands for birth and death; James 5:20; Genesis 49:27.

That is a most ingenious theory. No one can either finally prove it or disprove it, and it certainly would explain in the most natural way the reference in 1:1 to the twelve tribes in the Dispersion, the tribes scattered abroad. It would hold that some Christian came upon this Jewish tract, written under the name of Jacob to all the exiled Jews, and was so impressed with its moral worth that he made certain adjustments and additions to it and issued it as a Christian book. There is no doubt that this is an attractive theory – but it is possible for a theory to be too ingenious.

(2) Just as the Jews did, the Christians also wrote many books under the names of the great figures of the Christian faith. There are gospels issued under the name of Peter and Thomas and James himself; there is a letter under the name of Barnabas; there are gospels of Nicodemus and

Bartholomew; and there are Acts of John, Paul, Andrew, Peter, Thomas, Philip and others. The technical title for these books is *pseudonymous*, that is, written under a *false name*.

It has been suggested that James was a letter written by someone else under the name of the Lord's brother. That is apparently what Jerome thought when he said that this letter 'was issued by someone under James' name'. But, whatever else this work is, it cannot be that – because, whenever such a book was written, the author was careful to make quite clear who was supposed to have written it. If this had been pseudonymous, no possible doubt would have been left that the author was supposed to be James *the brother of our Lord*; but this fact is not mentioned at all.

(3) The New Testament scholar James Moffatt inclined to the theory that the writer was not the brother of our Lord, or any other well-known James, but simply a teacher called James of whose life and story we have no information whatever. That is by no means impossible, for the name James was just as common then as it is now; but it would be rather difficult to understand how such a book gained entry into the New Testament, and how it came to be connected with the name of the Lord's brother.

(4) The traditional view is that the book was written by James, the Lord's brother. We have already seen that it seems strange that such a book should have only two incidental references to Jesus, and none at all to the resurrection or to Jesus as the Messiah. A further and most serious difficulty is this. The book is written in good Greek. In his commentary, J. H. Ropes says that Greek must have been the native language of the man who wrote it; and J. B. Mayor, himself one of the greatest of Greek scholars, says: 'I should be inclined to rate the Greek of this epistle as approaching more nearly to the standard of classical purity than that of any other

book in the New Testament with the exception perhaps of the Epistle to the Hebrews.' Quite certainly, James' native language was Aramaic and not Greek, and quite certainly he would not be an expert in classical Greek. His orthodox Jewish upbringing would make him despise and avoid it as a hated Gentile language. It is next to impossible to think of James actually writing this letter.

(5) So we come to the fifth possibility. Let us remember how closely the Letter of James resembles a sermon. It is possible that this is, in substance, a sermon preached by James, taken down by someone else, translated into Greek, added to and decorated a little and then issued to the wider church so that everyone could benefit from it. That explains its form and how it came to be attached to the name of James. It even explains the scarcity of the references to Jesus, to the resurrection and to the messiahship of Jesus – for, in one single sermon, James could not go through the whole range of orthodoxy and is, in fact, pressing moral duty upon men and women, and not talking about theology. It seems to us that this is the one theory that explains the facts.

One thing is certain – we may approach this little letter feeling that it is one of the lesser books of the New Testament; but, if we study it faithfully, we will lay it down thanking God that it was preserved for our instruction and inspiration.

JAMES

GREETINGS

James 1:1

> James, the slave of God and of the Lord Jesus Christ,
> sends greetings to the twelve tribes who are scattered
> throughout the world

AT the very beginning of his letter, James describes himself
by the title in which lies his only honour and his only glory,
the slave of God and of the Lord Jesus Christ. With the
exception of Jude, he is the only New Testament writer to
describe himself by that term (*doulos*) without any qualification. Paul describes himself as the slave of Jesus Christ
and his apostle (cf. Romans 1:1; Philippians 1:1). But James
will go no further than to call himself the slave of God and of
the Lord Jesus Christ. There are at least four implications in
this title.

(1) It implies *absolute obedience*. Slaves know no law
but their master's word; they have no rights of their own;
they are the absolute possessions of their master; and they
are bound to give their master unquestioning obedience.

(2) It implies *absolute humility*. It is the word of someone
who thinks not of privileges but of duties, not of rights but of
obligations. It is the word of someone who has lost all sense
of self in the service of God.

(3) It implies *absolute loyalty*. It is the word of someone who has no self-interest, because whatever is done is done for God. Personal gain and preference do not enter into the calculations; all loyalty is to God.

(4) Yet, at the back of it, this word implies a certain *pride*. Far from being a title of dishonour, it was the title by which the greatest ones of the Old Testament were known. Moses was the *doulos* of God (1 Kings 8:53; Daniel 9:11; Malachi 4:4); so were Joshua and Caleb (Joshua 24:29; Numbers 14:24); so were the great patriarchs, Abraham, Isaac and Jacob (Deuteronomy 9:27); so was Job (Job 1:8); so was Isaiah (Isaiah 20:3); and *doulos* is distinctively the title by which the prophets were known (Amos 3:7; Zechariah 1:6; Jeremiah 7:25). By taking the title *doulos*, James sets himself in the great succession of those who found their freedom and their peace and their glory in perfect submission to the will of God. The only greatness to which the Christian can ever aspire is that of being the slave of God.

There is one unusual thing about this opening salutation. James sends greetings to his readers, using the word *chairein*, which is the regular opening word of salutation in secular Greek letters. Paul never uses it. He always uses the distinctively Christian greeting, 'Grace and peace' (Romans 1:7; 1 Corinthians 1:3; 2 Corinthians 1:2; Galatians 1:3; Ephesians 1:2; Philippians 1:2; Colossians 1:2; 1 Thessalonians 1:1; 2 Thessalonians 1:2; Philemon 3). This secular greeting occurs only twice in the rest of the New Testament, in the letter which Claudius Lysias, the Roman officer, wrote to Felix to ensure the safe journeying of Paul (Acts 23:26), and in the general letter issued after the decision of the Council of Jerusalem to allow the Gentiles into the Church (Acts 15:23). This is interesting, because it was James who presided over that Council (Acts 15:13). It may be that he used the most general greeting that he could find because his letter was going out to the widest public.

THE JEWS THROUGHOUT THE WORLD

James 1:1 (*contd*)

THE letter is addressed to *the twelve tribes who are scattered abroad*. Literally, the greeting is to the twelve tribes in the *Diaspora*, the technical word for the Jews who lived outside Palestine. All the millions of Jews who were, for one reason or another, outside the promised land were the Diaspora. This dispersal of the Jews throughout the world was of the very greatest importance for the spread of Christianity, because it meant that all over the world there were synagogues, from which the Christian preachers could make a beginning, and it meant that all over the world there were groups of men and women who themselves already knew the Old Testament and who had persuaded others among the Gentiles at least to be interested in their faith. Let us see how this dispersal took place.

Sometimes – and the process began in this way – the Jews were forcibly taken out of their own land and compelled to live as exiles in foreign lands. There were three such great movements.

(1) The first compulsory removal came when the people of the Northern Kingdom, who had their capital in Samaria, were conquered by the Assyrians and were carried away into captivity in Assyria (2 Kings 17:23; 1 Chronicles 5:26). These are the lost ten tribes who never returned. The Jews themselves believed that at the end of all things all Jews would be gathered together in Jerusalem, but until the end of the world these ten tribes, they believed, would never return. They

founded this belief on a rather fanciful interpretation of an Old Testament text. The Rabbis argued like this: 'The ten tribes never return for it is said of them, "He will cast them into another land, as at this day" (Deuteronomy 29:28). As then this day departs and never returns, so too are they to depart and never return. As this day becomes dark, and then again light, so too will it one day be light again for the ten tribes for whom it was dark.'

(2) The second compulsory removal was in about 580 BC. At that time, the Babylonians conquered the Southern Kingdom whose capital was at Jerusalem, and carried the 'elite of the land' away to Babylon (2 Kings 24:14–16; Psalm 137). In Babylon, the Jews behaved very differently; they stubbornly refused to be assimilated and to lose their national identity. They were said to be congregated mainly in the cities of Nehardea and Nisibis. It was actually in Babylon that Jewish scholarship flourished and produced the Babylonian Talmud, the immense sixty-volume exposition of the Jewish law. When the Jewish historian Josephus wrote his *Jewish Wars*, the first edition was not in Greek but in Aramaic, and was designed for the scholarly Jews in Babylon. He tells us that the Jews rose to such power there that at one time the province of Mesopotamia was under Jewish rule. Its two Jewish rulers were Asidaeus and Anilaeus, and on the death of Anilaeus it was said that no fewer than 50,000 Jews were massacred.

(3) The third compulsory transportation took place much later. When Pompey conquered the Jews and took Jerusalem in 63 BC, he took many Jews back to Rome as slaves. Their determination to stick rigidly to their own ceremonial law and their stubborn observance of the Sabbath made them difficult slaves, and most of them were freed. They took up residence in a kind of quarter of their own on the far side of

the Tiber. Before long, they were to be found flourishing all over the city. The Roman historian Dio Cassius says of them: 'They were often suppressed, but they nevertheless mightily increased, so that they achieved even the free exercise of their customs.' Julius Caesar was their great protector, and we read of them mourning all night long at his coffin. We read of them present in large numbers when Cicero, the Roman senator and orator, was defending Flaccus. In AD 19, the whole Jewish community was banished from Rome on the charge that they had robbed a wealthy female convert on pretence of sending the money to the Temple, and at that time 4,000 of them were conscripted to fight against the brigands in Sardinia; but they were soon received back. When the Jews of Palestine sent their deputation to Rome to complain of the rule of Archelaus, we read that the deputation was joined by 8,000 Jews resident in the city. Roman literature is full of contemptuous references to the Jews, for anti-semitism is no new thing, and the very number of the references is proof of the part that the Jews played in the life of the city.

Compulsory transportation took the Jews by the thousand to Babylon and to Rome. But far greater numbers left Palestine of their own free will for more comfortable and more profitable lands. Two lands in particular received thousands of Jews. Palestine was sandwiched between the two great powers, Syria and Egypt, and was therefore liable at any time to become a battle ground. For that reason, many Jews left it to take up residence either in Egypt or in Syria.

During the time of Nebuchadnezzar, there was a voluntary exodus of many Jews to Egypt (2 Kings 25:26). As far back as 650 BC, the Egyptian king Psammetichus was said to have had Jewish mercenaries in his armies. When Alexander the Great founded Alexandria, special privileges were offered to settlers there, and the Jews came in large numbers. Alexandria was divided into five administrative sections, and two of them were inhabited by Jews. In Alexandria alone, there were more than 1,000,000 Jews. The settlement of the Jews in Egypt went so far that in about 50 BC a temple, modelled on the Jerusalem one, was built at Leontopolis for the Egyptian Jews.

The Jews also went to Syria. The highest concentration was in Antioch, where the gospel was first preached to the Gentiles and where the followers of Jesus were first called Christians. In Damascus, we read of 10,000 of them being massacred at one time.

So, Egypt and Syria had very large Jewish populations. But they had spread far beyond that. In Cyrene in North Africa, we read that the population was divided into citizens, agriculturists, resident aliens and Jews. The German historian Theodor Mommsen, who wrote a history of Rome, writes: 'The inhabitants of Palestine were only a portion, and not the most important portion, of the Jews; the Jewish communities of Babylonia, Syria, Asia Minor and Egypt were far superior to those of Palestine.' That mention of Asia Minor leads us to another sphere in which the Jews were numerous. When Alexander's empire broke up on his death, Egypt fell to the Ptolemies, and Syria and the surrounding districts fell to Seleucus and his successors, known as the Seleucids. The Seleucids had two notable characteristics. They followed a deliberate policy of joining populations together into one, hoping to gain security by banishing national identity. And they founded a large number of cities. These cities needed citizens, and special attractions and privileges were offered to those who would settle in them. The Jews accepted citizenship of these cities by the thousand. All over Asia Minor, in the cities of the Mediterranean sea coast, in the great commercial centres, Jews were numerous and prosperous. There were also compulsory transportations. Antiochus the Great took 2,000 Jewish families from Babylon and settled them in Lydia and Phrygia. In fact, so great was the drift from Palestine that the Jews of Palestine complained against those who left the hardships of Palestine for the baths and feasts of Asia and Phrygia, and Aristotle tells of meeting a Jew in Asia Minor who was 'not only Greek in his language but in his very soul'.

It is quite clear that everywhere in the world there were Jews. Strabo, the Greek geographer, writes: 'It is hard to find a spot in the whole world which is not occupied and dominated by Jews.' Josephus, the Jewish historian, writes: 'There is no city, no tribe, whether Greek or barbarian, in which Jewish law and Jewish customs have not taken root.' The Sibylline Oracles, written around 140 BC, say that every land and every sea is filled with the Jews. There is a letter, said to be from Agrippa to Caligula, which the Jewish writer Philo quotes. In it, he says that Jerusalem is the capital not only of Judaea but of most countries by reason of the colonies it has sent out on fitting occasions into the neighbouring lands of Egypt, Phoenicia, Syria, Coelesyria, and the still more remote Pamphylia and Cilicia, into most parts of Asia as far as Bithynia, and into the most distant corners of Pontus, also to Europe, Thessaly, Boeotia, Macedonia, Aetolia, Attica, Argos, Corinth, and the most and best parts of the Peloponnese. And not only is the continent full of Jewish settlements, but also the more important islands – Euboea, Cyprus, Crete – to say nothing of the lands beyond the Euphrates, for all have Jewish inhabitants.

The Jewish Diaspora extended to the farthest limits of the world, and there was no greater factor in the spread of Christianity.

THE RECIPIENTS OF THE LETTER

James I:I (*contd*)

JAMES writes to the *twelve tribes in the Diaspora*. Who has he in mind as he writes? *The twelve tribes in the Diaspora* has three equally valid possible meanings.

(1) It could stand for all the Jews outside Palestine. We have seen that they were numbered by the million. There were actually far more Jews scattered throughout Syria and Egypt and Greece and Rome and Asia Minor and all the Mediterranean lands and far-off Babylon than there were in Palestine. Under the conditions of the ancient world, it would be quite impossible to send out a message to such a huge and scattered constituency.

(2) It could mean Christian Jews outside Palestine. In this instance, it would mean the Jews in the lands closely surrounding Palestine, perhaps particularly those in Syria and in Babylon. Certainly, if anyone was going to write a letter to these Jews, it would be James, for he was the acknowledged leader of Jewish Christianity.

(3) The phrase could have a third meaning. To the Christians, the Christian Church was the real Israel. At the end of Galatians, Paul sends his blessing to the *Israel of God* (Galatians 6:16). The nation of Israel had been the specially chosen people of God; but they had refused to accept their place and their responsibility and their task. When the Son of God came, they had rejected him. Therefore all the privileges which had once belonged to them passed over to the Christian Church, for it was in truth the chosen people of God. Paul (cf. Romans 9:7–8) had fully worked out the idea. It was his conviction that the true descendants of Abraham were not those who could trace their physical descent from him but those who had made the same venture

of faith as he had made. The true Israel was composed not of any particular nation or race but of those who accepted Jesus Christ in faith. So, this phrase may well mean the *wider Christian Church*.

We may choose between the second and the third meanings, each of which gives excellent sense. James may be writing to the Christian Jews scattered throughout the surrounding nations, or he may be writing to the new Israel, the Christian Church.

TESTED AND TRIUMPHANT

James 1:2-4

> My brothers, reckon it all joy whenever you become involved in all kinds of testings, for you are well aware that the testing of your faith produces unswerving constancy. And let constancy go on to work out its perfect work that you may be perfect and complete, deficient in nothing.

JAMES never suggested to his readers that Christianity would be for them an easy way. He warns them that they will find themselves involved in what the Authorized Version calls *divers temptations*. The word translated as *temptations* is *peirasmos*, whose meaning we must understand fully if we are to see the very essence of the Christian life.

Peirasmos is not *temptation* in our sense of the term; it is *testing* (*trial* in the Revised Standard Version). *Peirasmos* is trial or testing *directed towards an end*, and the end is that anyone who is tested should emerge stronger and purer from the experience. The corresponding verb *peirazein*, which the Authorized Version usually translates as *to tempt*, has the same meaning. The idea is not that of enticement into sin but of strengthening and purifying. For instance, a young bird is said to test (*peirazein*) its wings. The Queen of Sheba was said to come to test (*peirazein*) the wisdom of Solomon (1 Kings 10:1). God was said to test (*peirazein*) Abraham, when he appeared to be demanding the sacrifice of Isaac (Genesis 22:1). When Israel came into the promised land, God did not remove the people who were already there. He left them so that Israel might be tested (*peirazein*) in the struggle against them (Judges 2:22, 3:1, 3:4). The experiences in Israel were tests which contributed to the making of the people of Israel (Deuteronomy 4:34, 7:19).

Here is a great and uplifting thought. F. J. A. Hort, the New Testament scholar, writes: 'The Christian must expect to be jostled by trials on the Christian way.' All kinds of experiences will come to us. There will be the test of the sorrows and the disappointments which seek to take our faith away. There will be the test of the seductions which seek to lure us from the right way. There will be the tests of the dangers, the sacrifices and the unpopularity which are so much a part of the Christian way. But they are not meant to make us fall; they are meant to make us soar. They are not meant to defeat us; they are meant to be defeated. They are not meant to make us weaker; they are meant to make us stronger. Therefore we should not complain about them; we should rejoice in them. Christians are like athletes. The heavier the course of training they undergo, the more they are glad, because they know that it is preparing them all the better for victorious effort. As Robert Browning said in 'Rabbi Ben Ezra', we must 'welcome each rebuff that turns earth's smoothness rough', for every difficult experience is another step on the upward way.

THE RESULT OF TESTING

James 1:2–4 (*contd*)

JAMES describes this process of testing by the word *dokimion*. It is an interesting word. It is the word for *sterling coinage*, for money which is genuine and absolutely pure. The aim of testing is to purge us of all impurity.

If we meet this testing in the right way, it will produce *unswerving constancy* (or *steadfastness* as the Revised Standard Version translates it). The word is *hupomonē*, which the Authorized Version translates as *patience* – but patience is far too passive. *Hupomonē* is not simply the ability to bear things; it is the ability to turn them to greatness and to glory. The thing which amazed the non-Christians in the centuries of Christian persecution was that the martyrs did not die grimly, they died singing. One smiled in the flames; they asked him what he found to smile at there. 'I saw the glory of God,' he said, 'and was glad.' *Hupomonē* is the quality which makes people able not simply to suffer things but to overcome them. The effect of testing borne in the right way is strength to bear still more and to conquer in still harder battles.

This unswerving constancy in the end makes those who are tested three things.

(1) It makes them *perfect*. The Greek is *teleios*, which usually has the meaning of *perfection towards a given end*. A sacrificial animal is *teleios* if it is fit to offer to God. A scholar is *teleios* if he or she is mature. A person who is fully grown is *teleios*. This constancy, which comes from a positive response to testing, makes each one of us *teleios* in the sense of being fit for the task we were sent into the world to do. Here is a great thought. By the way in which we meet every experience in life, we are making ourselves either fit or unfit for the task which God meant us to do.

(2) It makes them *complete*. The Greek is *holoklēros*, which means *entire, perfect in every part*. It is used of the animal which is fit to be offered to God and of the priest who is fit to serve him. It means that the animal or the person has no disfiguring and disqualifying blemishes. Gradually, this unswerving constancy removes the weaknesses and the imperfections from a person's character. Daily, it enables us to conquer old sins, to shed old blemishes and to gain new virtues, until in the end we become entirely fit for the service of God and of one another.

(3) It makes them *deficient in nothing*. The Greek is *leipesthai*, and it is used of the defeat of an army, of the giving up of a struggle, of the failure to reach a standard that should have been reached. If we meet our testing in the right way, if day by day we develop this unswerving constancy, day by day we will live more victoriously and reach nearer to the standard of Jesus Christ himself.

GOD'S GIVING AND OUR ASKING

James 1:5–8

> If any of you is deficient in wisdom, let him ask it from God, who gives generously to all men and never casts up the gift, and it will be given to him. Let him ask in faith, with no doubts in his mind; for he who oscillates between doubts is like a surge of the sea, wind-driven and blown hither and thither. Let not that man think that he will receive anything from the Lord, a man with a divided mind, inconstant in all his ways.

THERE is a close connection between this passage and what has gone before. James has just told his readers that, if they use all the testing experiences of life in the right way, they will emerge from them with that unswerving constancy which is the basis of all the virtues. But immediately the question arises: 'Where can I find the wisdom and the understanding to use these testing experiences in the right way?' James' answer is: 'If you feel that you do not have the wisdom to use aright the experiences of this life – and no one truly possesses that wisdom   request it from God.'

Once thing stands out. For James, the Christian teacher with the Jewish background, wisdom is entirely practical. It is not philosophic speculation and intellectual knowledge; it is concerned with the business of living. The Stoics defined wisdom as 'knowledge of things human and divine'. But, in his commentary, J. H. Ropes defines this Christian wisdom as 'the supreme and divine quality of the soul whereby man knows and practises righteousness'. F. J. A. Hort defines it as 'that endowment of heart and mind which is needed for the right conduct of life'. In the Christian wisdom there is, of course, knowledge of the deep things of God, but it is essentially practical; it is such knowledge turned into action in the decisions and personal relationships of everyday life. When we ask God for that wisdom, we must remember two things.

(1) We must remember *how* God *gives*. He gives generously and never calculates the gift. 'All wisdom', said Jesus the son of Sirach, 'is from the Lord, and is with him forever' (Sirach [Ecclesiasticus] 1:1). But the Jewish wise men were well aware how the best gift in the world could be spoiled by the manner of the giving. They have much to say about how the fool gives. 'My child, do not mix reproach with your good deeds, or spoil your gift with harsh words . . . Indeed, does not a word surpass a good gift? Both are to be found in a gracious person. A fool is ungracious and abusive, and a gift of a grudging giver makes the eyes dim' (Sirach 18:15–18).

'A fool's gift will profit you nothing, for he looks for recompense sevenfold. He gives little, and upbraids much; he opens his mouth like a town crier. Today he lends, and tomorrow he asks it back; such a one is hateful to God and humans' (Sirach 20:14–15). The same writer warns against 'abusive words before friends' (Sirach 41:22). There is a kind of giver who gives only with a view to getting more than is given; such people give only to gratify their vanity and their sense of power by putting recipients under an obligation which they will never be allowed to forget; they give and then continuously calculate the value of the gift that they have given. But God gives with generosity. Philemon, the Greek poet, called God 'the lover of gifts', not in the sense of loving to receive gifts, but in the sense of loving to give them. Nor does God calculate the value of his gifts; he gives with all the splendour of his love, because it is his nature to give.

(2) We must remember *how the asker must ask*. We must ask without doubts. We must be sure of both the power and the desire of God to give. If we ask in doubt, our minds are like the broken water of the sea, driven hither and thither by any chance wind. J. B. Mayor describes the one who doubts as being like a cork carried by the waves, now near the shore, now far away. Such a person is unstable. Hort suggests that the picture is of someone who is drunk, staggering from side to side on the road and getting nowhere. James says vividly that such a person is *dipsuchos*, which literally means someone with two souls, or two minds. One believes, the other disbelieves, and the individual is a walking civil war in which trust and distrust of God wage a continual battle against each other.

If we are to use aright the experiences of life to develop a sterling character, we must ask for wisdom from God. And when we ask, we must remember the absolute generosity of

God and see to it that we ask believing that we shall receive
what God knows it is good and right for us to have.

AS EACH INDIVIDUAL NEEDS

James 1:9–11

> Let the lowly brother be proud of his exaltation; and let
> the rich brother be proud of his humiliation; for he will
> pass away like a flower of the field. The sun rises with
> the scorching wind and withers the grass, and the flower
> wilts, and the beauty of its form is destroyed. So the
> rich will wither away in all his ways.

As James saw it, Christianity brings to every individual what
he or she needs. As J. B. Mayor put it, 'As the despised poor
learns self-respect, so the proud rich learns self-abasement.'

(1) Christianity brings to the poor a new sense of their
own value. (a) They learn that they matter *in the Church*. In
the early Church, there were no class distinctions. It could
happen that the slave was the minister of the congregation,
preaching and dispensing the sacrament, while the master
was no more than a humble member. In the Church, the social
distinctions of the world are obliterated, and no individual
matters more than any other. (b) They learn that they matter
in the world. It is the teaching of Christianity that everyone
in this world has a task to do. Everyone is of use to God –
and, even if someone is confined to a bed of pain, the power
of that person's prayers can still act on the world. (c) They
learn that they matter *to God*. As Muretus the wandering
scholar said long ago, 'Call no man worthless for whom Christ
died.'

(2) Christianity brings to the rich a new sense of self-
abasement. The great peril of riches is that they tend to give

people a false sense of security. They feel that they are safe; they feel that they have the resources to cope with anything and to buy themselves out of any situation they may wish to avoid.

James draws a vivid picture, very familiar to the people of Palestine. In the desert places, if there is a shower of rain, the thin green shoots of grass will sprout, but one day's burning sunshine will make them vanish as if they had never been. The *scorching heat* is the *kausōn*. The *kausōn* was the south-east wind, the Simoon. It came straight from the deserts and burst on Palestine like a blast of hot air when an oven door is opened. In an hour, it could wipe out all vegetation.

This is a picture of what a life dependent on riches can be like. Those who put their trust in riches are trusting in things which the chances and changes of life can take from them at any moment. Life itself is uncertain. At the back of James' mind, there is Isaiah's picture: 'All people are grass, their constancy is like the flower of the field. The grass withers, the flower fades, when the breath of the Lord blows upon it; surely the people are grass' (Isaiah 40:6–7; cf. Psalm 103:15).

James' point is this. If life is so uncertain and human beings so vulnerable, calamity and disaster may come at any moment. Since that is so, people are fools to put all their trust in things – like wealth – which they may lose at any moment. They are only wise if they put their trust in things which they cannot lose.

So, James urges the rich to cease to put their trust in the things that their own power can amass. He urges them to admit their essential human helplessness and humbly to put their trust in God, who alone can give the things which abide forever.

THE CROWN OF LIFE

James 1:12

> Happy is the man who meets trial with steadfast constancy because, when he has shown himself of sterling worth, he will receive the crown of life which he has promised to those who love him.

To those who meet trials in the right way, there is joy here and hereafter.

(1) In this life, they become men and women of sterling worth. The word used is *dokimos*. They are like metal which is cleansed of all alloy. The weaknesses of character are eradicated; and they emerge strong and pure.

(2) In the life to come, they receive *the crown of life*. There is far more than one idea here. In the ancient world, the crown (*stephanos*) had at least four great associations.

(a) The crown of flowers was worn at times of joy, at weddings and at feasts (cf. Isaiah 28:1–2; Song of Solomon 3:11). The crown was the sign of festive joy.

(b) The crown was the mark of royalty. It was worn by kings and by those in authority. Sometimes this was the crown of gold; sometimes it was the linen strip, or head-band, worn around the brow (cf. Psalm 21:3; Jeremiah 13:18).

(c) The crown of laurel leaves was the victor's crown in the games, the prize which athletes coveted above all (cf. 2 Timothy 4:8).

(d) The crown was the mark of honour and of dignity. The instructions of parents can bring a crown of grace to those who listen to them (Proverbs 1:9); wisdom provides a crown of glory (Proverbs 4:9); in a time of disaster and dishonour, it can be said: 'The crown has fallen from our head' (Lamentations 5:16).

We do not need to choose between these meanings. They are all included. Christians have a *joy* that others can never have. Life for them is like always being at a feast. They have a *royalty* that others have never achieved, for, however humble their earthly circumstances, they are the children of God. They have a *victory* which others cannot win, for they meet life and all its demands in the conquering power of the presence of Jesus Christ. They have a new *dignity*, for they are always conscious that God considered them worth the life and death of Jesus Christ.

What is the crown? It is the *crown of life*, and that phrase means that it is *the crown which consists of life*. The Christian crown is a new kind of living which is life indeed; through Jesus Christ, Christians have entered into a life that is more abundant.

James says that if Christians meet the testings of life in the steadfast constancy which Christ can give, life becomes infinitely more splendid than ever it was before. The struggle is the way to glory, and the very struggle itself is a glory.

PUTTING THE BLAME ON GOD

James 1:13–15

> Let no man say when he is tempted: 'My temptation comes from God.' For God himself is untemptable by evil and tempts no man. But temptation comes to every man, because he is lured on and seduced by his own desire; then desire conceives and begets sin; and, when sin has reached its full development, it spawns death.

BEHIND this passage lies a Jewish way of belief to which all of us are to some extent prone. James is here rebuking those who put the blame for temptation on God.

Jewish thought was haunted by the internal conflict that is in every individual. It was the problem which haunted Paul: 'I delight in the law of God in my inmost self, but I see in my members another law at war with the law of my mind, making me captive to the law of sin that dwells in my members' (Romans 7:22–3). Every man and every woman was pulled in two directions. Purely as an interpretation of experience, the Jews arrived at the doctrine that in every individual there were two tendencies. They called them the *Yetser Hatob, the good tendency*, and the *Yetser Hara, the evil tendency*. This simply stated the problem; it did not explain it. In particular, it did not say where the evil tendency came from. So Jewish thought set out to try to explain that.

Ben Sirach, the writer of Ecclesiasticus, was deeply impressed with the havoc that the evil tendency causes. 'O inclination to evil [*Yetser Hara*], why were you formed to cover the land with deceit?' (Sirach [Ecclesiasticus] 37:3). In his view, the inclination to evil came from Satan, and the defence against it was an individual's own will. 'It was he [God] who created humankind in the beginning, and he left them in the power of their own free choice. If you choose, you can keep the commandments, and to act faithfully is a matter of your own choice' (Sirach 15:14–15).

There were Jewish writers who traced this evil tendency right back to the Garden of Eden. The story is told in the apocryphal work *The Life of Adam and Eve* that Satan took the form of an angel and, speaking through the serpent, put into Eve the desire for the forbidden fruit and made her swear that she would give the fruit to Adam as well. 'When he had made me swear,' says Eve, 'he ascended up into the tree. But in the fruit he gave me to eat *he placed the poison of his malice*, that is, of his lust. For lust is the beginning of all sin.

57

And he bent down the bough to the earth, and I took of the fruit and ate it.' In this view, it was Satan who succeeded in inserting the evil tendency into human beings, and that evil tendency is identified with physical lust. A later development of this story was that the beginning of all sin was in fact Satan's lust for Eve.

The Book of Enoch has two theories. One is that the fallen angels are responsible for sin (1 Enoch 85). The other is that human beings themselves are responsible for it. 'Sin has not been sent upon the earth, but man himself created it' (1 Enoch 98:4).

But every one of these theories simply pushes the problem one step further back. Satan may have put the evil tendency into men and women; the fallen angels may have put it into them; men and women may have put it into themselves. But where did it *ultimately* come from?

To meet this problem, certain of the Rabbis took a bold and dangerous step. They argued that, since God has created everything, he must have created the evil tendency also. So we get Rabbinic sayings such as the following. 'God said, It repents me that I created the evil tendency in man; for had I not done so, he would not have rebelled against me. I created the evil tendency; I created the law as a means of healing. If you occupy yourself with the law, you will not fall into the power of it. God placed the good tendency on a man's right hand, and the evil on his left.' The danger is obvious. It means that in the last analysis we can blame God for our own sin. We can say, as Paul said: 'It is no longer I that do it, but sin that dwells within me' (Romans 7:17). Of all strange doctrines, surely the strangest is that God is ultimately responsible for sin.

AVOIDING RESPONSIBILITY

James 1:13–15 (*contd*)

FROM the beginning of time, it has been a human instinct to blame others for our own sin. The ancient writer who wrote the story of the first sin in the Garden of Eden was a first-rate psychologist with a deep knowledge of the human heart. When God challenged Adam with his sin, Adam's reply was: 'The woman whom you gave to be with me, she gave me fruit from the tree, and I ate.' And when God challenged Eve with her action, her answer was: 'The serpent tempted me, and I ate.' Adam said: 'Don't blame me; blame Eve.' Eve said: 'Don't blame me; blame the serpent' (cf. Genesis 3:12–13).

Human beings have always been experts in evasion. Robert Burns wrote in 'A Prayer in the Prospect of Death':

> Thou know'st that Thou hast formed me
> With passions wild and strong;
> And list'ning to their witching voice
> Has often led me wrong.

In effect, he is saying that his conduct was as it was because God made him as he was. The blame is laid on God. So we blame one another, we blame our circumstances, we blame the way in which we are made, for the sins of which we are guilty.

James sternly rebukes that view. To him, what is responsible for sin is a person's own evil desire. Sin would be helpless if there was nothing in human beings to which it could appeal. Desire is something which can be nourished or stifled. It can be controlled and even, by the grace of God, eliminated if dealt with it at once. But people can allow their thoughts to follow certain tracks, and their steps to take them into certain

59

places and their eyes to linger on certain things, and so stimulate desire. They can so hand themselves over to Christ and be so engaged on good things that there is no time or place left for evil desire. It is idle hands for which Satan finds mischief to do; it is undisciplined minds and uncommitted hearts that are vulnerable. If someone encourages desire for long enough, there is an inevitable consequence. Desire becomes action.

Further, it was the Jewish teaching that sin produced death. *The Life of Adam and Eve* says that the moment Eve ate of the fruit she caught a glimpse of death. The word which James uses in verse 15, and which the Authorized and the Revised Standard Versions translate as *brings forth* death, is an animal word for birth; and it means that sin *spawns* death. Overcome by desire, human beings become less than human and sink to the level of animals.

The great value of this passage is that it urges upon us a personal responsibility for sin. No one was ever born without desire for some wrong thing. And, if we deliberately encourage and nourish that desire until it becomes fully grown and monstrously strong, it will inevitably result in the action which is sin – and that is the way to death. Such a thought – and all human experience admits it to be true – must drive us to the grace of God, which is the only thing that can make and keep us clean, and which is available to all.

GOD'S CONSTANCY FOR GOOD

James 1:16–18

> My dear brothers, do not be deceived. Every good gift and every perfect boon comes down from the Father of lights, with whom there is none of that changeableness

which comes from changing shadows. Of his own
purpose he has begotten us by the word of truth so that
we might be, as it were, the first fruits of his created
things.

ONCE again, James stresses the great truth that every gift that
God sends is good. Verse 17 might well be translated: 'All
giving is good.' That is to say, there is nothing which comes
from God which is not good. There is a strange phenomenon
here in the Greek. The phrase which we have translated as
'Every good gift and every perfect boon' is, in fact, a perfect
hexameter line of poetry – that is, a line with six stresses in
it. Either James had a rhythmic ear for a fine cadence or he is
quoting from some work that we do not know.

What he is stressing is the unchangeableness of God. To
do so, he uses two terms from astronomy. The word he uses
for changeableness is *parallagē*, and the word for the turn of
the shadow is *tropē*. Both these words have to do with the
variation which the heavenly bodies show, the variation in
the length of the day and of the night, the apparent variation
in the course of the sun, the phases of waxing and waning,
the different brilliance of the stars and the planets at different
times. Variability is characteristic of all created things. God
is the creator of the lights of heaven – the sun, the moon, the
stars. The Jewish morning prayer says: 'Blessed be the Lord
God who has formed the lights.' The lights change, but the
one who created them never changes.

Further, his purpose is altogether gracious. *The word of
truth* is the gospel, and by the sending of that gospel it is
God's purpose that men and women should be reborn into a
new life. The shadows are ended and the certain word of
truth has come.

That rebirth is a rebirth into the family and the possession
of God. In the ancient world, it was the law that all first fruits

were sacred to God. They were offered in grateful sacrifice to God because they belonged to him. So, when we are reborn by the true word of the gospel, we become the property of God, just as the first fruits of the harvest did.

James insists that, far from ever proving a temptation, God's gifts are invariably good. In all the chances and changes of a changing world, they never vary. And God's supreme object is to re-create life through the truth of the gospel, so that all people should know that they belong by right to him.

WHEN TO BE QUICK AND WHEN TO BE SLOW

James 1:19–20

> All this, my dear brothers, you already know. Let every man be quick to hear, slow to speak, slow to anger; for the anger of man does not produce the righteousness which God desires.

THERE are few among the wise who have not been impressed by the dangers of being too quick to speak and too unwilling to listen. A most interesting list could be compiled of the things in which it is best to be quick and the things in which it is best to be slow. In the Sayings of the Jewish Fathers, we read: 'There are four characters in scholars. Quick to hear and quick to forget; his gain is cancelled by his loss. Slow to hear and slow to forget; his loss is cancelled by his gain. Quick to hear and slow to forget; he is wise. Slow to hear and quick to forget; this is an evil lot.' The Roman poet Ovid encourages people to be slow to punish, but swift to reward. The Jewish writer Philo tells them to be swift to benefit others and slow to harm them.

In particular, the wise teachers were impressed by the necessity of being slow to speak. Rabbi Simeon said: 'All my days I have grown up among the wise, and have not found aught good for a man but silence . . . Whoso multiplies words occasions sin.' Jesus, the son of Sirach, writes: 'Be quick to hear, but deliberate in answering. If you know what to say, answer your neighbour; but if not, put your hand over your mouth' (Sirach 5:11–12). Proverbs is full of the perils of speech which is too hasty. 'When words are many, transgression is not lacking, but the prudent are restrained in speech' (Proverbs 10:19). 'Those who guard their mouths preserve their lives; those who open wide their lips come to ruin' (Proverbs 13:3). 'Even fools who keep silent are considered wise' (Proverbs 17:28). 'Do you see someone who is hasty in speech? There is more hope for a fool than for anyone like that' (Proverbs 29:20).

The scholar F. J. A. Hort says that those who are really good will be much more anxious to listen to God than arrogantly, loudly and stridently to shout their own opinions. The classical writers had the same idea. Zeno of Elea said: 'We have two ears but only one mouth, that we may hear more and speak less.' When the Cynic philosopher Demonax was asked how anyone might rule best, he answered: 'Without anger, speaking little, and listening much.' One of the earliest philosophers of ancient Greece, Bias, said: 'If you hate quick speaking, you will not fall into error.' The tribute was once paid to a great linguist that he could be silent in seven different languages. Many of us would do well to listen more and to speak less.

It is James' advice that we should also be *slow to anger*. He is probably meeting the arguments of some that there is a place for the blazing anger of rebuke. That is undoubtedly true; the world would be a poorer place without those who blazed against the abuses and the tyrannies of sin. But too often this is made an excuse for petulant and self-centred irritation.

Teachers will be tempted to be angry with slow and backward scholars and pupils, and still more with those who are lazy. But, except on the rarest occasions, they will achieve more by encouragement than by the lash of the tongue. *Preachers* will be tempted to anger. But 'don't scold' is always good advice to them; they lose their power whenever they do not make it clear by every word and gesture that they love their people. When anger gives the impression of dislike or contempt in the pulpit, it will not convert the souls of men and women. *Parents* will be tempted to anger. But a parent's anger is much more likely to produce a still more stubborn resistance than it is to control and direct. The accent of love always has more power than the accent of anger; and when anger becomes constant irritability, petulant annoyance, carping nagging, it always does more harm than good.

To be slow to speak, slow to anger, quick to listen is a good policy for life.

THE TEACHABLE SPIRIT

James 1:21

> So then strip yourself of all filthiness and of the excrescence of vice, and in gentleness receive the inborn word which is able to save your souls.

JAMES uses a series of vivid words and pictures.

He tells his readers to strip themselves of all vice and filthiness. The word he uses for *strip* is the word used for stripping off one's clothes. He tells his hearers to get rid of all defilement as they would strip off soiled garments or as a snake casts off its skin.

Both the words he uses for *defilement* are vivid. The word we have translated as *filthiness* is *ruparia*, and it can be used for the filth which soils clothes or soils the body. But it has one very interesting connection. It is derived from *rupos*; and, when *rupos* is used in a medical sense, it means wax in the ear. It is just possible that it still retains that meaning here, and that James is telling his readers to get rid of everything which would stop their ears to the true word of God. When wax gathers in the ear, it can make us deaf; and our sins can make us deaf to God. Further, James talks of the *excrescence* (*perisseia*), the ugly growth, of vice. He thinks of vice as tangled undergrowth or a cancerous tumour which must be cut away.

He bids them receive the *inborn word* in gentleness. The word for *inborn* is *emphutos*, and it has two possible general meanings.

(1) It can mean *inborn* in the sense of *innate* as opposed to acquired. If James uses it in that way, he is thinking of much the same thing as Paul was thinking of when he spoke of the Gentiles doing the works of the law by nature because they have a kind of law in their hearts (Romans 2:14–15); it is the same picture as the Old Testament picture of the law 'very near to you; it is in your mouth and in your heart' (Deuteronomy 30:14). It is practically equal to our word *conscience*. If this is its meaning here, James is saying that there is an instinctive knowledge of good and evil in the human heart whose guidance we should at all times obey.

(2) It can mean *inborn* in the sense of *implanted*, as a seed is planted in the ground. In 2 Esdras [4 Ezra] 9:31, we read of God saying: 'For I sow my law in you . . . and you shall be glorified in it forever.' If James is using the word in this sense, the idea may well go back to the parable of the sower (Matthew 13:1–8), which tells how the seed of the word is sown into the hearts of men and women. Through his prophets and his preachers, and above all through Jesus

Christ, God sows his truth into our hearts, and those who are wise will receive it and welcome it.

It may well be that we are not required to make a choice between these two meanings. It may well be that James is implying that knowledge of the true word of God comes to us from *two* sources, from the depths of our own being, and from the Spirit of God and the teaching of Christ and human preaching. From inside and from outside come voices telling us the right way; and those who are wise will listen and obey.

They will receive the word with *gentleness*. *Gentleness* is an attempt to translate the untranslatable word *prautēs*. This is a great Greek word which has no precise English equivalent. Aristotle defined it as the mid-point between excessive anger and excessive angerlessness; it is the quality of the person whose feelings and emotions are under perfect control. Andronicus Rhodius, the Greek philosopher, commenting on Aristotle, writes: '*Prautēs* is moderation in regard to anger . . . You might define *prautēs* as serenity and the power, not to be led away by emotion, but to control emotion as right reason dictates.' The Platonic *definitions* say that *prautēs* is the regulation of the movement of the soul caused by anger. It is the temperament (*krasis*) of a soul in which everything is mixed in the right proportions.

No one can ever find one English word to translate what is a one-word summary of the truly teachable spirit. The teachable spirit is *docile* and *easily controlled*, and therefore humble enough to learn. The teachable spirit is *without resentment* and *without anger* and is, therefore, able to face the truth, even when it hurts and condemns. The teachable spirit is not blinded by its own overriding *prejudices* but is clear-eyed to the truth. The teachable spirit is not seduced by *laziness* but is so self-controlled that it can willingly and faithfully accept the discipline of learning. *Prautēs* describes the perfect conquest and control of everything in a person's nature which would be a hindrance to seeing, learning and obeying the truth.

HEARING AND DOING

James 1:22–4

Prove yourselves to be doers of the word, and not only hearers, for those who think that hearing is enough deceive themselves. For, if a man is a hearer of the word and not a doer of it, he is like a man who looks in a mirror at the face which nature gave him. A glance and he is gone; and he immediately forgets what kind of man he is.

AGAIN James presents us with two of the vivid pictures of which he is such a master. First of all, he speaks of those who go to the church meeting and listen to the reading and expounding of the word, and who think that that listening has made them Christians. They have shut their eyes to the fact that what is read and heard in church must then be lived out. It is still possible to identify church attendance and Bible-reading with Christianity, but this is to take ourselves less than half the way; the really important thing is to turn that to which we have listened into action.

Second, James says such people are like those who look at themselves in a mirror – ancient mirrors were made not of glass but of highly polished metal – see the smuts which disfigure their faces and the dishevelment of their hair, and go away and forget what they actually look like, and so fail to do anything about it. Listening to the true word reveals to individuals what they are and what they ought to be. They see what is wrong and what must be done to put it right; but, if they are only hearers, they remain just as they are, and all the hearing has been to no avail.

James does well to remind us that what is heard in the holy place must be lived in the market place – or there is no point in hearing at all.

THE TRUE LAW

James 1:25

> He who looks into the perfect law, which is the law in the observance of which a man finds freedom, and who abides in it and shows himself not a forgetful hearer but an active doer of the word, will be blessed in all his action.

THIS is the kind of passage in James which Martin Luther disliked so much. He disliked the idea of law altogether, for with Paul he would have said: 'Christ is the end of the law' (Romans 10:4). 'James', said Luther, 'drives us to law and works.' And yet beyond all doubt there is a sense in which James is right. There is an ethical law which Christians must seek to put into action. That law is to be found first in the Ten Commandments and then in the teaching of Jesus.

James calls that law two things.

(1) He calls it the *perfect law*. There are three reasons why the law is perfect. (a) It is God's law, given and revealed by him. The way of life which Jesus laid down for his followers is in accordance with the will of God. (b) It is perfect in that it cannot be bettered. The Christian law is the law of love, and the demand of love can never be satisfied. We know well, when we love someone, that even if we gave them all the world and served them for a lifetime, we still could not satisfy or deserve their love. (c) But there is still

another sense in which the Christian law is perfect. The Greek word is *teleios*, which nearly always describes perfection towards some given end. Now, if men and women obey the law of Christ, they will fulfil the purpose for which God sent them into the world; they will be the people they ought to be and will make the contribution to the world they ought to make. They will be perfect in the sense that they will, by obeying the law of God, achieve their God-given destiny.

(2) He calls it the *law of liberty*; that is, the law in the keeping of which people find their true liberty. All the great philosophers and scholars have agreed that it is only in obeying the law of God that an individual becomes truly free. 'To obey God', said Seneca, 'is liberty.' 'The wise man alone is free,' said the Stoics, 'and every foolish man is a slave.' Philo said: 'All who are under the tyranny of anger or desire or any other passion are altogether slaves; all who live with the law are free.' As long as human beings have to obey their own passions and emotions and desires, they are nothing less than slaves. It is when we accept the will of God that we become really free – for then we are free to be what we ought to be. God's service is perfect freedom, and in doing his will is our peace.

TRUE WORSHIP

James 1:26–7

> If anyone thinks that he is a worshipper of God and yet does not bridle his tongue, his worship is an empty thing. This is pure and undefiled worship, as God the Father sees it, to visit the orphans and the widows, and to keep oneself unspotted from the world.

WE must be careful to understand what James is saying here. The Revised Standard Version translates the phrases at the beginning of verse 27: '*Religion* that is pure and undefiled is . . .' The word translated as *religion* is *thrēskeia*, and its meaning is not so much *religion* as *worship* in the sense of the outward expression of religion in ritual and liturgy and ceremony. What James is saying is: 'The finest ritual and the finest liturgy you can offer to God is service of the poor and personal purity.' To James, real worship did not lie in elaborate vestments or in magnificent music or in a carefully planned service; it lay in the practical service of others and in the purity of one's own personal life. It is perfectly possible for a church to be so taken up with the beauty of its buildings and the splendour of its liturgy that it has neither the time nor the money for practical Christian service – and that is what James is condemning.

In fact, James is condemning only what the prophets had condemned long ago. God, said the psalmist, is 'father of orphans and protector of widows' (Psalm 68:5). It was Zechariah's complaint that the people pulled away their shoulders and made their hearts as unyielding as stone at the demand to render true justice, to show mercy and compassion to one another, not to oppress the widow, the fatherless, the stranger and the poor, and not to entertain evil thoughts against another within the heart (cf. Zechariah 7:6–10). It was Micah's complaint that all ritual sacrifices were useless if the people did not do justice and love kindness and walk humbly before God (cf. Micah 6:6–8).

All through history, people have tried to make ritual and liturgy a substitute for sacrifice and service. They have made religion splendid *within* the church at the expense of neglecting it *outside* the church. This is by no means to say that it is wrong to seek to offer the noblest and the most splendid worship within God's house, but it is to say that all such worship is empty and idle unless it sends people out to love God by loving one another and to walk more purely in the tempting ways of the world.

FAVOURITISM

James 2:1

> My brothers, you cannot really believe that you have faith in our glorious Lord Jesus Christ, and yet continue to have respect of persons.

'RESPECT of persons' is the New Testament phrase for undue and unfair favouritism; it means pandering to others because they are rich or influential or popular. It is a fault which the New Testament consistently condemns. It is a fault of which the orthodox Jewish leaders completely acquitted Jesus. Even they were bound to admit that there was no favouritism with him (Luke 20:21; Mark 12:14; Matthew 22:16). After his vision of the sheet with the clean and unclean animals upon it, the lesson that Peter learned was that with God there is no partiality (Acts 10:34). It was Paul's conviction that both Gentiles and Jews stand under the same judgment in the sight of God, for with God there is no favouritism (Romans 2:11). This is a truth which Paul urges on his people again and again (Ephesians 6:9; Colossians 3:25).

The word itself is curious – *prosōpolēmpsia*. The noun comes from the expression *prosōpon lambanein*. *Prosōpon* is the *face*, and *lambanein* here means *to lift up*. The expression in Greek is a literal translation of a Hebrew phrase. To lift up someone's countenance was to regard that person with favour, in contrast perhaps to *casting down the person's countenance*.

71

Originally, it was not a bad word at all; it simply meant *to accept a person with favour*. Malachi asks if the governor will be pleased with the people and *will accept their persons*, will show them favour, if they bring him blemished offerings (Malachi 1:8–9). But the word rapidly acquired a bad sense. It soon began to mean not so much to favour a person as to show favouritism, to allow oneself to be unduly influenced by a person's social status or prestige or power or wealth. Malachi goes on to condemn that very sin when God accuses the people of not keeping his ways and of showing partiality (Malachi 2:9). The great characteristic of God is his complete impartiality. In the law, it was written: 'You shall not render an unjust judgment; you shall not be partial to the poor or defer to the great: with justice you shall judge your neighbour' (Leviticus 19:15). There is a necessary emphasis here. A person may be unjust because of the snobbery which flatters and panders to the rich, and may be equally unjust because of the inverted snobbery which glorifies the poor. 'The Lord', said Ben Sirach, 'is the judge and with him there is no partiality' (Sirach [Ecclesiasticus] 35:15).

The Old and New Testaments unite in condemning that partiality of judgment and favouritism of treatment which comes from giving undue weight to a person's social standing, wealth or worldly influence. And it is a fault to which everyone has a tendency in some degree. 'The rich and the poor have this in common:' says Proverbs, 'the Lord is the maker of them all' (Proverbs 22:2). 'It is not right', says Ben Sirach, 'to despise one who is intelligent but poor, and it is not proper to honour one who is sinful' (Sirach 10:23). We do well to remember that it is just as much a sign of favouritism to pander to the mob as it is to flatter a tyrant.

THE PERIL OF SNOBBERY WITHIN
THE CHURCH

James 2:2–4

> For, if a man comes into your assembly with his fingers
> covered with gold rings and dressed in elegant clothes
> and a poor man comes in dressed in shabby clothes,
> and you pay special attention to the man who is dressed
> in elegant clothes and you say to him: 'Will you sit
> here, please?' and you say to the poor man: 'You stand
> there!' or 'Squat on the floor beside my footstool!' have
> you not drawn distinctions within your minds, and have
> you not become judges whose thoughts are evil?'

IT is James' fear that snobbery may invade the Church. He
draws a picture of two men entering the Christian assembly.
The one is well dressed, and his fingers are covered with
gold rings. In the ancient world, the more ostentatious people
wore rings on every finger except the middle one, and wore
far more than one on each finger. 'We adorn our fingers
with rings,' said Seneca, 'and we distribute gems over every
joint.' The early Christian theologian Clement of Alexandria
recommends that Christians should wear only one ring, and
that it should be worn on the little finger. It ought to have on
it a religious emblem, such as a dove, a fish or an anchor, and
the justification for wearing it is that it might be used as a
seal.

So, into the Christian assembly comes an elegantly dressed
man wearing many rings. The other is a poor man dressed in
poor clothes because he has no others to wear, and unadorned
by any jewels. The rich man is ushered to a special seat with
all ceremony and respect, while the poor man is told to
stand, or to squat on the floor, beside the footstool of the
well-to-do.

That the picture is not exaggerated is seen from certain instructions in some early service order books. In his commentary, J. H. Ropes quotes a typical passage from the Ethiopic *Statutes of the Apostles*: 'If any other man or woman enters in fine clothes, either a man of the district or from other districts, being brethren, thou, presbyter, while thou speakest the word which is concerning God, or while thou hearest or readest, thou shalt not respect persons, nor leave thy ministering to command places for them, but remain quiet, for the brethren shall receive them, and if they have no place for them, the lover of brothers and sisters, will rise, and leave a place for them . . . And if a poor man or woman of the district or of other districts should come in and there is no place for them, thou, presbyter, make place for such with all thy heart, even if thou wilt sit on the ground, that there should not be the respecting of the person of man but of God.' Here is an identical picture. It is even suggested that, when a rich man entered, the leader of the service might stop the service and escort the man to a special seat.

There is no doubt that there must have been social problems in the early Church. The Church was the only place in the ancient world where social distinctions did not exist. There must have been a certain initial awkwardness when a master found himself sitting next to his slave or when a master arrived at a service in which his slave was actually the leader and the dispenser of the sacrament. The gap between the slave, who in law was nothing more than a living tool, and the master was so wide as to cause problems of approach on either side. Further, in its early days the Church was predominantly poor and humble, and therefore if a rich man was converted and came to the Christian fellowship, there must have been a very real temptation to make a fuss of him and treat him as a special trophy for Christ.

The Church must be the one place where all distinctions are wiped out. There can be no distinctions of rank and prestige when we meet in the presence of the King of glory. There can be no distinctions of merit when we meet in the presence of the supreme holiness of God. In his presence, all earthly distinctions are less than the dust and all earthly righteousness is as filthy rags. In the presence of God, all are one.

In verse 4, there is a problem of translation. The word *diekrithēte* can have two meanings. (1) It can mean 'You are wavering in your judgments if you act like that.' That is to say, 'If you pay special honour to the rich, you are torn between the standards of the world and the standards of God, and you can't make up your mind which you are going to apply.' (2) It may mean 'You are guilty of making class distinctions which in the Christian fellowship should not exist.' We prefer the second meaning, because James goes on to say: 'If you do that, you are judges whose thoughts are evil.' That is to say, 'You are breaking the commandment of him who said, "Judge not that you be not judged"' (Matthew 7:1).

THE RICHES OF POVERTY
AND THE POVERTY OF RICHES

James 2:5–7

> Listen, my dear brothers. Did God not choose those who are poor by the world's valuation to be rich because of their faith and to be heirs of the kingdom which he has promised to those who love him? But you dishonour the poor man. Do not the rich oppress you, and is it not they who drag you to the law courts? And is it not they who abuse the fair name by which you have been called?

'GOD', said the American president Abraham Lincoln, 'must love the common people because he made so many of them.' Christianity has always had a special message for the poor. In Jesus' first sermon in the synagogue at Nazareth, his claim was: 'He has anointed me to bring good news to the poor' (Luke 4:18). His answer to John's puzzled inquiries as to whether or not he was God's chosen one culminated in the claim: 'The poor have good news brought to them' (Matthew 11:5). The first of the beatitudes was: 'Blessed are the poor in spirit, for theirs is the kingdom of heaven' (Matthew 5:3). And Luke is even more definite: 'Blessed are you who are poor, for yours is the kingdom of God' (Luke 6:20). During the ministry of Jesus, when he was banished from the synagogues and took to the open road and the hillside and the seaside, it was the crowds of ordinary men and women to whom his message came. In the days of the early Church, it was to the crowds that the street preachers preached. In fact, the message of Christianity was that those who mattered to no one else mattered intensely to God. 'Consider your own call, brothers and sisters,' wrote Paul to the Corinthians, 'not many of you were wise by human standards, not many were powerful, not many were of noble birth' (1 Corinthians 1:26).

It is not that Christ and the Church do not want the great and the rich and the wise and the mighty; we must beware of an inverted snobbery, as we have already seen. But it was the simple fact that the gospel offered so much to the poor, and demanded so much from the rich, that it was the poor who were swept into the Church. It was, in fact, the ordinary people who heard Jesus gladly and the rich young ruler who went sorrowfully away because he had great possessions. James is not shutting the door on the rich – far from it. He is saying that the gospel of Christ is especially dear to the poor and that in it there is a welcome for those who have no one to welcome them, and that through it there is a value set on those whom the world regards as valueless.

In the society that James inhabited, the rich oppressed the poor. They dragged them to the law courts. No doubt this was for debt. At the bottom end of the social scale, people were so poor that they could hardly live, and money-lenders were plentiful and well practised in extortion. In the ancient world, there was a custom of instant arrest. If a creditor met a debtor on the street, he could seize him by the neck of his robe, nearly throttling him, and literally drag him to the law courts. That is what the rich did to the poor. They had no sympathy; all they wanted was every last penny, every last cent. It is not riches that James is condemning; it is the management of riches without sympathy.

It is the rich who abuse the name by which the Christians are called. It may be the name *Christian* by which the followers of Christ were called first of all at Antioch and which was given initially as a joke. It may be the name of Christ, which was pronounced over a Christian at baptism. The word James uses for *called* (*epikaleisthai*) is the word used for a wife taking her husband's name in marriage or for children being called after their father. Christians take the name of Christ; they are called after Christ. It is as if they were married to Christ, or born and christened into the family of Christ.

The rich and the masters would have many reasons for insulting the name *Christian*. Slaves who became Christians would have a new *independence*; they would no longer cringe at their master's power, punishment would cease to terrorize them and they would meet their master with a new strength and confidence. They would have a new *honesty*. That would make them better slaves, but it would also mean they could no longer be their master's instruments in sharp practice and petty dishonesty as once they might have been. They would have a new *sense of worship*, and on the Lord's Day they would insist on putting work aside in order that they might worship with the people of God. There would be ample opportunity for a master to find reasons for insulting the name of Christian and cursing the name of Christ.

THE ROYAL LAW

James 2:8–11

> If you perfectly keep the royal law, as the Scripture has it: 'You must love your neighbour as yourself', you do well. But if you treat people with respect of persons, such conduct is sin and you stand convicted by the law as transgressors. For, if a man keeps the whole law and yet fails to keep it in one point, he becomes guilty of transgressing the law as a whole. For he who said 'Do not commit adultery' also said 'Do not kill'. If you do not commit adultery but kill, you become a transgressor of the law.

THE connection of thought with the previous passage is this. James has been condemning those who pay special attention to the rich man who enters the church. 'But', they might answer, 'the law tells me to love my neighbour as myself. Therefore we are duty-bound to welcome this man when he comes to church.' 'Very well,' answers James, 'if you are really welcoming the man because you love him as you do yourself, and you wish to give him the welcome you yourself would wish to receive, that is fine. But, if you are giving him this special welcome because he is rich, that is favouritism and that is wrong – and, far from keeping the law, you are in fact breaking it. You don't love your neighbour, or you would not neglect the poor man. What you love is wealth – and that is not what the law commands.'

James calls the great commandment to love our neighbour as ourselves the *royal law*. There can be various meanings of the phrase. It may mean the law which is of *supreme excellence*; it may mean *the law which is given by the King of Kings*; it may mean *the supreme law*; it may mean *the law that gives the regal quality to people and is fit for royalty*. To keep that greatest law is to become king of oneself and a king among others. It is a law fit for those who are royal, and able to make others royal.

James goes on to lay down a great principle about the law of God. To break any part of it is to become a trans- gressor. The Jews were very apt to regard the law as a series of detached commandments. To keep one was to gain credit; to break one was to incur debt. People could add up the ones they kept and subtract the ones they broke and so emerge with a credit or a debit balance. There was a Rabbinic saying: 'Whoever fulfils only one law, good is appointed to him; his days are prolonged and he will inherit the land.' Again, many of the Rabbis held that 'the Sabbath weighs against all precepts', and to keep it was to keep the law.

As James saw it, the *whole* law was the will of God; to break any part of it was to infringe that will and therefore to be guilty of sin. That is perfectly true. To break any part of the law is to become a transgressor in principle. Even under human justice, people become criminals when they have broken one law. So James argues: 'No matter how good you may be in other directions, if you treat people with favouritism, you have acted against the will of God and you are a transgressor.'

There is a great truth here which is both relevant and practical. We may put it much more simply. Men and women may be in nearly all respects good people, and yet they may spoil themselves by one fault. They may be moral in their action, pure in their speech, meticulous in their devotion. But they may be hard and self-righteous, rigid and unsympathetic, and, if so, their goodness is spoiled.

We do well to remember that, though we may claim to have done many good things and to have resisted many evil things, there may be something in us by which everything is spoiled.

THE LAW OF LIBERTY AND THE LAW OF MERCY

James 2:12–13

> So speak and so act as those who are going to be judged under the law of liberty. For he who acts without mercy will have judgment without mercy. Mercy triumphs over judgment.

As he comes to the end of a section, James reminds his readers of two great facts of the Christian life.

(1) Christians live under the law of liberty, and it is by the law of liberty that they will be judged. What he means is this. Unlike the Pharisees and the orthodox Jews, Christians are not men and women whose lives are governed by the external pressure of a whole series of rules and regulations imposed on them from outside. They are governed by the inner compulsion of love. They follow the right way, the way of love to God and love to other people, not because any external law compels them to do so nor because any threat of punishment frightens them into doing so, but because the love of Christ within their hearts makes them want to do so.

(2) Christians must always remember that only those who show mercy will find mercy. This is a principle which runs

through all Scripture. Ben Sirach wrote: 'Forgive your neighbour the wrong he has done, and then your sins will be pardoned when you pray. Does anyone harbour anger against another, and expect healing from the Lord? If one has no mercy to another like himself, can he then seek pardon for his own sins?' (Sirach 28:2–5). Jesus said: 'Blessed are the merciful, for they will receive mercy' (Matthew 5:7). 'If you forgive others their trespasses, your heavenly Father will also forgive you; but if you do not forgive others, neither will your Father forgive your trespasses' (Matthew 6:14–15). 'Do not judge, so that you may not be judged. For with the judgment you make you will be judged' (Matthew 7:1–2). He tells of the condemnation which fell upon the unforgiving servant, and ends the parable by saying: 'So, my heavenly Father will also do to every one of you, if you do not forgive your brother or sister from your heart' (cf. Matthew 18:23–35).

Scripture teaching is agreed that those who would find mercy must themselves be merciful. And James goes even further, for in the end he says that mercy triumphs over judgment – by which he means that in the day of judgment those who have shown mercy will find that their mercy has even blotted out their own sin.

FAITH AND WORKS

James 2:14–26

> My brothers, what use is it if a man claims to have faith and has no deeds to show? Are you going to claim that his faith is able to save him? If a brother or sister has nothing to wear, and if they have not enough for their daily food, and if one of you says to them 'Go in

peace! Be warmed and fed!' and yet does not give them the essentials of bodily existence, what use is that? So, if faith too has no deeds to show, by itself it is dead.

But someone may well say: 'Have you faith?' My answer is: 'I have deeds. Show me your faith apart from your deeds, and I will show you my faith by means of my deeds.' You say that you believe that there is one God. Excellent! The demons also believe the same thing – and shudder in terror.

Do you wish for proof, you empty creature, that faith without deeds is ineffective? Was not our father Abraham proved righteous in virtue of deeds when he was ready to offer Isaac his own son upon the altar? You see how his faith co-operated with his deeds and how his faith was completed by his deeds, and so there was fulfilled the passage of Scripture which says: 'Abraham believed in God, and it was reckoned to him for righteousness, for he was called the friend of God.' You see that it is by deeds that a man is proved righteous, and not only by faith.

In the same way, was Rahab the harlot not also proved righteous by deeds, when she received the messengers and sent them away by another way? For just as the body without breath is dead, so faith without works is dead.

THIS is a passage which we must take as a whole before we look at it in parts, for it is so often used in an attempt to show that James and Paul held completely different views. It is apparently Paul's emphasis that we are saved by faith alone and that deeds do not come into the process at all. 'For we hold that a person is justified by faith apart from works prescribed by the law' (Romans 3:28). 'A person is justified not by works of the law but through faith in Jesus Christ . . .

because no one will be justified by the works of the law'
(Galatians 2:16). It is often argued that James is not simply
differing from Paul but is flatly contradicting him. This is a
matter we must investigate.

(1) We begin by noting that James' emphasis is in fact a
universal New Testament emphasis. It was the preaching of
John the Baptist that men and women should prove the reality
of their repentance by the excellence of their deeds (Matthew
3:8; Luke 3:8). It was Jesus' preaching that people should so
live that the world might see their good works and give the
glory to God (Matthew 5:16). He insisted that it was by their
fruits that men and women must be known and that a faith
which expressed itself in words only could never take the
place of one which expressed itself in the doing of the will of
God (Matthew 7:15–21).

Nor is this emphasis missing from Paul himself. Apart
from anything else, there can be few teachers who have
ever stressed the ethical effect of Christianity as Paul does.
However doctrinal and theological his letters may be, they
never fail to end with a section in which the expression of
Christianity in deeds is insisted upon. Apart from that general
custom, Paul repeatedly makes clear the importance he
attaches to deeds as part of the Christian life. He speaks of
God who will render to all according to their works (Romans
2:6). He insists that we shall all give account of ourselves
to God (Romans 14:12). He urges people to put off the
works of darkness and put on the armour of light (Romans
13:12). We shall all receive our own reward according to
our labour (1 Corinthians 3:8). We must all appear before
the judgment seat of Christ so that everyone may receive
good or evil, according to what he or she has done in the
body (2 Corinthians 5:10). Christians have to put off the old
nature and all its deeds (Colossians 3:9).

The fact that Christianity must be demonstrated ethically is an essential part of the Christian faith throughout the New Testament.

(2) The fact remains that James reads as if his views disagreed with those of Paul – for, in spite of all that we have said, Paul's main emphasis is upon grace and faith and James' upon action and works. But this must be said – what James is condemning is not Paulinism but a distortion of it. The essential Pauline position in one sentence was: 'Believe on the Lord Jesus, and you will be saved' (Acts 16:31). But, clearly, the significance we attach to this demand will entirely depend on the meaning we attach to *believe*. There are two kinds of belief.

There is belief which is purely intellectual. For instance, I believe that the square on the hypotenuse of a right-angled triangle equals the sum of the squares on the other two sides; and, if I had to, I could prove it – but it makes no difference to my life and living. I accept it, but it has no effect upon me.

There is another kind of belief. I believe that five and five make ten, and, therefore, I will resolutely refuse to pay more than ten pounds or ten dollars for two items marked at half that sum. I take that fact not only into my mind but also into my life and action.

What James is arguing against is the first kind of belief, the acceptance of a fact without allowing it to have any influence upon life. The devils are intellectually convinced of the existence of God; they, in fact, tremble before him, but their belief does not alter them in the slightest. What Paul held was the second kind of belief. For him, to believe in Jesus meant to take that belief into every section of life and to live by it.

It is easy to distort Paulinism and to remove all strength and effective meaning from *believe*; and it is not really

Paulinism but a misunderstood form of it that James condemns. He is condemning those who claim to be Christians
without putting their claims into practice – and with that
condemnation Paul would have entirely agreed.

(3) Even allowing for that, there is still a difference
between James and Paul – *they begin at different times in the
Christian life*. Paul begins *at the very beginning*. He insists
that no one can ever earn the forgiveness of God. The initial
step must come from the free grace of God; we can only
accept the forgiveness which God offers us in Jesus Christ.

James begins much later *with the professing Christians*,
those who claim to be already forgiven and in a new
relationship with God. Such people, James rightly says, must
live new lives, for they are new creatures. They have been
justified; they must now show that they are *sanctified*. With
that, Paul would have entirely agreed.

The fact is that no one can be saved by works, but equally
no one can be saved without producing works. By far the
best analogy is that of a great human love. When we are
loved, we become certain that we do not deserve to be loved;
but we are also certain that we must spend our lives trying to
be worthy of that love.

The difference between James and Paul is a difference of
starting point. Paul starts with the great basic fact of the
forgiveness of God which no one can earn or deserve; James
starts with the professing Christians and insists that
individuals must prove their Christianity by their deeds. We
are not saved *by* deeds; we are saved *for* deeds; these are the
twin truths of the Christian life. Paul's emphasis is on the
first and James' is on the second. In fact, they do not contradict
but complement each other, and the message of both is
essential to the Christian faith in its fullest form. As the
Scottish paraphrase has it:

> Let all who hold this faith and hope
>   In holy deeds abound;
> Thus faith approves itself sincere,
>   By active virtue crown'd.

PROFESSING THE FAITH
AND PUTTING IT INTO PRACTICE

James 2:14–17

> My brothers, what use is it if a man claims to have faith
> and has no deeds to show? Are you going to claim that
> his faith is able to save him? If a brother or sister has
> nothing to wear, and if they have not enough for their
> daily food, and if one of you says to them 'Go in peace!
> Be warmed and fed!' and yet does not give them the
> essentials of bodily existence, what use is that? So, if
> faith too has no deeds to show, by itself it is dead.

THE one thing that James cannot stand is a claim to faith
without putting it into practice, words without deeds. He
chooses a vivid illustration of what he means. Suppose a
person has neither clothes for protection nor food for sustenance, and suppose a so-called friend expresses the sincerest
sympathy for such a sad plight, and suppose that sympathy
stops with words and no effort is made to ease the plight of
the unfortunate individual, what use is that? What use is
sympathy without some attempt to turn that sympathy into
practical effect? Faith without deeds is dead. This is a passage
which would appeal particularly to a Jew.

(1) To a Jew, almsgiving was of supreme importance – so
much so that righteousness and almsgiving mean one and the
same thing. Charitable giving was considered to be a person's
one defence when the time came to be judged by God. 'As

water extinguishes a blazing fire,' writes Ben Sirach, 'so almsgiving atones for sin' (Sirach 3:30). In Tobit, it is written: 'Do not turn your face away from anyone who is poor and the face of God will not be turned away from you' (Tobit 4:7). When the leaders of the Jerusalem church agreed that Paul should go to the Gentiles, the one specific instruction given to him was not to forget the poor (Galatians 2:10). This stress on practical help was one of the great and lovely marks of Jewish piety.

(2) There was a strain of Greek religion to which this stress on sympathy and almsgiving was quite alien. The Stoics aimed at *apatheia*, the complete absence of feeling. The aim of life was serenity. Emotion disturbs serenity. The way to perfect calm was to annihilate all emotion. Pity was a mere disturbance of the detached philosophic calm in which people should aim to live. So Epictetus lays it down that only the one who disobeys the divine command will ever feel grief or pity (*Discourses*, 3:24, 43). When Virgil in the *Georgics* (2:498) draws the picture of the perfectly happy man, he has no pity for the poor and no grief for the sorrowing, for such emotions would only upset his own serenity. This is the very opposite of the Jewish point of view. For the Stoics, blessedness meant being wrapped up in their own philosophic detachment and calm; for the Jews, it meant actively sharing in the misfortunes of others.

(3) In his approach to this subject, James is profoundly right. There is nothing more dangerous than the repeated experiencing of a fine emotion with no attempt to put it into action. It is a fact that every time we feel a generous impulse without taking action, we become less likely ever to take action. In a sense, it is true to say that we have no right to feel sympathy unless we at least attempt to put that sympathy into action. An emotion is not something in which

to luxuriate; it is something which at the cost of effort and of toil and of discipline and of sacrifice must be turned into the stuff of life.

NOT 'EITHER OR', BUT 'BOTH AND'

James 2:18–19

> But someone may well say: 'Have you faith?' My answer is: 'I have deeds. Show me your faith apart from your deeds, and I will show you my faith by means of my deeds.' You say that you believe there is one God. Excellent! The demons also believe the same thing – and shudder in terror.

JAMES is thinking of a possible objector who says: 'Faith is a fine thing, and works are fine things. They are both perfectly genuine manifestations of real religion. But an individual does not necessarily possess both. One person will have faith and another will have works. Well, then, you carry on with your works and I will carry on with my faith; and we are both being truly religious in our own way.' The objector's view is that faith and works are alternative expressions of the Christian religion. James will have none of it. It is not a case of *either* faith *or* works; it is necessarily a case of *both* faith *and* works.

In many ways, Christianity is falsely represented as an 'either or' when it must properly be a 'both and'.

(1) In the well-proportioned life, there must be *thought* and *action*. It is tempting and it is common to think that it is possible to be either *primarily engaged in thought* or *in action*. The thoughtful individual will sit in a study thinking great thoughts; the person who needs to be involved in action will be out in the world doing great deeds. But that is wrong. The

thinker is only half a person unless the thoughts are turned into deeds, and will scarcely even inspire others to action unless he or she comes down into the battle and shares the arena with them. As Rudyard Kipling had it in his poem 'The Glory of the Garden':

> Our England is a garden and such gardens are not made
> By singing, 'O how beautiful', and sitting in the shade;
> While better men than we began their working lives
> By digging weeds from garden paths with broken dinner knives.

Nor can anyone really take effective action unless the great principles on which those deeds are founded have been carefully thought out.

(2) In the well proportioned life, there must be *prayer* and *effort*. Again it is tempting to divide people into two classes – the saints who spend life secluded on their knees in constant devotion, and the toilers who labour in the dust and the heat of the day. But it will not do. It is said that Martin Luther was close friends with another monk. The other was as fully persuaded of the necessity of the Reformation as Luther was. So they made an arrangement. Luther would go down into the world and fight the battle there; the other would remain in his cell praying for the success of Luther's labours. But one night the monk had a dream. In it he saw a single reaper engaged in the impossible task of reaping an immense field by himself. The lonely reaper turned his head, and the monk saw that his face was the face of Martin Luther, and he knew that he must leave his cell and his prayers and go to help. It is, of course, true that there are some who, because of age or physical weakness, can do nothing other than pray; and their prayers are indeed a strength and a support. But if any able-bodied person thinks that prayer can be a substitute for effort,

that person's prayers are merely a way of escape. Prayer and
effort must go hand in hand.

(3) In any well-balanced life, there must be *faith* and
deeds. It is only through deeds that faith can prove and
demonstrate itself, and it is only through faith that deeds will
be attempted and done. Faith is bound to overflow into action,
and action begins only when we have faith in some great
cause or principle which God has presented to us.

THE PROOF OF FAITH

James 2:20–6

> Do you wish for proof, you empty creature, that faith
> without deeds is ineffective? Was not our father
> Abraham proved righteous in virtue of deeds when he
> was ready to offer Isaac his son upon the altar? You see
> how his faith co-operated with his deeds and how his
> faith was completed by his deeds, and so there was
> fulfilled the passage of Scripture which says: 'Abraham
> believed in God, and it was reckoned to him for
> righteousness, for he was called the friend of God.' You
> see that it is by deeds that a man is proved righteous,
> and not only by faith.
>
> In the same way, was Rahab the harlot not also
> proved righteous by deeds, when she received the
> messengers and sent them away by another way? For
> just as the body without breath is dead, so faith without
> works is dead.

JAMES offers two illustrations of the point of view on which
he is insisting. Abraham is the great example of faith, but
Abraham's faith was proved by his willingness to sacrifice
Isaac at the apparent demand of God. Rahab was a famous
figure in Jewish legend. She had sheltered the spies sent to

spy out the promised land (Joshua 2:1–21). Later legend said that she became a convert to the Jewish faith, that she married Joshua and that she was a direct ancestor of many priests and prophets, including Ezekiel and Jeremiah. It was her treatment of the spies which proved that she had faith.

Paul and James are both right here. Unless Abraham had had faith, he would never have answered the summons of God. Unless Rahab had had faith, she would never have taken the risk of identifying her future with the fortunes of Israel. And yet, unless Abraham had been prepared to obey God to the uttermost, his faith would have been unreal, and unless Rahab had been prepared to risk all to help the spies, her faith would have been useless.

These two examples show that faith and deeds are not opposites; they are, in fact, inseparables. No one will ever be moved to action without faith, and our faith is not genuine unless it moves us to action. Faith and deeds are opposite sides of our experience of God.

THE TEACHER'S PERIL

James 3:1

> My brothers, it is a mistake for many of you to become teachers, for you must be well aware that those of us who teach will receive a greater condemnation.

In the early Church, the teachers were of prime importance. Wherever they are mentioned, they are mentioned with honour. In the church at Antioch, they are ranked with the prophets who sent out Paul and Barnabas on the first missionary journey (Acts 13:1). In Paul's list of those who hold great gifts within the Church, they come second only to the apostles and to the prophets (1 Corinthians 12:28; cf.

Ephesians 4:11). The apostles and the prophets were always
on the move. Their field was the whole Church, and they did
not stay long in any one congregation. But the teachers
worked within a congregation, and their supreme importance
was that it must have been to them that the converts were
handed over for instruction in the facts of the Christian gospel
and for education in the Christian faith. It was the awe-
inspiring responsibility of the teachers that they could put
the stamp of their own faith and knowledge on those who
were entering the Church for the first time.

In the New Testament itself, we get glimpses of teachers
who failed in their responsibility and became false teachers.
There were teachers who tried to turn Christianity into another
kind of Judaism and tried to introduce circumcision and the
keeping of the law (Acts 15:24). There were teachers who
lived out nothing of the truth which they taught, whose lives
were a contradiction of what they taught and who did nothing
but bring dishonour on the faith they represented (Romans
2:17–29). There were some who tried to teach before they
themselves knew anything (1 Timothy 1:6–7), and others who
pandered to the false desires of the crowd (2 Timothy 4:3).

But, quite apart from the false teachers, it is James' conviction that teaching is a dangerous occupation for anyone.
The instrument of teaching is speech, and its agent is the
tongue. As J. H. Ropes puts it, James is concerned to point
out 'the responsibility of teachers and the dangerous character
of the instrument they have to use'.

Christian teachers entered into a perilous heritage. In the
Church, they took the place of the Rabbis in Judaism. There
were many great and saintly Rabbis, but the Rabbi was treated
in a way that was liable to ruin the character of any man. His
very name means 'My great one'. Everywhere he went, he
was treated with the utmost respect. It was actually held that

a man's duty to his Rabbi exceeded his duty to his parents, because his parents only brought him into the life of this world but his teacher brought him into the life of the world to come. It was also said that if a man's parents and a man's teacher were captured by an enemy, the Rabbi must be ransomed first. It was true that a Rabbi was not allowed to take money for teaching and that he was supposed to support his physical needs by working at a trade; but it was also held that it was a specially pious and meritorious work to take a Rabbi into the household and to support him with every care. It was desperately easy for a Rabbi to become the kind of person whom Jesus depicted – a spiritual tyrant who made a great show of piety, someone who loved to have the highest place at any function, a person who gloried in the almost subservient respect shown to him in public (cf. Matthew 23:4–7). No profession is more liable to give rise to spiritual and intellectual pride.

There are two dangers which all teachers must avoid. Because of their position, they will be teaching either those who are young in years or those who are children in the faith. They must struggle, therefore, throughout their lives to avoid two things. They must take every care that they are teaching the truth, and not their own opinions or even their own prejudices. It is fatally easy for teachers to distort the truth and to teach not God's version but their own. They must take great care that they do not contradict their teaching by their lives, continually, as it were, having to say not 'Do as I do' but 'Do as I say.' They must never get into the position where their scholars and students cannot hear what they say for listening to what they are. As the Jewish Rabbis themselves said, 'Not learning but doing is the foundation, and he who multiplies words multiplies sin' (*Sayings of the Fathers*, 1:18).

It is James' warning that teachers have of their own choice entered into a special position and are, therefore, under the greater condemnation if they fail in their task. The people to whom James was writing coveted the prestige given to teachers; James demanded that they should never forget the responsibility.

THE UNIVERSAL DANGER

James 3:2

> There are many things in which we all slip up; but if a man never slips up in his speech, he is a perfect man, able to keep the whole body also on the rein.

JAMES sets down two ideas which were woven into Jewish thought and literature.

(1) There is no one in this world who does not sin in some way or other. The word James uses means *to slip up*. 'Life', said Lord Fisher, the great naval commander, 'is strewn with orange peel.' Sin is so often not deliberate but the result of a slip-up when we are off our guard. This universality of sin runs all through the Bible. 'There is no one who is righteous, not even one', quotes Paul. 'For all have sinned and fall short of the glory of God' (Romans 3:10; cf. 3:23). 'If we say that we have no sin,' says John, 'we deceive ourselves, and the truth is not in us' (1 John 1:8). 'Surely there is no one on earth so righteous as to do good without ever sinning', said the preacher (Ecclesiastes 7:20). 'There is no one', says the Jewish sage, 'among those that have been born who has not acted wickedly; among those who have existed there is no one who has not done wrong' (2 Esdras 8:35). There is no room for pride in human life, for there is not a man or woman upon earth who has not some blot of which to be ashamed.

Even the Greek and Roman writers have the same conviction of sin. 'It is the nature of man to sin both in private and in public life,' said Thucydides (3:45). 'We all sin,' said Seneca, 'some more grievously, some more lightly' (*On Clemency*, 1:6).

(2) There is no sin into which it is easier to fall and none which has graver consequences than the sin which is the result of something uttered. Again, this idea is woven into Jewish thought. Jesus warned people that they would give account for every word they spoke. 'By your words you will be justified, and by your words you will be condemned' (Matthew 12:37). 'A soft answer turns away wrath, but a harsh word stirs up anger ... A gentle tongue is a tree of life, but perverseness in it breaks the spirit' (Proverbs 15:1–4).

Of all Jewish writers, Jesus ben Sirach, the writer of Ecclesiasticus, was most impressed with the terrifying potentialities of the tongue. 'Honour and dishonour come from speaking, and the tongue of mortals may be their downfall. Do not be called double-tongued and do not lay traps with your tongue; for shame comes to the thief, and severe condemnation to the double-tongued ... and do not become an enemy instead of a friend; for a bad name incurs shame and reproach; so it is with the double-tongued sinner' (Sirach [Ecclesiasticus] 5:13–6:1). 'Happy are those who do not blunder with their lips' (14:1). 'Who has not sinned with his tongue?' (19:16). 'Who will set a guard over my mouth, and an effective seal upon my lips, so that I may not fall because of them and my tongue may not destroy me?' (22:27).

He has a lengthy passage which is so nobly and passionately expressed that it is worth quoting in full:

> Curse the gossips and the double-tongued,
>   for they destroy the peace of many,

Slander has shaken many,
    and scattered them from nation to nation;
it has destroyed strong cities, and overturned the
    houses of the great.
Slander has driven virtuous women from their homes,
    and deprived them of the fruit of their toil.
Those who pay heed to slander will not find rest,
    nor will they settle down in peace.
The blow of a whip raises a welt, but a blow of the
    tongue crushes the bones.
Many have fallen by the edge of the sword,
    but not as many as have fallen because of the tongue.
Happy is the one who is protected from it,
    who has not been exposed to its anger,
who has not borne its yoke,
    and has not been bound with its fetters.
For its yoke is a yoke of iron,
    and its fetters are fetters of bronze;
its death is an evil death,
    and Hades is preferable to it.
. . .
As you fence in your property with thorns,
    so make a door and a bolt for your mouth.
As you lock up your silver and gold,
    so make balances and scales for your words.
Take care not to err with your tongue,
    and fall victim to one lying in wait.

                                        (28:13–26)

LITTLE BUT POWERFUL

James 3:3–5a

If we put bits into horses' mouths to make them obedient
to us, we can control the direction of their whole body
as well. Look at ships, too. See how large they are and
how they are driven by rough winds, and see how their

course is altered by a very small rudder, wherever the
pressure of the steersman desires. So, too, the tongue is
a little member of the body, but it makes arrogant claims
for itself.

IT might be argued against James' terror of the tongue that it
is a very small part of the body to make such a fuss about and
to which to attach so much importance. To combat that
argument, James uses two pictures.

(1) We put a bit into the mouth of a horse, knowing that if
we can control its mouth we can control its whole body. So
James says that if we can control the tongue we can control
the whole body, but if the tongue is uncontrolled the whole
life is set on the wrong path.

(2) A rudder is very small in comparison with the size of
a ship; and yet, by exerting pressure on that little rudder, the
steersman can alter the course of the ship and direct it to
safety. Long before James wrote, Aristotle had used this same
picture when he was talking about the science of mechanics:
'A rudder is small and it is attached to the very end of the
ship, but it has such power that by this little rudder, and by
the power of one man – and that a power gently exerted – the
great bulk of ships can be moved.' The tongue also is small,
yet it can direct the whole course of a person's life.

The Jewish writer Philo called the mind the charioteer and
steersman of an individual's life; it is when the mind controls
every word and is itself controlled by Christ that life is safe.

James is not for a moment saying that silence is better than
speech. He is not pleading for a life where speech is forbidden,
as it would be for Trappist monks. He is pleading for the
control of the tongue. Aristippus, the Greek philosopher, had
a wise saying: 'The conqueror of pleasure is not the man who
never uses it. He is the man who uses pleasure as a rider guides
a horse or a steersman directs a ship, and so directs them

wherever he wishes.' Abstention from anything is never a complete substitute for control in its use. James is pleading not for the silence that comes from a fear of saying something wrong or hurtful but for a wise use of speech.

A DESTRUCTIVE FIRE

James 3:5b–6

> See how great a forest how little a fire can set alight. And the tongue is a fire; in the midst of our members the tongue stands for the whole wicked world, for it defiles the whole body and sets on fire the ever-recurring cycle of creation, and is itself set on fire by hell.

THE damage the tongue can cause is like that caused by a forest fire. The picture of the forest fire is common in the Bible. It is the prayer of the psalmist that God may make the wicked like chaff before the wind, and that his tempest may destroy them as fire consumes the forest and the flame sets the mountains ablaze (cf. Psalm 83:13–14). Isaiah says: 'wickedness burned like a fire, consuming briers and thorns; it kindled the thickets of the forest' (Isaiah 9:18). Zechariah speaks of 'a blazing pot on a pile of wood, like a flaming torch among sheaves' (Zechariah 12:6). The picture was one the Jews of Palestine knew well. In the dry season, the scanty grass and low-growing thorn bushes and scrub were as dry as tinder. If they were set on fire, the flames spread like a wave which there was no stopping.

The picture of the tongue as a fire is also a common Jewish picture. 'Scoundrels concoct evil, and their speech is like a scorching fire', says the writer of the Proverbs (Proverbs 16:27). 'A hasty quarrel kindles a fire' (Sirach 28:11). There are two reasons why the damage that the tongue can do is like a fire.

(1) It is wide-ranging. The tongue can damage at a distance. A chance word dropped at one end of the country or the town can end up by bringing grief and hurt at the other. The Jewish Rabbis had this picture: 'Life and death are in the hand of the tongue. Has the tongue a hand? No, but as the hand kills, so the tongue. The hand kills only at close quarters; the tongue is called an arrow because it kills at a distance. An arrow kills at forty or fifty paces, but of the tongue it is said (Psalm 73:9): "They set their mouths against the heavens, and their tongue struts through the earth." It ranges over the whole earth and reaches to heaven.' That, indeed, is the peril of the tongue. It is possible to ward off a blow with the hand, for the striker must be physically present. But when someone drops a malicious word, or repeats a scandalous and untrue story, about a complete stranger or about someone who lives hundreds of miles away, it can cause infinite harm.

(2) It is uncontrollable. In the tinder-dry conditions of Palestine, a forest fire was almost immediately out of control – and no one can control the damage of the tongue. 'Three things come not back – the spent arrow, the spoken word and the lost opportunity.' There is nothing so impossible to kill as a rumour; there is nothing so impossible to obliterate as an idle and malicious story. Before we speak, let us remember that once a word is spoken it is gone from our control; and let us think before we speak because, although we cannot get it back, we will most certainly answer for it.

THE CORRUPTION WITHIN

James 3:5b–6 (*contd*)

WE must spend a little longer on this passage, because in it there are two particularly difficult phrases.

(1) The tongue, says the Revised Standard Version, is an *unrighteous world*. That ought to be *the* unrighteous world. In our bodies, that is to say, the tongue stands for the whole wicked world. In Greek, the phrase is *ho kosmos tēs adikias*, and we shall best discover its sense by remembering that *kosmos* can have two meanings.

(a) It can mean *adornment*, although this is less usual. The phrase, therefore, could mean that the tongue is *the adornment of evil*. That would mean that it is the organ which can make evil attractive. By the tongue, people can make the worse appear the better reason; by the tongue, people can excuse and justify their wicked ways; by the tongue, people can persuade others into sin. There is no doubt that this makes excellent sense; but it is doubtful if the phrase really can mean that.

(b) *Kosmos* can mean *world*. In almost every part of the New Testament, *kosmos* means the world, with more than a suggestion of *the evil world*. The world cannot receive the Spirit (John 14:17). Jesus reveals himself to the disciples but not to the world (John 14:22). The world hates him and therefore hates his disciples (John 15:18–19). Jesus' kingdom is not of this world (John 18:36). Paul condemns the wisdom of this world (1 Corinthians 1:20). Christians must not be conformed to this world (Romans 12:2). When *kosmos* is used in this sense, it means *the world without God*, the world in its ignorance of, and often its hostility to, God. Therefore, if we call the tongue the evil *kosmos*, it means that it is that part of the body which is without God. An uncontrolled tongue is like a world hostile to God. It is the part of us which disobeys him.

(2) The second difficult phrase is what the Revised Standard Version translates as *the cycle of nature* (*trochos geneseōs*). It literally means *the wheel of being*.

In the ancient world, the picture of the wheel was used to describe life in four different ways.

(a) The wheel is a circle, a rounded and complete whole – and, therefore, the wheel of life can mean *the totality of life*.

(b) Any particular point in the wheel is always moving up or down. Therefore, the wheel of life can stand for *the ups and downs of life*. In this sense, the phrase very nearly means the wheel of fortune, always changing and always variable.

(c) The wheel is circular; it is always turning back upon itself in exactly the same circle; therefore, the wheel came to stand for *the cyclical repetition of life*, the weary round of an existence which is constantly repeating itself without advancing.

(d) The phrase had one particular technical use. The Orphic religion, which was one of the mystery religions, believed that the human soul was continually undergoing a process of birth and death and rebirth, and the aim of life was to escape from this treadmill into infinite being. So the Orphic devotee who had achieved this state could say: 'I have flown out of the sorrowful, weary wheel.' In this sense, the wheel of life can stand for *the weary treadmill of constant reincarnation*.

It is unlikely that James knew anything about Orphic reincarnation. It is not at all likely that any Christian would think in terms of a cyclical life which was not going anywhere. It is not likely that a Christian would be afraid of the chances and changes of life. Therefore, the phrase most probably means *the whole of life and living*. What James is saying is that the tongue can kindle a destructive fire which can destroy all life; and the tongue itself is kindled with the very fire of hell. Here indeed is its terror.

BEYOND ALL TAMING

James 3:7–8

> Every kind of beast and bird, and reptile and fish, is and
> has been tamed for the service of mankind; but no man
> can tame the tongue. It is a restless evil, full of deadly
> poison.

THE idea of the taming of the animal creation in the service of
human beings is one which often occurs in Jewish literature.
We find it in the creation story. God said of man: 'Have
dominion over the fish of the sea and over the birds of the air
and over every living thing that moves upon the earth' (Genesis
1:28). It is, in fact, to that verse that James is most probably
looking back. The same promise is repeated to Noah: 'The
fear and dread of you shall rest on every animal of the earth,
and on every bird of the air, on everything that creeps on the
ground, and on all the fish of the sea; into your hand they are
delivered' (Genesis 9:2). The writer of Ecclesiasticus repeats
the same idea: 'He [God] put the fear of them in all living
beings, and gave them dominion over beasts and birds' (Sirach
[Ecclesiasticus] 17:4). The psalmist thought on the same lines:
'You have given them dominion over the works of your hands;
you have put all things under their feet, all sheep and oxen,
and also the beasts of the field, the birds of the air, and the fish
of the sea, whatever passes along the paths of the seas' (Psalm
8:6–8). The Roman world knew of tame fish in the fish ponds
which were in the open central hall or atrium of a Roman
house. The serpent was the emblem of Aesculapius, the god
of medicine, and in his temples tame serpents glided about
and were supposed to be incarnations of the god. People who
were ill slept in the temples of Aesculapius at night; and, if
one of these tame serpents glided over them, it was supposed
to be the healing touch of the god.

Human ingenuity has tamed every wild creature in the sense of controlling and making useful; that, says James, is what no one has ever been able to do with the tongue.

BLESSING AND CURSING

James 3:9–12

> With it we bless the Lord and Father and with it we curse the men who have been made in the likeness of God. From the same mouth there emerge blessing and cursing. These things should not be so, my brothers. Surely the one stream from the same cleft in the rock does not gush forth fresh and salt water? Surely, brothers, a fig tree cannot produce olives, nor a vine figs, nor can salt water produce fresh water?

WE know only too well from experience that there is a split in human nature. In human beings there is something of the ape and something of the angel, something of the hero and something of the villain, something of the saint and much of the sinner. It is James' conviction that nowhere is this contradiction more evident than in the tongue.

With it, he says, we bless God. This was especially relevant to a Jew. Whenever the name of God was mentioned, a Jew had to respond: 'Blessed be he!' Three times a day, devout Jews had to repeat the *Shemoneh Esreh*, the famous eighteen prayers called *Eulogies*, every one of which begins: 'Blessed be thou, O God.' God was indeed *eulogētos, the Blessed One*, the one who was continually blessed. And yet the very mouths and tongues which had frequently and piously blessed God were the very same mouths and tongues which cursed their neighbours. To James, there was something unnatural about this; it was as unnatural as for a stream to gush out both fresh and salt water or a bush to bear different kinds of fruit. Unnatural and wrong such things might be, but they were tragically common.

Peter could say: 'Even though I must die with you, I will not deny you' (Matthew 26:35) – and that very same tongue of his denied Jesus with oaths and curses (Matthew 26:69 – 75). The John who said: 'Little children, love one another' was the same who had once wanted to call down fire from heaven in order to destroy a Samaritan village (Luke 9:51– 6). Even the tongues of the apostles could say very different things.

John Bunyan tells us of Talkative: 'He was a saint abroad and a devil at home.' Many people speak with perfect courtesy to strangers and may even preach love and gentleness, and yet snap with impatient irritability at their own families. It has not been unknown for someone to speak with piety on Sunday and to curse a team of workers on Monday. It has not been unknown for someone to utter the most pious sentiments one day and to repeat the most questionable stories the next. It has not been unknown for someone to speak with sweet graciousness at a religious meeting and then to go outside to destroy another person's reputation with a malicious tongue.

These things, said James, should not be. Some drugs are both poisons and cures; they are benefits to a patient when wisely controlled by a doctor, but harmful when used unwisely. The tongue can bless or curse; it can wound or soothe; it can speak the fairest or the foulest things. It is one of life's hardest and plainest duties to see that the tongue does not contradict itself but speaks only such words as we would want God to hear.

THE ONE WHO OUGHT NEVER
TO BE A TEACHER

James 3:13–14

> Who among you is a man of wisdom and of under-
> standing? Let him show by the loveliness of his
> behaviour that all he does is done with gentleness. If in
> your hearts you have a zeal that is bitter, and selfish
> ambition, do not be arrogantly boastful about your
> attainments, for you are false to the truth.

JAMES goes back, as it were, to the beginning of the chapter.
His argument runs like this: 'Is there anyone among you
who wishes to be a real sage and a real teacher? Then let that
person live a life of such beautiful graciousness that it will be
proved to all that gentleness is enthroned as the controlling
power within the heart. For, if you have a fanatical bitterness
and are obviously controlled by selfish and personal ambition,
then, whatever claims you make in your arrogance, all you
are doing is to be false to the truth which you profess to
teach.'

James uses two interesting words. His word for *zeal* is
zēlos. *Zēlos* need not be a bad word. It could mean the desire
to emulate which we feel when confronted with some picture
of greatness and goodness. But there is a very narrow dividing
line between a fine desire to imitate and an unworthy sense
of envy. The word he uses for *selfish ambition* is *eritheia*,
again a word which was not necessarily understood in a bad
sense. It originally meant *spinning for hire* and was used of
serving women. Then it came to mean any work done for
pay. Then it came to mean the kind of work done solely for
what could be got out of it. Then it entered politics and came
to mean that selfish ambition which was out for self and for
nothing else and was ready to use any means to gain its ends.

Scholars and teachers are always susceptible to a double temptation.

(1) They are susceptible to the temptation to *arrogance*. Arrogance was the sin which troubled the Rabbis. The greatest of the Jewish teachers were well aware of that. In the *Sayings of the Fathers*, we read: 'He that is arrogant in decision is foolish, wicked, puffed up in spirit.' It was the advice of one of the wise men: 'It rests with your colleagues to choose whether they will adopt your opinion: it is not for you to force it upon them.' Few are in such constant spiritual peril as teachers and preachers. They are used to being listened to and to having their words accepted. Quite unconsciously, they tend to say, as Shakespeare had it in *The Merchant of Venice*:

> I am Sir Oracle,
> And when I ope my lips let no dog bark!

It is very difficult to be a teacher or a preacher and to remain humble, but it is absolutely necessary.

(2) They are susceptible to the temptation to *bitterness*. We know how easily 'learned discussion can produce passion'. The *odium theologicum* is notorious. The seventeenth-century writer and physician Sir Thomas Browne has a passage on the savagery of scholars to each other: 'Scholars are men of peace, they bear no arms, but their tongues are sharper than Actius's razor; their pens carry farther, and give a louder report than thunder: I had rather stand the shock of a basilisco [a kind of cannon], than the fury of a merciless pen.' Dr H. F. Stewart of Trinity College, Cambridge, said that the arguments of the French philosopher Pascal with the Jesuits reminded him of Alan Breck's fight with the crew of the *Covenant* in Robert Louis Stevenson's *Kidnapped*: 'The sword in his hand flashed like quicksilver into the middle of our flying enemies,

and at every flash came the scream of a man hurt.' One of the most difficult things in the world is to argue without passion and to meet arguments without wounding. To be utterly convinced of one's own beliefs without at the same time being bitter to those of others is no easy matter, and yet it is a first requirement for Christian teachers and scholars.

We may find in this passage four characteristics of the wrong kind of teaching.

(1) It is *fanatical*. The truth it holds is held with un-balanced violence rather than with reasoned conviction.

(2) It is *bitter*. It regards its opponents as enemies to be annihilated rather than as friends to be persuaded.

(3) It is *selfishly ambitious*. It is, in the end, more eager to display itself than to display the truth, and it is interested more in the victory of its own opinions than in the victory of the truth.

(4) It is *arrogant*. Its attitude is pride in its knowledge rather than humility in its ignorance. Genuine scholars will be far more aware of what they do not know than of what they know.

THE WRONG KIND OF WISDOM

James 3:15–16

> Such wisdom is not the wisdom which comes down from above, but is earthly, characteristic of the natural man, inspired by the devil. For where there is envy and selfish ambition, there is disorder and every evil thing.

THIS so-called bitter and arrogant wisdom is very different from real wisdom. James first of all describes it in itself, and then he describes its effects. In itself, it is three things.

(1) It is *earthly*. Its standards and sources are earthly. It measures success in worldly terms, and its aims are worldly aims.

(2) It is *characteristic of the natural man*. The word James uses is difficult to translate. It is *psuchikos*, which comes from *psuchē*. The ancient scholars divided human beings into three parts – body, soul and spirit. The body (*sōma*) is our physical flesh and blood; the soul (*psuchē*) is the physical life which we share with the animals; the spirit (*pneuma*) is that which only human beings possess, which differentiates them from the animals, which makes them rational creatures and kin to God. This is a little confusing for us, because we are in the habit of using *soul* in the same sense as people in the past used *spirit*. James is saying that this wrong kind of wisdom is no more than an animal instinct; it is the kind of wisdom which makes an animal snap and snarl with no other thought than that of prey or personal survival.

(3) It is *devilish*. Its source is not God but the devil. It produces the kind of situation which the devil delights in, not God.

James then describes the effects of this arrogant and bitter wisdom. The most notable thing about it is that it produces disorder. That is to say, instead of bringing people together, it drives them apart. Instead of producing peace, it brings out strife. There is a kind of person who is undoubtedly clever, with an acute brain and a skilful tongue; but the effect of such a person, nevertheless, in any committee, in any church, in any group, is to cause trouble and to disturb personal relationships. It is a sobering thing to remember that the wisdom that person possesses is devilish rather than divine.

THE TRUE WISDOM (1)

James 3:17–18

> The wisdom which comes from above is first pure, then
> peaceable, considerate, willing to yield, full of mercy
> and of good fruits, undivided in mind, without hypocrisy.
> For the seed which one day produces the reward which
> righteousness brings can only be sown when personal
> relationships are right and by those whose conduct
> produces such relationships.

THE Jewish sages were always agreed that the true wisdom
came from above. It was not the result of human attainment
but the gift of God. Wisdom describes this wisdom as 'the
breath of the power of God, and a pure emanation of the
glory of the Almighty' (Wisdom of Solomon 7:25). The
same book prays: 'Give me the wisdom that sits by your
throne' (Wisdom 9:4); and again: 'Send her forth from the
holy heavens, and from the throne of your glory' (Wisdom
9:10). Ben Sirach began his book with the sentence: 'All
wisdom is from the Lord, and it remains with him forever'
(Sirach 1:1); and he makes Wisdom say: 'I came forth from
the mouth of the Most High' (Sirach 24:3). With one voice,
the Jewish sages agreed that wisdom came to men and women
from God.

James uses eight words to describe this wisdom, and every
one has a great picture in it.

(1) The true wisdom is *pure*. The Greek is *hagnos*, and its
root meaning is *pure enough to approach the gods*. At first, it
had only a ceremonial meaning and meant nothing more than
having gone through the right ritual cleansings. So, for
instance, the Greek dramatist Euripides can make one of his
characters say: 'My hands are pure, but my heart is not.' At
this stage, *hagnos* describes ritual, but not necessarily moral,

purity. But, as time went on, the word came to describe the moral purity which alone can approach the gods. On the Temple of Aesculapius at Epidaurus, there was the inscription at the entrance: 'He who would enter the divine temple must be pure [*hagnos*]; and purity is to have a mind which thinks holy thoughts.' The true wisdom is so cleansed of all ulterior motives and of self that it has become pure enough to see God. Worldly wisdom might well wish to escape God's sight; the true wisdom is able to bear his very scrutiny.

(2) The true wisdom is *eirēnikos*. We have translated this as *peaceable*, but it has a very special meaning. *Eirēnē* means *peace*, and when it is used in a human context its basic meaning is *right relationships between individuals, and between individuals and God*. The true wisdom produces right relationships. There is a kind of clever and arrogant wisdom which separates people from one another, and which makes them look with superior contempt on others. There is a kind of cruel wisdom which takes a delight in hurting others with clever but cutting words. There is a kind of depraved wisdom which seduces men and women away from their loyalty to God. But the true wisdom at all times brings people closer to one another and to God.

(3) The true wisdom is *epieikēs*. Of all Greek words in the New Testament, this is one of the most untranslatable. Aristotle defined it as that 'which is just beyond the written law' and as 'justice and better than justice' and as that 'which steps in to correct things when the law itself becomes unjust'. The person who is *epieikēs* is someone who knows when it is actually wrong to apply the strict letter of the law. Such a person knows how to forgive when strict justice dictates that there is a perfect right to condemn. Such a person knows how to make allowances, when not to stand upon individual rights, and how to soften justice with mercy, and

always remembers that there are greater things in the world than rules and regulations. It is impossible to find an English word to translate this quality. The poet Matthew Arnold called it 'sweet reasonableness', and it is the ability to extend to others the kindly consideration we would wish to receive ourselves.

THE TRUE WISDOM (2)

James 3:17–18 (*contd*)

(4) The true wisdom is *eupeithēs*. Here we must make a choice between two meanings. (a) *Eupeithēs* can mean *always ready to obey*. The first of the eighteenth-century churchman William Law's rules for life was: 'To fix it deep in my mind that I have but one business upon my hands, to seek for eternal happiness by doing the will of God.' If we take the word in this sense, it means that the truly wise are always ready to obey whenever God's voice comes to them. (b) *Eupeithēs* can mean *easy to persuade*, not in the sense of being pliable and weak, but in the sense of not being stubborn and of being willing to listen to reason and to appeal. Coming as it does after *epieikēs*, it probably bears this second meaning here. The true wisdom is not rigid but is willing to listen and skilled in knowing when wisely to yield.

(5) We take the next two terms together. The true wisdom is *full of mercy* (*eleos*) *and good fruits*. *Eleos* is a word which acquired a new meaning in Christian thought. The Greeks defined it as *pity for the one who is suffering unjustly*; but Christianity means far more than that by *eleos*. (a) In Christian thought, *eleos* means mercy for those who are in trouble, even if the trouble is their own fault. Christian pity is the reflection of God's pity, and that went out to men and women not only when they were suffering unjustly but also when

they were suffering through their own fault. We are so apt to say, of someone in trouble, 'It is his own fault' or 'She brought it on herself', and therefore to feel no responsibility ourselves. Christian mercy is mercy for all who are in trouble, even if they have brought that trouble on themselves. (b) In Christian thought, *eleos* means mercy which produces good fruits, that is, which results in practical help. Christian pity is not merely an emotion; it is action. We can never say that we have truly pitied anyone until we have given our help.

(6) The true wisdom is *adiakritos, undivided*. This means that it is not wavering and swaying; it knows its own mind, chooses its course and abides by it. There are those who think that it is clever never to make one's mind up about anything. They speak about having an open mind and about suspending judgment. But Christian wisdom is based on Christian certainties which come to us from God through Jesus Christ.

(7) The true wisdom is *anupokritos, without hypocrisy*. That is to say, it is not a pose and does not deal in deception. It is honest; it never pretends to be what it is not; and it never acts a part to gain its own ends.

(8) Finally, James says something which every Christian church and every Christian group should have written on its heart. The Revised Standard Version correctly translates the Greek literally: 'The harvest of righteousness is sown in peace by those who make peace.' This is a highly compressed sentence. Let us remember that peace, *eirēnē*, means *right relationships between individuals*. So, what James is saying is this: 'We are all trying to reap the harvest which a good life brings. But the seeds which bring the rich harvest can never flourish in any atmosphere other than one of right relationships between individuals. And the only people who can sow these seeds and reap the reward

are those whose life work it has been to produce such right relationships.'

That is to say, nothing good can ever grow in an atmosphere where people are at variance with one another. A group where there is bitterness and strife is a barren soil in which the seeds of righteousness can never grow and out of which no reward can ever come. Those who disturb personal relationships and are responsible for strife and bitterness have cut themselves off from the reward which God gives to those who live a godly life.

HUMAN PLEASURE OR GOD'S WILL?

James 4:1-3

> Whence come feuds and whence come fights among you? Is this not their source – do they not arise because of these desires for pleasures which carry on their constant warring campaign within your members? You desire but you do not possess; you murder; you covet but you cannot obtain. You fight and war but you do not possess, because you do not ask. You ask but you do not receive, because you ask wrongly, for your only desire is to spend what you receive on your own pleasures.

JAMES is setting before his people a basic question – whether their aim in life is to submit to the will of God or to gratify their own desires for the pleasures of this world. He warns that, if pleasure is the policy of life, nothing but strife and hatred and division can possibly follow. He says that the result of the overriding search for pleasure is *polemoi* (wars) and *machai* (battles). He means that the feverish search for pleasure results in long-drawn-out resentments, which are like wars, and sudden explosions of enmity, which are like battles. The ancient moralists would have thoroughly agreed with him.

When we look at human society, we so often see a seething mass of hatred and strife. The Jewish scholar Philo writes: 'Consider the continual war which prevails among men even in times of peace, and which exists not only between nations and countries and cities, but also between private houses, or, I might rather say, is present with every individual man; observe the unspeakable raging storm in men's souls that is excited by the violent rush of the affairs of life; and you may well wonder whether anyone can enjoy tranquillity in such a storm, and maintain calm amid the surge of this billowing sea.'

The root cause of this endless and bitter conflict is nothing other than desire. Philo points out that the Ten Commandments culminate in the forbidding of covetousness or desire, for desire is the worst of all the passions of the soul. 'Is it not because of this passion that relations are broken, and this natural goodwill changed into desperate enmity? that great and populous countries are desolated by domestic dissensions? and land and sea filled with ever new disasters by naval battles and land campaigns? For the wars famous in tragedy . . . have all flowed from one source – desire either for money or glory or pleasure. Over these things the human race goes mad.' Lucian, the Greek satirist, writes: 'All the evils which come upon man – revolutions and wars, stratagems and slaughters – spring from desire. All these things have as their fountain-head the desire for more.' Plato writes: 'The sole cause of wars and revolutions and battles is nothing other than the body and its desires.' Cicero, the Roman orator, writes: 'It is insatiable desires which overturn not only individual men, but whole families, and which even bring down the state. From desires there spring hatred, schisms, discords, seditions and wars.' Desire is at the root of all the evils which ruin life and cause divisions.

The New Testament is clear that this overriding desire for the pleasures of this world is always a threatening danger to the spiritual life. It is the cares and riches and pleasures of this life which combine to choke the good seed (Luke 8:14). People can become slaves to passions and pleasures – and, when that happens, malice and envy and hatred enter into life (cf. Titus 3:3).

The ultimate choice in life lies between pleasing oneself and pleasing God, and a world in which people seek first and foremost to please themselves is a battle ground of savagery and division.

THE CONSEQUENCES OF THE LIFE DOMINATED BY PLEASURE

James 4:1–3 (*contd*)

THIS life dominated by pleasure has certain inevitable consequences.

(1) It sets people at each other's throats. Desires, as James sees it, are fundamentally warring powers. He does not mean that they war within a person – although that is also true – but that they set individuals warring against each other. The basic desires are for the same things – for money, for power, for prestige, for worldly possessions, for the gratification of physical lusts. When everyone is striving to possess the same things, life inevitably becomes a competitive arena. People trample each other down in the rush to grasp what they want. They will do anything to eliminate a rival. Obedience to the will of God draws people together, for it is that will that they should love and serve one another; obedience to the craving

for pleasure drives them apart, for it drives them to rivalry for the same things.

(2) The craving for pleasure drives people to shameful deeds. It drives them to envy and to enmity – and even to murder. Before reaching the point of action, there must be a certain driving emotion in the heart. People may restrain themselves from the things that the desire for pleasure incites them to do, but as long as that desire is in their hearts they are not safe. It may at any time burst free and lead to ruinous action.

The steps of the process are simple and terrible. We allow ourselves to desire something. That thing begins to dominate our thoughts; we find ourselves involuntarily thinking about it in our waking hours and dreaming of it when we sleep. It begins to be what is aptly called a *ruling passion*. We begin to form imaginary schemes to obtain it; and these plans may well involve ways of eliminating those who stand in our way. For some time, all this may go on in the mind. Then one day the imaginings may blaze into action; and we may find ourselves taking the terrible steps necessary to obtain our desire. Every crime in this world has come from desire which was first only a feeling in the heart but which, being nourished long enough, in the end resulted in action.

(3) The craving for pleasure in the end shuts the door of prayer. If our prayers are simply for the things which will gratify our desires, they are essentially selfish – and, therefore, it is not possible for God to answer them. The true end of prayer is to say to God: 'Your will be done.' The prayer of the person who is dominated by pleasure is: 'My desires be satisfied.' It is one of the grim facts of life that a selfish person can hardly ever pray aright; no one can ever pray aright until self has been removed from the centre of life and God has been put there instead.

In this life, we have to choose whether to make our main object our own desires or the will of God. And, if we choose our own desires, we have thereby separated ourselves from other people and from God.

INFIDELITY TO GOD

James 4:4–7

> Renegades to your vows, do you not know that love for this world is enmity to God? Whoever makes it his aim to be the friend of this world thereby becomes the enemy of God. Do you think that the saying of Scripture is only an idle saying: 'God jealously yearns for the spirit which he has made to dwell within us'? But God gives the more grace. That is why Scripture says: 'God sets himself against the haughty, but gives grace to the humble.' So, then, submit yourselves to God. Resist the devil and he will flee from you; draw near to God and he will draw near to you.

THE Authorized Version makes this passage even more difficult than it is. In it, the warning is addressed to *adulterers* and *adulteresses*. In the correct text, the word occurs only in the feminine. Further, the word is not intended to be taken literally; the reference is not to physical but to spiritual adultery. The whole idea is based on the common Old Testament concept of Yahweh as the husband of Israel and Israel as the bride of God. 'Your Maker is your husband, the Lord of hosts is his name' (Isaiah 54:5). 'Instead as a faithless wife leaves her husband, so you have been faithless to me, O house of Israel, says the Lord' (Jeremiah 3:20). This idea of Yahweh as the husband and the nation of Israel as the wife explains the way in which the Old Testament constantly expresses spiritual infidelity in terms of physical adultery. To make a covenant with the gods of a strange land and to sacrifice to them and to intermarry with their people is to 'prostitute themselves to their gods' (Exodus 34:15–16). It is God's forewarning to Moses that the day will come when the people 'will begin to prostitute themselves to the foreign gods in their midst, the gods of the land into which they are going', and that they will forsake him (Deuteronomy 31:16). It is Hosea's complaint that the people have played the whore and forsaken God (Hosea 9:1). It is in this spiritual sense that the New Testament speaks of 'an *adulterous* generation' (Matthew 16:4; Mark 8:38). And the picture came into Christian thought in the idea of the Church as the bride of Christ (2 Corinthians 11:1–2; Ephesians 5:24–8; Revelation 19:7, 21:9).

This form of expression may offend some delicate modern ears, but the picture of Israel as the bride of God and of God as the husband of Israel has something very precious in it. It means that to disobey God is like breaking the marriage vow. It means that all sin is sin against love. It means that our relationship to God is not like the distant relationship of king and subject or master and slave, but like the intimate relationship of husband and wife. It means that when we sin we break God's heart, as the heart of one partner in a marriage may be broken by the desertion of the other.

FRIENDSHIP WITH THE WORLD
AND ENMITY WITH GOD

James 4:4–7 (*contd*)

In this passage, James says that love of the world is enmity or hostility with God and that whoever is the friend of the world thereby becomes the enemy of God. It is important to understand what he means.

(1) This is not spoken out of contempt for the world. It is not spoken from the point of view which, to use an image from Thomas Taylor's hymn, regards earth as 'a desert drear' and which cannot see anything good in the natural world. There is a story of a Puritan who was out for a walk in the country with a friend. The friend noticed a very lovely flower at the roadside and said: 'That is a lovely flower.' The Puritan replied: 'I have learned to call nothing lovely in this lost and sinful world.' That is not James' point of view; he would have agreed that this world is the creation of God; and like Jesus he would have rejoiced in its beauty.

(2) We have already seen that the New Testament often uses the word *kosmos* in the sense of *the world apart from God*. There are two New Testament passages which well illustrate what James means. Paul writes: 'The mind that is set on the flesh is hostile to God . . . those who are in the flesh cannot please God' (Romans 8:7–8). What he means is that those who insist on assessing everything by purely human standards are necessarily at variance with God. The second passage is one of the most poignant epitaphs on the Christian life in all literature: 'Demas, in love with this present world, has deserted me' (2 Timothy 4:10). The idea is that of *worldliness*. If material things are the things to which we dedicate our lives, clearly we cannot dedicate our lives to God. In that sense, those who have dedicated their lives to the world are at enmity with God.

(3) The best commentary on this saying is that of Jesus: 'No one can serve two masters' (Matthew 6:24). There are two attitudes to the things of this world and the things of time. We may be so dominated by them that the world becomes our master. Or we may so use them as to serve our neighbours

and prepare ourselves for eternity, in which case the world is not our master but our servant. We may either use the world or be used by it. To use the world as the servant of God and of others is to be the friend of God, for that is what God meant the world to be. To use the world as the controller and dictator of life is to be at enmity with God, for that is precisely what God never meant the world to be.

GOD THE JEALOUS LOVER

James 4:4–7 (*contd*)

VERSE 5 is exceedingly difficult. To begin with, it is cited as a quotation from Scripture; but there is no part of Scripture of which it is, in fact, anything like a recognizable quotation. We may assume either that James is quoting from some book now lost which he regarded as Scripture, or that he is summing up in one sentence what is the eternal sense of the Old Testament and is not meaning to quote any particular passage.

Further, the translation is difficult. There are two alternative renderings which in the end give much the same sense: 'He [that is, God] jealously yearns for the devotion of the spirit which he has made to dwell within us', or 'The Spirit which God has made to dwell within us jealously yearns for the full devotion of our hearts.'

In either case, the meaning is that God is the jealous lover who will not tolerate a rival. The Old Testament was never afraid to apply the word *jealous* to God. Moses says of God and the people: 'They made him jealous with strange gods' (Deuteronomy 32:16). He hears God say: 'They made me jealous with what is no God' (Deuteronomy 32:21). In insisting on his sole right to worship, God in the Ten

Commandments says: 'I the Lord your God am a jealous God' (Exodus 20:5). 'You shall worship no other god, because the Lord, whose name is Jealous, is a jealous God' (Exodus 34:14). Zechariah hears God say: 'Thus says the Lord of hosts: I am jealous for Zion with great jealousy' (Zechariah 8:2). *Jealous* comes from the Greek *zēlos*, which has in it the idea of burning heat. The idea is that God loves human beings with such a passion that he cannot bear any other love within the hearts of men and women.

It may be that *jealous* is a word which nowadays we find it difficult to connect with God, for it has acquired a significance and association with undesirable feelings; but behind it is the amazing truth that God is the lover of our souls. There is a sense in which love must be spread among all people and over all God's children, but there is also a sense in which love gives and demands an exclusive devotion to one person. It is profoundly true that we can be in love only with one person at any one time; if we think otherwise, we do not know the meaning of love.

THE GLORY OF HUMILITY
AND THE TRAGEDY OF PRIDE

James 4:4-7 (*contd*)

JAMES goes on to meet an almost inevitable reaction to this picture of God as the jealous lover. If God is like that, how can anyone give to him the devotion he demands? James' answer is that, if God makes a great demand, he gives great grace to fulfil it; and the greater the demand, the greater the grace God gives.

But grace has a constant characteristic – we cannot receive it until we have realized our need of it and have come to God humbly pleading for help. Therefore, it must always remain true that God sets himself against the proud and gives lavishly of his grace to the humble. 'God opposes the proud, but gives grace to the humble.' This is a quotation from Proverbs 3:34, and it is made again in 1 Peter 5:5.

What is this destructive pride? The word for *proud* is *huperēphanos*, which literally means *one who shows himself above other people*. Even the Greeks hated pride. The philosopher Theophrastus described it as 'a certain contempt for all other people'. Theophylact, the Christian writer, called it 'the citadel and summit of all evils'. Its real terror is that it is a thing of the heart. It means *haughtiness*; but those who suffer from it might well appear to be walking in downcast humility, while all the time there is in their hearts a vast contempt for other people.

This pride shuts itself off from God for three reasons. (1) *It does not know its own need*. It so admires itself that it recognizes no need to be supplied. (2) *It cherishes its own independence*. It will be indebted or obligated to no one and not even to God. (3) *It does not recognize its own sin*. It is occupied with thinking of its own goodness and never realizes that it has any sin from which it needs to be saved. A pride like that cannot receive help, because it does not know that it needs help, and therefore it cannot ask.

The humility for which James pleads is not a cringing subservience. It has two great characteristics.

(1) It knows that if anyone takes a resolute stand against the devil, the devil will be proved to be a coward. 'The devil', as the author of *The Shepherd of Hermas* puts it, 'can wrestle against the Christian, but he cannot throw him.' This is a truth of which the Christians were fond, for Peter says the same thing (1 Peter 5:8–9). The great example and inspiration is Jesus in his own temptations. In them, Jesus showed

that the devil is not invincible; when he is confronted with the word of God, he can be put to flight. Christians have the humility that knows that they must fight their battles with the tempter, not in their own power, but in the power of God.

(2) It knows that it has the greatest privilege of all – access to God. This is a tremendous thing, for the right of approach to God under the old order of things belonged only to the priests (Exodus 19:22). The office of the priest was to come near to God for sin-stained people (Ezekiel 44:13). But, through the work of Jesus Christ, anyone can come boldly before the throne of God, certain of finding mercy and grace to help in time of need (Hebrews 4:16). There was a time when only the high priest might enter the Holy of Holies; but we have a new and a living way, a better hope by which we draw near to God (Hebrews 7:19).

Christians must have humility, but it is a humility which gives them unfailing courage and which knows that the way to God is open to the most fearful saint.

GODLY PURITY

James 4:8–10

> Cleanse your hands, you sinners, and purify your hearts, you double-minded. Be afflicted and mourn and weep. Let your laughter be turned to sorrow, and your joy to gloom. Humble yourself before God and then he will exalt you.

IN James' thought, the ethical demand of Christianity is never far away. He has talked about the grace which God gives to the humble and which enables people to meet great demands. But James is sure that there is something needed beyond asking and passive receiving. He is sure that moral effort is a prime necessity.

His appeal is addressed to *sinners*. The word used for *sinner* is *hamartōlos*, which means the hardened sinner, the one whose sin is obvious and notorious. Suidas, the tenth-century scholar who compiled works of reference, defines *hamartōloi* as 'those who choose to live in company with disobedience to the law, and who love a corrupt life'. From such people, James demands a moral reform which will embrace both their outward conduct and their inner desires. He demands both clean hands and a pure heart (Psalm 24:4).

The phrase *cleanse your hands* originally denoted nothing more than ceremonial cleansing, the ritual washing with water which made people ceremonially fit to approach the worship of God. The priests had to wash and bathe themselves before they entered on their service (Exodus 30:19–21; Leviticus 16:4). Orthodox Jews had to perform the ceremony of washing their hands before they ate (Mark 7:3). But people came to see that God required much more than an outward washing; and so the phrase came to stand for moral purity. 'I wash my hands in innocence', says the psalmist (Psalm 26:6). It is Isaiah's demand that the people should 'wash yourselves; make yourselves clean', and that is equated with ceasing to do evil (Isaiah 1:16). In the letter to Timothy, the men are urged to lift holy hands to God in prayer (1 Timothy 2:8). The history of the phrase shows a deepening consciousness of what God demanded. People began by thinking in terms of an outward washing, a ritual practice, and ended by seeing that the demand of God was moral, not ritual.

Biblical thought demands a fourfold cleansing. It demands a cleansing of the *lips* (Isaiah 6:5–6). It demands a cleansing of the *hands* (Psalm 24:4). It demands a cleansing of the *heart* (Psalm 73:13). It demands a cleansing of the *mind* (James

Elohim — Triune creator + Sovereign
of the Universe, of life + all
nations.

Jehovah: God of revelation — God of
his covenant people.

El- Shaddai — mighty — sufficient
+ satisfying one.

Adonai — sovereign Lord, the
master of our lives + service

Jireh — one who provides sacrificial
lamb of our redemption.

Rophe — Healer of life's sicknesses + sorrows

Nissi — Standard of our victory in life's
conflicts,
m'Kaddesh —

Printed as a Special Service Project by
Students of the Graphic Arts Lab—Fairfax High School

4:8). That is to say, the ethical demand of the Bible is that a person's words and deeds and emotions and thoughts should all be purified. Inwardly and outwardly, men and women must be clean, for only the pure in heart shall see God (Matthew 5:8).

THE GODLY SORROW

James 4:8–10 (*contd*)

IN his demand for a godly sorrow, James is going back to the fact that Jesus had said: 'Blessed are those who mourn, for they will be comforted' (Matthew 5:4; cf. Luke 6:20–6). We must not read into this passage something James does not mean. He is not denying the joy of the Christian life. He is not demanding that people should live a life filled with gloom in a shadowed world. He is doing two things. He is pleading for a sober life in place of frivolity, and is doing so with all the intensity of one whose natural instincts are puritan, and he is describing not the *end* but the *beginning* of the Christian life. He demands three things.

(1) He demands what he calls *affliction*. The verb is *talaiporein*, and it can describe – the Greek historian Thucydides uses it in this way – the experiences of an army whose food has all gone and who have no shelter from the stormy weather. What James is demanding is a voluntary restraint from lavish luxury and excessive comfort. He is talking to people who are in love with the world, and he is pleading with them not to make luxury and comfort the standards by which they judge all life. It is discipline which produces the scholar; it is rigorous training which creates the athlete; and it is a wise abstinence which produces the Christian who knows how to use the world and its gifts aright.

(2) He demands that they should *mourn*, that their laughter should be turned to sorrow and their joy to gloom. Here, James is describing the *first* step of the Christian life which is taken when people are confronted with God and with their own sin. That is a daunting experience. When John Wesley, the founder of Methodism, preached to the miners of Kingswood, they were moved to such grief that the tears made streaks as they ran down the grime of their faces. But that is by no means the end of the Christian life. The terrible sorrow of the realization of sin moves on to the thrilling joy of sins forgiven. But, to get to the second stage, it is necessary to go through the first. James is demanding that these self-satisfied, luxury-loving, unworried hearers of his should be confronted with their sins and should be ashamed, grief-stricken and afraid, for only then can they reach out for grace and go on to a joy far greater than their earthbound pleasures.

(3) He demands that they should *weep*. It is perhaps not reading too much into this to say that James may well be thinking of *tears of sympathy*. Up to this time, these luxury-loving people have lived in utter selfishness, quite insensitive to what the Italian poet, Petrarch, called 'a rain of tears'. James is insisting that the griefs and the needs of others should pierce the armour of their own pleasure and comfort. We are not truly Christians until we become aware of the poignant cry of that humanity for which Christ died.

So, in words deliberately chosen to waken the sleeping soul, James demands that his hearers should substitute the way of restraint for the way of luxury, that they should become aware of their own sins and mourn for them, and that they should become conscious of the world's need and weep for it.

THE GODLY HUMILITY

James 4:8–10 (*contd*)

JAMES concludes with the demand for a godly humility. All through the Bible, there runs the conviction that it is only the humble who can know the blessings of God. God will save the humble person (Job 22:29). A person's pride will bring humiliation, but whoever is humble in spirit will obtain honour (Proverbs 29:23). God dwells on high, but he is also with whoever is of a humble and a contrite spirit (Isaiah 57:15). Those who fear the Lord will humble their souls in his sight, and the greater people are, the more they ought to humble themselves if they are to find favour in the sight of God (Sirach 2:17, 3:18). Jesus himself repeatedly declared that it was only those who humbled themselves who would be exalted (Matthew 23:12; Luke 14:11).

Only when people realize their own ignorance will they ask God's guidance. Only when they realize their own poverty in the things that matter will they pray for the riches of God's grace. Only when people realize their weakness in necessary things will they come to draw upon God's strength. Only when they realize their own sin will they realize their need of a Saviour and of God's forgiveness.

In life, there is one sin which can be said to be the basis of all others, and that is forgetting that we are creatures and that God is creator. When we realize our essential creatureliness, we realize our essential helplessness and go to the only source from which our helplessness can find assistance.

Such a dependence brings forth the only real independence, for then we face life not in our own strength but in God's, and we are given victory. As long as we regard ourselves as independent of God, we are on the way to ultimate collapse and to defeat.

THE SIN OF JUDGING OTHERS

James 4:11–12

> Stop talking harshly about each other. He who speaks
> harshly of his brother, or who judges his brother,
> speaks harshly of the law and judges the law; and, if
> you judge the law, you are not a doer of the law but a
> judge of it. One is law-giver and judge, he who is able
> to save and to destroy. Who are you to judge your
> neighbour?

THE word James uses for *to speak harshly of*, or *to slander*, is
katalalein. Usually this verb means to slander someone when
he or she is not there to offer a defence. This sin of slander
(the noun is *katalalia*) is condemned all through the Bible.
It is the psalmist's accusation against the wicked: 'You sit
and speak against your kin; you slander your own mother's
child' (Psalm 50:20). The psalmist hears God saying: 'One
who secretly slanders a neighbour I will destroy' (Psalm
101:5). Paul lists it among the sins which are characteristic of
the unredeemed evil of the non-Christian world (Romans
1:30), and it is one of the sins which he fears he will find
in the warring church of Corinth (2 Corinthians 12:20). It
is significant to note that, in both these passages, *slander*
comes in immediate connection with *gossip*. *Katalalia* is
the sin of those who meet in corners and gather in little
groups and pass on confidential titbits of information which
destroy the good name of those who are not there to defend
themselves. The same sin is condemned by Peter (1 Peter 2:1).

This is a much-needed warning. People are slow to realize
that there are few sins which the Bible so unsparingly
condemns as the sin of irresponsible and malicious gossip.
There are few activities in which the average person finds more
delight than this; to tell and to listen to the slanderous story –

especially about some famous person – is for most people a fascinating activity. We do well to remember what God thinks of it. James condemns it for two fundamental reasons.

(1) It is a breach of the royal law that we should love our neighbour as ourselves (James 2:8; Leviticus 19:18). Obviously we cannot love our neighbours as ourselves and speak slanderous evil about them. Now, if people break a law knowingly, they set themselves above the law. That is to say, they have made themselves judges of the law. But the duty of everyone is not to judge the law but to obey it. So those who speak evil of their neighbours have appointed themselves as judges of the law and taken to themselves the right to break it, and therefore they stand condemned.

(2) It is an infringement of the prerogative of God. To slander our neighbours is, in fact, to pass judgment upon them. And no human being has any right to judge any other human being; the right of judgment belongs to God alone.

It is God alone who is able to save and to destroy. This great prerogative runs all through Scripture. 'I kill and I make alive', says God (Deuteronomy 32:39). 'The Lord kills and brings to life', says Hannah in her prayer (1 Samuel 2:6). 'Am I God, to give death or life?' is the shocked question of the Israelite king to whom Naaman came with a demand for a cure for his leprosy (2 Kings 5:7). Jesus warns that we should not fear those who at the worst can only kill the body, but should fear those who can destroy both body and soul (Matthew 10:28). As the psalmist had it, it is to God alone that the issues of life and of death belong (Psalm 68:20). To judge another is to take to ourselves a right to do what God alone has the right to do, and anyone who deliberately infringes the prerogatives of God is indeed reckless.

We might think that to speak evil of our neighbour is not a very serious sin. But Scripture would say that it is one of the worst of all sins because it breaks the royal law and is an infringement of the rights of God.

THE MISTAKEN CONFIDENCE

James 4:13–17

> Come now, you who say: 'Today, or tomorrow, we will go into this city, and we will spend a year there, and we will trade and make a profit.' People like you do not know what will happen tomorrow. What is your life like? You are like a mist which appears for a little time and then disappears. And yet you talk like that instead of saying: 'If the Lord wills, we shall live, and we shall do this or that.' As it is, you make your arrogant claims in your braggart ways. All such arrogant claims are evil. So then, if a man knows what is good and does not do it, that to him is sin.

HERE again is a contemporary picture which James' readers would recognize, and in which they might well see their own portrait. The Jews were the great traders of the ancient world, and in many ways that world gave them every opportunity to practise their commercial abilities. This was an age of the founding of cities; and often, when cities were founded and their founders were looking for citizens to occupy them, citizenship was offered freely to the Jews, for where the Jews came, money and trade followed. So the picture is of a man looking at a map. He points at a certain spot on it and says: 'Here is a new city where there are great trade chances. I'll go there; I'll start at the bottom; I'll trade for a year or so; I'll make my fortune and come back rich.' James' answer is that no one has a right to make confident plans for the future, for we do not know what even a day may bring. As Thomas à Kempis had it in his book *The Imitation of Christ*: 'Man proposes, but God disposes.'

The essential uncertainty of the future was deeply impressed on the minds of men and women of all nations. The Hebrew sage wrote: 'Do not boast about tomorrow, for you do not know what a day may bring' (Proverbs 27:1). Jesus told his story of the rich but foolish man who made his fortune and built up his plans for the future but forgot that his soul might be required of him that very night (Luke 12:16–21). Ben Sirach wrote: 'One becomes rich through diligence and self-denial, and the reward allotted to him is this: when he says "I have found rest, and now I shall feast on my goods!" he does not know how long it will be until he leaves them to others and dies' (Sirach 11:18–19). Seneca said: 'How foolish it is for a man to make plans for his life, when not even tomorrow is in his control.' And again: 'No man has such rich friends that he can promise himself tomorrow.' The Rabbis had a proverb: 'Care not for the morrow, for you know not what a day may bring forth. Perhaps you may not find tomorrow.' Dennis Mackail was a friend of the writer Sir James Barrie. He tells that, as Barrie grew older, he would never make an arrangement for even a social engagement at any distant date. 'Short notice now!' he would always say.

James goes on. This uncertainty of life is not a cause either for fear or for inaction. It is a reason for realizing our complete dependence on God. It has always been the mark of serious-minded people that they make their plans in such dependence. Paul writes to the Corinthians: 'I will come to you soon, if the Lord wills' (1 Corinthians 4:19). 'I hope to spend some time with you, if the Lord permits' (1 Corinthians 16:7). Xenophon, the Greek historian, writes: 'May all these things be, if the gods so will. If anyone wonders that we often find the phrase written, "if the gods will", I would have him to know that, once he has experienced the risks of life, he will not wonder nearly so much.' Plato relates a conversation between Socrates and Alcibiades. Alcibiades says: 'I will do so if you wish, Socrates.' Socrates answers: 'Alcibiades, that is not the way to talk. And how ought you to speak? You ought to say: "If *God* so wishes."' The second-century Christian author Minucius Felix writes: 'God grant it – it comes instinctively to the ordinary man to speak like that.' Among the Arabs, the expression: 'Insh' Allah – if Allah wills' is constantly used. The curious thing is that there seems to have been no corresponding phrase which the Jews used. In this, they had to learn.

The true Christian way is not to be terrorized into fear and paralysed into inaction by the uncertainty of the future, but to commit the future and all our plans into the hands of God, always remembering that these plans may not be within God's purpose.

Anyone who does not remember that is guilty of arrogant boasting. The word is *alazoneia*. *Alazoneia* was originally the characteristic of the wandering quack who offered cures which were no cures and boasted of things that he was not able to do. The future is not within our hands, and no one can arrogantly claim to have the power to decide it.

James ends with a threat. Anyone who knows that a thing is wrong and still continues to do it commits sin. James is in effect saying: 'You have been warned; the truth has been placed before your eyes.' To continue now in the self-confident habit of seeking to dispose of one's own life is sin for anyone who has been reminded that the future is not in our hands but in God's.

THE WORTHLESSNESS OF RICHES

James 5:1-3

> Come now, you rich, weep and wail at the miseries
> which are coming upon you. Your wealth is rotten and
> your garments are food for moths. Your gold and silver
> are corroded clean through with rust, and their rust is
> proof to you of how worthless they are. It is a rust which
> will eat into your very flesh like fire. It is a treasure
> indeed that you have amassed for yourselves in the last
> days!

In the first six verses of this chapter, James has two aims –
first, to show the ultimate worthlessness of all earthly
riches, and, second, to show the detestable character of those
who possess them. By doing this, he hopes to prevent his
readers from placing all their hopes and desires on earthly
things.

If you knew what you were doing, he says to the rich, you
would weep and wail for the terror of the judgment that is
coming upon you at the day of the Lord. The vividness of the
picture is increased by the word which James uses for *to wail*.
It is the verb *ololuzein*, which is onomatopoeic; that is, it
carries its meaning in its very sound. It means even more
than to wail; it means *to shriek*, and in the Authorized Version
is often translated as *to howl*; and it depicts the frantic terror
of those on whom the judgment of God has come (Isaiah
13:6, 14:31, 15:2-3, 16:7, 23:1, 23:14, 65:14; Amos 8:3). We
might well say that it is the word which describes those
undergoing the tortures of the damned.

All through this passage, the words are vivid and pictorial
and carefully chosen. In the middle east, there were three
main sources of wealth, and James has a word for the decay
of each of them.

There were corn and grain. That is the wealth which becomes rotten (*sēpein*).

There were garments. In this part of the world, garments were wealth. Joseph gave changes of garments to his brothers (Genesis 45:22). It was for a beautiful mantle from Shinar that Achan brought disaster on the nation and death on himself and his family (Joshua 7:21). It was changes of garments that Samson promised to anyone who would solve his riddle (Judges 14:12). It was garments that Naaman brought as a gift to the prophet of Israel and to obtain which Gehazi sinned (2 Kings 5:5, 5:22). It was Paul's claim that he had coveted no one's money or clothing (Acts 20:33). These garments, which are so splendid, will be food for moths (*sētobrōtos*; cf. Matthew 6:19).

The climax of the world's inevitable decay comes at the end. Even their gold and silver will be rusted clean through (*katiasthai*). The point is that gold and silver do not actually rust; so James in the most vivid way is giving a warning that even the most precious and apparently most indestructible things are doomed to decay.

This rust is proof of the impermanence and ultimate valuelessness of all earthly things. More, it is a dreadful warning. The desire for these things is like a terrible rust eating into people's bodies and souls. Then comes a grim sarcasm. It is a fine treasure indeed that all who concentrate on these things are heaping up for themselves at the last. The only treasure they will possess is a consuming fire which will wipe them out.

It is James' conviction that to concentrate on material things is not only to concentrate on a decaying delusion; it is to concentrate on self-produced destruction.

THE SOCIAL PASSION OF THE BIBLE

James 5:1-3 (*contd*)

NOT even the most cursory reader of the Bible can fail to be impressed with the social passion which blazes through its pages. No book condemns dishonest and selfish wealth with such searing passion as it does. The book of the prophet Amos was called 'The Cry for Social Justice' by the Old Testament scholar J. E. McFadyen. Amos condemns those who store up violence and robbery in their palaces (Amos 3:10). He condemns those who tread on the poor and themselves have houses of hewn stone and pleasant vineyards – which in the wrath of God they will never enjoy (Amos 5:11). He lets loose his wrath on those who give short weight and short measure, who buy the poor for silver and the needy for a pair of shoes, and who palm off on the poor the refuse of their wheat. 'I will never forget any of their deeds', says God (Amos 8:4-7). Isaiah warns those who build up great estates by adding house to house and field to field (Isaiah 5:8). The sage insists that those who trust in riches shall fall (Proverbs 11:28). Luke quotes Jesus as saying: 'Woe to you that are rich!' (Luke 6:24). It is only with difficulty that those who have riches enter into the kingdom of God (Luke 18:24). Riches are a temptation and a snare; the rich are liable to foolish and hurtful desires which end in ruin, for the love of money is the root of all evils (1 Timothy 6:9-10).

In the intertestamental literature, there is the same note. 'Woe to you who acquire silver and gold in unrighteousness . . . They shall perish with their possessions, and in shame will their spirits be cast into the furnace of fire' (1 Enoch 97:8, 98:3). In the Wisdom of Solomon, there is a savage passage in which the sage makes the selfish rich speak of their own way of life as compared with that of the righteous.

'Come, therefore, let us enjoy the good things that exist; and make use of the creation to the full as in youth. Let us take our fill of costly wine and perfumes and let no flower of spring pass by us. Let us crown ourselves with rosebuds before they wither. Let none of us fail to share in our revelry; everywhere let us leave signs of enjoyment; because this is our portion, and this our lot. Let us oppress the righteous poor man; let us not spare the widow or regard the grey hairs of the aged . . . Let us lie in wait for the righteous man, because he is inconvenient to us and opposes our actions; he reproaches us for sins against the law, and accuses us of sins against our training' (Wisdom of Solomon 2:6–12).

One of the mysteries of social history is how the Christian religion ever came to be regarded as 'the opium of the people' or to seem an other-worldly affair. There is no book in any literature which speaks so explosively of social injustice as the Bible, nor any book which has proved so powerful a social dynamic. It does not condemn wealth as such; but there is no book which more strenuously insists on wealth's responsibility and on the perils which surround those who are abundantly blessed with this world's goods.

THE WAY OF SELFISHNESS AND ITS END

James 5:4–6

> Look you, the pay of the reapers who reaped your estates, the pay kept back from them by you, cries against you, and the cries of those who reaped have come to the ears of the Lord of hosts. On the earth you have lived in soft luxury and played the wanton; you have fattened your hearts for the day of slaughter. You condemned, you killed the righteous man, and he does not resist you.

Here is condemnation of selfish riches and warning of where they must end.

(1) The selfish rich have gained their wealth by injustice. The Bible is always sure that the labourer deserves to be paid (Luke 10:7; 1 Timothy 5:18). The day labourer in Palestine lived on the very verge of starvation. His wage was small; it was impossible for him to save anything; and if the wage was withheld from him, even for a day, he and his family simply could not eat. That is why the merciful laws of Scripture again and again insist on the prompt payment of wages to the hired labourer. 'You shall not withhold the wages of poor and needy labourers ... You shall pay them their wages daily before sunset, because they are poor and their livelihood depends on them; otherwise they might cry to the Lord against you, and you would incur guilt' (Deuteronomy 24:14–15). 'You shall not keep for yourself the wages of a labourer until morning' (Leviticus 19:13). 'Do not say to your neighbour, "Go, and come again; tomorrow I will give it" – when you have it with you' (Proverbs 3:28). 'Woe to him who builds his house by unrighteousness, and his upper rooms by injustice; who makes his neighbours work for nothing, and does not give them their wages' (Jeremiah 22:13). 'Those who oppress the hired workers in their wages' are under the judgment of God (Malachi 3:5). 'To take away a neighbour's living is to commit murder; to deprive an employee of wages is to shed blood' (Sirach 34:26–7). 'Do not keep over until the next day the wages of those who work for you, but pay them at once' (Tobit 4:14).

The law of the Bible is nothing less than the charter of the labourer. The social concern of the Bible speaks in the words of the law and of the prophets and of the sages alike. Here, it is said that the cries of the harvesters have reached the ears of the Lord of hosts! The hosts are the hosts of heaven, the stars and the heavenly powers. It is the teaching of every part of the Bible that the Lord of the universe is concerned for the rights of those who labour.

(2) The selfish rich have used their wealth selfishly. They have lived in soft luxury and lived for lust and pleasure. The word translated as *to live in soft luxury* is *truphein*. It comes from a root which means *to break down*, and it describes the soft living which in the end saps and destroys a person's moral strength. The word translated as *to play the wanton* is *spatalan*. It is a much worse word; it means to live shameless, debauched and lustful lives. It is the condemnation of the selfish rich that they have used their possessions to gratify their own love of comfort and to satisfy their own lusts, and that they have forgotten all duty to other people.

(3) But anyone who chooses this pathway has also chosen its end. The end of specially fattened cattle is that they will be slaughtered for some feast; and those who have sought this easy luxury and selfish wantonness are like men and women who have fattened themselves for the day of judgment. The end of their pleasure is grief, and the goal of their luxury is death. Selfishness always leads to the destruction of the soul.

(4) The selfish rich have killed the unresisting righteous one. It is doubtful to whom this refers. It could be a reference to Jesus. 'You rejected the Holy and Righteous One and asked to have a murderer given to you' (Acts 3:14). It is Stephen's charge that the Jews always killed God's messengers even before the coming of the righteous one (Acts 7:52). It is Paul's declaration that God chose the Jews to see the righteous one although they rejected him (Acts 22:14). Peter says that Christ suffered for our sins, the just for the unjust (1 Peter 3:18). The suffering servant of the Lord offered

no resistance. He opened not his mouth and like a sheep before his shearers he was dumb (Isaiah 53:7), a passage which Peter quotes in his picture of Jesus (1 Peter 2:23). It may well be that James is saying that in their oppression of the poor and the righteous, the selfish rich have crucified Christ again. Every wound that selfishness inflicts on Christ's people is another wound inflicted on Christ.

It may be that James is thinking not especially of Jesus when he speaks about the righteous one but of the evil person's instinctive hatred of the good person. We have already quoted the passage in the Wisdom of Solomon which describes the conduct of the rich. That passage goes on:

> He (the righteous man) professes to have knowledge
>   of God,
> and calls himself a child of the Lord.
> He became to us a reproof of our thoughts;
> the very sight of him is a burden to us,
> because his manner of life is unlike that of others,
> and his ways are strange.
> We are considered by him as something base,
> and he avoids our ways as unclean;
> he calls the last end of the righteous happy,
> and boasts that God is his father.
> Let us see if his words are true,
> and let us test what will happen at the end of his life;
> for if the righteous man is God's child, he will help
>   him
> and will deliver him from the hand of his adversaries.
> Let us test him with insult and torture,
> so that we may find out how gentle he is,
> and make trial of his forbearance.
> Let us condemn him to a shameful death,
> for, according to what he says, he will be protected.
>
> (Wisdom of Solomon 2:13–20)

These, says the sage, are the words of those whose wickedness has blinded them.

Alcibiades, the friend of Socrates, for all his great talents often lived a riotous and debauched life. And there were times when he said to Socrates: 'Socrates, I hate you, for every time I see you, you show me what I am.' Those who are evil would gladly eliminate the good, for they remind them of what they are and of what they ought to be.

WAITING FOR THE COMING OF THE LORD

James 5:7–9

> Brothers, have patience until the coming of the Lord. Look you, the farmer waits for the precious fruit of the earth, patiently waiting for it until it receives the early and the late rains. So do you too be patient. Make firm your hearts, for the coming of the Lord is near. Brothers, do not complain against each other, that you may not be condemned. Look you, the judge stands at the door.

THE early Church lived in expectation of the immediate second coming of Jesus Christ, and James encourages his people to wait with patience for the few years which remain. The farmer has to wait for the crops until the early and the late rains have come. The early and the late rains are often spoken of in Scripture, for they were all-important to the farmer of Palestine (Deuteronomy 11:14; Jeremiah 5:24; Joel 2:23). The early rain was the rain of late October and early November, without which the seed would not germinate. The late rain was the rain of April and May, without which the grain would not mature. The farmer needs to wait patiently for the working of nature; and Christians need to wait patiently until Christ comes.

During that waiting, they must confirm their faith. They must not blame one another for the troubles of the situation in which they find themselves – for, if they do, they will be breaking the commandment which forbids Christians to judge one another (Matthew 7:1); and if they break that commandment, they will be condemned. James has no doubt of the nearness of the coming of Christ. The judge is at the door, he says, using a phrase which Jesus himself had used (Mark 13:29; Matthew 24:33).

It so happened that the early Church was mistaken. Jesus Christ did not return within a generation. But it will be of interest to gather up the New Testament's teaching about the second coming so that we may see the essential truth at its heart.

We may first note that the New Testament uses three different words to describe the second coming of Jesus Christ

(1) The most common is *parousia*, a word which has come into English as it stands. It is used in Matthew 24:3, 27, 37, 39; 1 Thessalonians 2:19, 3:13, 4:15, 5:23; 2 Thessalonians 2:1; 1 Corinthians 15:23; 1 John 2:28; 2 Peter 1:16, 3:4). In secular Greek, this is the ordinary word for someone's presence or arrival. But it has two other usages, one of which became quite technical. It is used of the invasion of a country by an army; and especially it is used of the visit of a king or a governor to a province of his empire. So, when this word is used of Jesus, it means that his second coming is the final invasion of earth by heaven and the coming of the King to receive the final submission and adoration of his subjects.

(2) The New Testament also uses the word *epiphaneia* (Titus 2:13; 2 Timothy 4:1; 2 Thessalonians 2:9). In ordinary Greek, this word has two special usages. It is used of the appearance of a god to the worshipper, and it is used of the accession of an emperor to the imperial power of Rome. So,

when this word is used of Jesus, it means that his second coming is God appearing to his people, both to those who are waiting for him and to those who are taking no interest in him.

(3) Finally, the New Testament uses the word *apokalupsis* (1 Peter 1:7, 1:13). *Apokalupsis* in ordinary Greek means an *unveiling* or a *laying bare*, and when it is used of Jesus it means that his second coming is the laying bare of the power and glory of God come upon men and women.

Here, then, we have a series of great pictures. The second coming of Jesus is the arrival of the King; it is God appearing to his people and mounting his eternal throne; it is God directing on the world the full blaze of his heavenly glory.

THE COMING OF THE KING

James 5:7-9 (*contd*)

WE may now gather up briefly the teaching of the New Testament about the second coming and the various uses it makes of the idea.

(1) The New Testament is clear that no one knows the day or the hour when Christ will come again. So secret, in fact, is that time that Jesus himself does not know it; it is known only to God (Matthew 24:36; Mark 13:32). From this basic fact, one thing is clear. Human speculation about the time of the second coming is not only useless, it is blasphemous – for surely no one should seek to gain a knowledge which is hidden from Jesus Christ himself and exists only in the mind of God.

(2) The one thing that the New Testament does say about the second coming is that it will be as sudden as the lightning and as unexpected as a thief in the night (Matthew 24:27, 37,

39; 1 Thessalonians 5:2; 2 Peter 3:10). We cannot wait to get ready when it comes; we must be ready for its coming.

So, the New Testament urges certain duties upon Christians.

(1) They must be constantly on the watch (1 Peter 4:7). They are like servants whose master has gone away and who, not knowing when he will return, must have everything ready for his return, whether it comes in the morning, at midday or in the evening (Matthew 24:36–51).

(2) Long delay must not produce despair or forgetfulness (2 Peter 3:4). God does not see time as human beings do. To him, 1,000 years are just the same as a period on watch in the night; and, even if the years pass on, it does not mean that he has either changed or abandoned his design.

(3) The time given to prepare for the coming of the King must be used. Christians must be sober (1 Peter 4:7). They must strengthen themselves in holiness (1 Thessalonians 3:13). By the grace of God, they must become blameless in body and in spirit (1 Thessalonians 5:23). They must put off the works of darkness and put on the armour of light now that the night is far gone and the day is near (Romans 13:11–14). They must use the time given to them to make themselves such that they can greet the coming of the King with joy and without shame.

(4) When that time comes, they must be found in fellowship. Peter uses the thought of the second coming to urge people to love and mutual hospitality (1 Peter 4:8–9). Paul commands that all things be done in love – *Maran atha* – the Lord is at hand (1 Corinthians 16:14, 16:22). He says that our *forbearance* must be known to all because the Lord is at hand (Philippians 4:5). The word translated as *forbearance* is *epieikēs*, which means the spirit that is more ready to offer forgiveness than to demand justice. The writer

to the Hebrews demands mutual help, mutual Christian fellowship and mutual encouragement because the day is coming near (Hebrews 10:24–5). The New Testament is sure that in view of the coming of Christ we must have our personal relationships right with our neighbours. The New Testament would urge that we should never end a day with an unhealed rift between ourselves and another person, in case Christ should come in the night.

(5) John uses the second coming as a reason for urging people to abide in Christ (1 John 2:28). Surely the best preparation for meeting Christ is to live close to him every day.

Much of the imagery attached to the second coming is Jewish and is part of the traditional apparatus of the last things in ancient Jewish thought. There are many things which we are not meant to take literally. But the great truth behind all the temporary pictures of the second coming is that this world is not purposeless but that it is going somewhere, that there is one divine far-off event to which the whole creation moves.

THE TRIUMPHANT PATIENCE

James 5:10–11

Brothers, take as an example of patience in hardship the prophets who spoke in the name of the Lord. Look you, we count those who endure blessed. You have heard of Job's steadfast endurance and you have seen the conclusion of his troubles which the Lord gave to him, and you have proof that the Lord is very kind and merciful.

It is always a comfort to feel that others have gone through what we have to go through. James reminds his readers that God's prophets could never have done their work and borne their witness if they had not patiently endured. He reminds them that Jesus himself had said that the one who endured to the end was blessed and would be saved (Matthew 24:13).

Then he quotes the example of Job, of whom they had often heard in the synagogue discourses. We generally speak of the *patience* of Job, which is the word the Authorized Version uses. But *patience* is far too passive a word. There is a sense in which Job was anything but patient. As we read the tremendous drama of his life, we see him passionately resenting what has happened to him, passionately questioning the conventional arguments of his so-called friends, passionately agonizing over the terrible thought that God might have forsaken him. Few have spoken such passionate words as he did, but the great fact about Job is that, in spite of all the agonizing questionings which tore at his heart, he never lost his faith in God. 'See, he will kill me; I have no hope' (Job 13:15). 'Even now, in fact, my witness is in heaven, and he that vouches for me is on high' (Job 16:19). 'For I know that my Redeemer lives' (Job 19:25). Job's is no unquestioning submission; he struggled and questioned, and sometimes even defied, but the flame of his faith was never extinguished.

The word used of him is that great New Testament word *hupomonē*, which describes not a passive patience but that gallant spirit which can confront the tides of doubt and sorrow and disaster and come out with faith still stronger on the other side. There may be a faith which never complained or questioned; but still greater is the faith which was tortured by questions and still believed. It was the faith which held on grimly that came out on the other side, for 'The Lord blessed the latter days of Job more than his beginning' (Job 42:12).

There will be moments in life when we think that God has forgotten; but, if we cling to the remnants of faith, at the end we, too, shall see that God is very kind and very merciful.

THE NEEDLESSNESS AND
THE FOLLY OF OATHS

James 5:12

> Above all things, my brothers, do not swear, neither by heaven nor by earth nor by any other oath. Let your yes be a simple yes and your no a simple no, lest you fall under judgment.

JAMES is repeating the teaching of Jesus in the Sermon on the Mount (Matthew 5:33–7), teaching which was very necessary in the days of the early Church. James is thinking not of what we call bad language but of confirming a statement or a promise or an undertaking by an oath. In the ancient world, there were two evil practices.

(1) There was a distinction – especially in the Jewish world – between oaths which were binding and oaths which were not binding. Any oath in which the name of God was directly used was considered to be definitely binding, but any oath in which direct mention of the name of God was not made was held not to be binding. The idea was that, once God's name was definitely used, he became an active partner in the transaction, but he did not become a partner unless his name was introduced in this way. The result of this was that it became a matter of skill and sharp practice to find an oath which was not binding. This made a mockery of the whole practice of confirming anything by an oath.

(2) There was at this time an extraordinary amount of oath-taking. This in itself was quite wrong. For one thing, the value of an oath depends to a large extent on the fact of it being very seldom necessary to take one. When oaths became

commonplace, they ceased to be respected as they ought to be. For another thing, the practice of taking frequent oaths was nothing other than a proof that lying and cheating was widespread. In an honest society, no oath is needed; it is only when people cannot be trusted to tell the truth that they have to be put on oath.

In this, the ancient writers on morals thoroughly agreed with Jesus. The Jewish writer Philo says: 'Frequent swearing is bound to beget perjury and impiety.' The Rabbis said: 'Accustom not yourself to vows, for sooner or later you will swear false oaths.' The Jewish sect of the Essenes forbade all oaths. They held that if an oath was required to make someone tell the truth, that person was already branded as untrustworthy. The great Greeks held that the best guarantee of any statement was not an oath but the character of the person who made it, and that the ideal was to make ourselves so respected that no one would ever think of demanding an oath from us because there could be no doubt that we would always speak the truth.

The New Testament view is that every word is spoken in the presence of God and ought therefore to be true, and it would agree that Christians must be known to be men and women of such honour that it will be quite unnecessary ever to put them on oath. The New Testament would not entirely condemn oaths, but it would deplore the human tendency to lying, which on occasion makes oaths necessary.

A SINGING CHURCH

James 5:13-15

> Is any among you in trouble? Let him pray. Is any in
> good spirits? Let him sing a hymn. Is any among you

> sick? Let him call in the elders of the Church; and let
> them anoint him with oil in the name of the Lord, and
> pray over him; and the believing prayer will restore to
> health the ailing person, and the Lord will enable him
> to rise from his bed; and even if he has committed sin,
> he will receive forgiveness.

HERE we have set out before us certain dominant characteristics of the early Church.

It was a *singing church*; the early Christians were always ready to burst into song. In Paul's description of the meetings of the church at Corinth, we find singing an integral part (1 Corinthians 14:15, 14:26). When he thinks of the grace of God going out to the Gentiles, it reminds him of the joyous saying of the psalmist: 'I will confess you among the Gentiles, and sing praises to your name' (Romans 15:9; cf. Psalm 18:49).

It is characteristic of the Christians that they speak to each other in psalms and hymns and spiritual songs, singing and making melody in their hearts to the Lord (Ephesians 5:19). The word of Christ dwells in them, and they teach and admonish each other in psalms and hymns and spiritual songs, singing with thankfulness in their hearts to the Lord (Colossians 3:16). There was a joy in the hearts of the Christians which burst from their lips in songs of praise for the mercy and the grace of God.

The fact is that the non-Christian world has always been sad and weary and frightened. Matthew Arnold wrote a poem entitled 'Oberman Once More', describing its bored weariness.

> On that hard Pagan world disgust
> And secret loathing fell;
> Deep weariness and sated lust
> Made human life a hell.

In his cool hall, with haggard eyes,
   The Roman noble lay;
He drove abroad in furious guise
   Along the Appian Way;
He made a feast, drank fierce and fast,
   And crowned his hair with flowers –
No easier nor no quicker passed
   The impracticable hours.

In contrast with that weary mood, the characteristic of Christians is singing joy. That was what impressed John Bunyan when he heard four poor old women talking, as they sat at a door in the sun: 'Methought they spake, as if joy did make them speak.' When Thomas Bilney, the sixteenth-century Protestant martyr, grasped the wonder of redeeming grace, he said: 'It was as if dawn suddenly broke on a dark night.' Archibald Lang Fleming, the first Bishop of the Arctic, tells of the saying of an Inuit hunter: 'Before you came, the road was dark and we were afraid. Now we are not afraid, for the darkness has gone away and all is light as we walk the Jesus way.'

The Church has always been a singing church. When Pliny, governor of Bithynia, wrote to Trajan, the Roman emperor, in AD 111 to tell him of this new sect of Christians, he said that his information was that 'they are in the habit of meeting on a certain fixed day before it is light, when they sing in alternate verses a hymn to Christ as God'. Since the fall of Jerusalem in AD 70, there has been no music in orthodox Jewish synagogues, for, when they worship, they remember a tragedy; but in the Christian Church, from the beginning until now, there has been the music of praise, for Christians remember an infinite love and enjoy a present glory.

A HEALING CHURCH

James 5:13-15 (*contd*)

ANOTHER great characteristic of the early Church was that it was a *healing* church. Here, it inherited its tradition from Judaism. When a Jew was ill, he went to the Rabbi rather than to the doctor; and the Rabbi anointed him with oil – which Galen the Greek doctor called 'the best of all medicines' – and prayed over him. Few communities can have been so devotedly attentive to their sick as the early Church was. Justin Martyr writes in the second century that countless people possessed by demons were healed by the Christians when all other exorcists had been unable to cure them and drugs had had no effect. Irenaeus, writing late in the second century, tells us that the sick were still healed by having hands laid on them. Tertullian, writing mid-way through the third century, says that no less a person than the Roman emperor, Alexander Severus, was healed by anointing at the hands of a Christian called Torpacion and that in his gratitude he kept Torpacion as a guest in his palace until the day of his death.

One of the earliest books concerning church administration is the *Canons of Hippolytus*, from the late second or early third century. It is there laid down that those who have the gift of healing are to be ordained as presbyters after investigation has been made to ensure that they really do possess the gift and that it comes from God. That same book gives the noble prayer used at the consecration of the local bishops, part of which runs: 'Grant unto him, O Lord . . . the power to break all the chains of the evil power of the demons, to cure all the sick, and speedily to subdue Satan beneath his feet.' In the *Clementine Letters*, the duties of the deacons are laid down, and they include the rule: 'Let the deacons of the

Church move about intelligently and act as eyes for the bishop
... Let them find out those who are sick in the flesh, and
bring such to the notice of the main body who know nothing
of them, that they may visit them, and supply their wants.' In
the *First Epistle of Clement*, the prayer of the Church is: 'Heal
the sick; raise up the weak; cheer the faint-hearted.' A very
early church code lays it down that each congregation must
appoint at least one widow to take care of women who are
sick. For many centuries, the Church consistently used
anointing as a means of healing the sick. In fact, it is important
to note that in the early centuries the sacrament of unction, or
anointing, was always designed as a means of cure, and not
as a preparation for death as it now is in the Roman Catholic
Church. It was not until AD 852 that this sacrament did, in
fact, become the Sacrament of Extreme Unction, administered
to prepare for death.

The Church has always cared for the sick; and the gift of
healing has always resided in the Church. The social gospel
is not something added on to Christianity; it is the very
essence of the Christian faith and life.

A PRAYING CHURCH

James 5:16–18

> Confess your sins to each other, and pray for each other,
> that you may be healed. The prayer of a good man,
> when it is set to work, is very powerful. Elijah was a
> man with the same emotions as ourselves, and he prayed
> earnestly that it should not rain, and for three years and
> six months no rain fell upon the earth. And he prayed
> again and the heaven gave rain; and the earth put forth
> her fruit.

THIS passage contains three basic ideas of Jewish religion.

(1) There is the idea that all sickness is due to sin. It was a deeply rooted Jewish belief that where sickness and suffering existed, there must have been sin. 'There is no death without guilt,' said the Rabbis, 'and no suffering without sin.' The Rabbis, therefore, believed that before people could be healed of their sickness their sins must be forgiven by God. Rabbi Alexandrai said: 'No man gets up from his sickness until God has forgiven him all his sins.' That is why Jesus began his healing of the paralytic by saying: 'Son, your sins are forgiven' (Mark 2:5). The Jews always identified suffering with sin. Nowadays we cannot make this automatic identification; but this remains true – that no one can know any health of soul or mind or body without being right with God.

(2) There is the idea that, to be effective, confession of sin has to be made to other people, and especially to the person wronged, as well as to God. In a very real sense, it is easier to confess sins to God than to confess them to another person, and yet in sin there are two barriers to be removed – the barrier it sets up between us and God, and the barrier it sets up between us and other people. If both these barriers are to be removed, both kinds of confession must be made. This was, in fact, the custom of the Moravian Church, and John Wesley took it over for his earliest Methodist classes. They used to meet two or three times a week 'to confess their faults to one another and to pray for one another that they might be healed'. This is clearly a principle which must be used wisely. It is quite true that there may be cases where confession of sin to each other may do infinitely more harm than good; but, where a barrier has been erected because of some wrong which has been done, people must put themselves right both with God and with one another.

(3) Above all, there is the idea that no limits can be set to the power of prayer. The Jews had a saying that the one who prays surrounds his house with a wall stronger than iron. They said: 'Penitence can do something, but prayer can do everything.' To them, prayer was nothing less than contacting the power of God; it was the channel through which the strength and grace of God were brought to bear on the troubles and problems of life. How much more must this be so for a Christian?

In *Morte d'Arthur*, Tennyson wrote:

> More things are wrought by prayer
> Than this world dreams of. Wherefore, let thy voice
> Rise like a fountain for me night and day.
> For what are men better than sheep or goats
> That nourish a blind life within the brain,
> If, knowing God, they lift not hands of prayer
> Both for themselves and those who call them friend?
> For so the whole round earth is every way
> Bound by gold chains about the feet of God.

As the Jews saw it, and as indeed it is, to cure the ills of life we need to be right with God and right with one another, and we need to bring to bear upon others through prayer the mercy and the might of God.

Before we leave this passage, there is one interesting technical fact that we must note. It quotes Elijah as an example of the power of prayer. This is an excellent illustration of how Jewish Rabbinic interpretation developed the meaning of Scripture. The full story is in 1 Kings 17–18. The *three years and six months* – a period also quoted in Luke 4:25 – is a deduction from 1 Kings 18:1. Further, the Old Testament narrative does not say that either the coming or the cessation of the drought was due to the prayers of Elijah; he was merely the prophet who announced its coming and its going. But the Rabbis always studied Scripture under the microscope. In 1 Kings 17:1, we read: 'As the Lord the God of Israel lives, *before whom I stand*, there shall be neither dew nor rain these years, except by my word.' Now the Jewish attitude of prayer was *standing before God*, and so in this phrase the Rabbis found what was to them an indication that the drought was the result of the prayers of Elijah. In 1 Kings 18:42, we read that Elijah went up to Carmel, *bowed himself down upon the earth* and put his face between his knees. Once again, the Rabbis saw here the attitude of agonizing prayer, and so found what was to them an indication that it was the prayer of Elijah which brought the drought to an end.

THE TRUTH WHICH MUST BE DONE

James 5:19–20

> My brothers, if any among you wanders from the truth and if anyone turns him again to the right way, let him know that he who has turned a sinner from his wandering way will save his brother's soul from death and will hide a multitude of his own sins.

IN this passage, there is set down the great differentiating characteristic of Christian truth. It is something from which people can *wander*. It is not only intellectual, philosophical and abstract; it is always moral truth.

This comes out very clearly when we go to the New Testament and look at the expressions which are used in connection with truth. Truth is something which people must *love* (2 Thessalonians 2:10); it is something which people must *obey* (Galatians 5:7); it is something which must be *openly stated* (2 Corinthians 4:2); it is something which must be *spoken in love* (Ephesians 4:15); it is something which must be *testified to* (John 18:37); it is something which must be *manifested in a life of love* (1 John 3:19); it is something which *liberates* (John 8:32); and it is something which is *the gift of the Holy Spirit*, sent by Jesus Christ (John 16:13–14).

Clearest of all is the phrase in John 3:21, *those who do what is true*. That is to say, *Christian truth is something which must be done*. It is not only the object of the search of the mind; it is always moral truth leading to action. It is not only something to be studied but something to be done; not only something to which we must submit only our minds but something to which we must submit our entire lives.

THE SUPREME HUMAN ACHIEVEMENT

James 5:19–20 (*contd*)

JAMES finishes his letter with one of the greatest and most uplifting thoughts in the New Testament, and yet one which occurs more than once in the Bible. Suppose someone goes wrong and strays away, and suppose a fellow Christian rescues that person from error and brings the sinner back to the right path. That Christian has not only saved the other person's soul but has covered a multitude of his or her own sins. In other words, to save another's soul is the surest way to save one's own.

J. B. Mayor points out that Origen, the third-century biblical scholar, has a wonderful passage in one of his Homilies in which he indicates these six ways in which people may gain forgiveness of their sins – by baptism, by martyrdom, by almsgiving (Luke 11:41), by the forgiveness of others (Matthew 6:14), by love (Luke 7:47) and by converting a sinner from evil ways. God will forgive much to anyone who has been the means of leading another brother or sister back to him.

This is a thought which shines forth every now and then from the pages of Scripture. Jeremiah says: 'If you utter what is precious, and not what is worthless, you shall serve as my mouth' (Jeremiah 15:19). Daniel writes: 'Those who are wise shall shine like the brightness of the sky, and those who lead many to righteousness, like the stars for ever and ever' (Daniel 12:3). The advice to the young Timothy is: 'Pay close attention to yourself and to your teaching . . . for in doing this you will save both yourself and your hearers' (1 Timothy 4:16).

There is a saying of the Jewish fathers: 'Whosoever makes a man righteous, sin prevails not over him.' Clement of Alexandria says that true Christians reckon that which benefits their neighbours to be their own salvation. It is told that a zealous evangelical lady once asked William Wilberforce, the liberator of the slaves in the British Empire, if his soul was saved. 'Madame,' he answered, 'I have been so busy trying to save the souls of others that I have had no time to think of my own.' It has been said that those who bring sunshine into the lives of others cannot keep it from themselves, and certainly those who bring the lives of others to God cannot keep God out of their own. The highest honour God can give is bestowed upon those who lead others to God; for everyone who does that does nothing less than share in the work of Jesus Christ, the Saviour of all.

The Letters of Peter

INTRODUCTION TO THE
FIRST LETTER OF PETER

The Catholic or General Epistles

First Peter belongs to that group of New Testament letters which are known as the Catholic or General Epistles. Two explanations of that title have been offered.

(1) It is suggested that these letters were so called because they were addressed to the wider Church, as distinct from the Pauline letters which were addressed to individual churches. But that is not so. James is addressed to a definite, though widely scattered, community. It is written to the twelve tribes in the Dispersion, the tribes that are scattered throughout the world (James 1:1). It needs no argument that 2 and 3 John are addressed to definite communities; and, although 1 John has no specific address, it is clearly written with the needs and perils of a particular community in mind. First Peter itself is written to the strangers scattered abroad through Pontus, Galatia, Cappadocia, Asia and Bithynia (1 Peter 1:1). It is true that these General Epistles have a wider range than the letters of Paul; at the same time, they all have a definite community in mind.

(2) So we must turn to the second explanation – that these letters were called Catholic or General because they were accepted as Scripture by the whole Church as distinct from that large number of letters which enjoyed a local and

temporary authority but which were never universally accepted as Scripture. At the time when these letters were being written, there was an outbreak of letter-writing in the Church. We still possess many of the letters which were written then – the letter of Clement of Rome to Corinth, the letter of Barnabas, the letters of Ignatius and the letters of Polycarp. All were regarded as very precious in the churches to which they were written but were never regarded as having authority throughout the Church; on the other hand, the Catholic or General Epistles gradually won a place in Scripture and were accepted by the whole Church. Here is the true explanation of their title.

The Lovely Letter

Of all the General Epistles, it is probably true that 1 Peter is the best known and loved, and the most read. No one has ever been in any doubt about its charm. In his commentary on these letters, James Moffatt writes of it: 'The beautiful spirit of the pastoral shines through any translation of the Greek text. "Affectionate, loving, lowly, humble," are Izaak Walton's quaternion of adjectives for the Epistles of James, John and Peter, but it is 1 Peter which deserves them pre-eminently.' It is written out of the love of a pastor's heart to help people who were experiencing troubled times and for whom worse things still lay ahead. 'The key-note', says Moffatt, 'is steady encouragement to endurance in conduct and innocence in character.' It has been said that its distinctive characteristic is *warmth*. The biblical scholar E. J. Goodspeed wrote: '1 Peter is one of the most moving pieces of persecution literature.' Even today, it is one of the easiest letters in the New Testament to read, for it has never lost its captivating appeal to the human heart.

THE LETTERS OF PETER (1)

The Modern Doubt

Until a comparatively short time ago, few would have raised any doubts about the authenticity of 1 Peter. The nineteenth-century French theologian Joseph Ernest Renan, who was by no means a conservative critic, wrote of it: 'The First Epistle is one of the writings of the New Testament which are most anciently and most unanimously cited as genuine.' But more recently the Petrine authorship of the letter has been widely questioned. The commentary by F. W. Beare, published in 1947, goes as far as saying: 'There can be no possible doubt that "Peter" is a pseudonym.' That is to say, Beare has no doubt that someone else wrote this letter under the name of Peter. In fairness, we shall go on to investigate that view; but first we shall set out the traditional view – which we ourselves unhesitatingly accept – of the date and authorship of this letter. This is that 1 Peter was written from Rome by Peter himself, about the year AD 67, in the days immediately following the first persecution of the Christians by Nero, to the Christians in those parts of Asia Minor named in the address. What is the evidence for this early date and, therefore, for the Petrine authorship?

The Second Coming

When we go to the letter, we find that expectation of the second coming of Christ is in the very forefront of its thought. Christians are being kept for the salvation which is to be revealed at the last time (1:5). Those who keep the faith will be saved from the coming judgment (1:7). Christians are to hope for the grace which will come at the revelation of Jesus Christ (1:13). The day of visitation is expected (2:12). The end of all things is at hand (4:7). Those who suffer with Christ will also rejoice with Christ when his glory is revealed (4:13).

Judgment is to begin at the household of God (4:17). The writer himself is sure that he will be a sharer in the glory to come (5:1). When the chief shepherd shall appear, the faithful Christian will receive a crown of glory (5:4).

From beginning to end of the letter, the second coming is in the forefront of the writer's mind. It is the motive for steadfastness in the faith, for the loyal living of the Christian life and for gallant endurance amid the sufferings that have come and will come upon them.

It would be untrue to say that the second coming ever dropped out of Christian belief; but it did recede from the forefront of Christian belief as the years passed and Christ did not return. It is, for instance, significant that in Ephesians, one of Paul's later letters, there is no mention of it. On this basis, it is reasonable to suppose that 1 Peter is early and comes from the days when the Christians vividly expected the return of their Lord at any moment.

Simplicity of Organization

It is clear that 1 Peter comes from a time when the organization of the Church is very simple. There is no mention of deacons, nor of the *episkopos*, the bishop, who begins to emerge in the Pastoral Epistles and becomes prominent in Ignatius' letters in the first half of the second century. The only church officials mentioned are the elders. 'As an elder myself . . . I exhort the elders among you' (5:1). For this reason, also, it is reasonable to suppose that 1 Peter comes from an early date.

The Theology of the Early Church

What is most significant of all is that the theology of 1 Peter is the theology of the very early Church. E. G. Selwyn has made a detailed study of this in his commentary, and he has proved beyond all question that the theological ideas of

1 Peter are exactly the same as those we meet in the recorded sermons of Peter in the early chapters of Acts.

The preaching of the early Church was based on five main ideas. One of the greatest contributions of C. H. Dodd to New Testament scholarship was his formulation of these. They form the framework of all the sermons of the early Church, as recorded in Acts, and they are the foundation of the thought of all the New Testament writers. The summary of these basic ideas has been given the name *kērugma*, which means the announcement or the proclamation of a herald.

These are the fundamental ideas which the Church in its first days proclaimed. We shall take them one by one and shall set down after each, first, the references in the early chapters of Acts and, second, the references in 1 Peter; and we will make the significant discovery that the basic ideas of the sermons of the early Church and the theology of 1 Peter are precisely the same. We are not claiming, of course, that the sermons in Acts are word-for-word reports of what was actually preached, but we believe that they give correctly the *substance* of the message of the first preachers.

(1) The age of fulfilment has dawned; the messianic age has begun. This is God's last word. A new order is being inaugurated, and the elect are summoned to join the new community (Acts 2:14–16, 3:12–26, 4:8–12, 10:34–43; 1 Peter 1:3, 1:10–12, 4:7).

(2) This new age has come through the life, death and resurrection of Jesus Christ, all of which are in direct fulfilment of the prophecies of the Old Testament and are, therefore, the result of the definite plan and foreknowledge of God (Acts 2:20–31, 3:13–14, 10:43; 1 Peter 1:20–1).

(3) By virtue of the resurrection, Jesus has been exalted to the right hand of God and is the messianic head of the

new Israel (Acts 2:22–6, 3:13, 4:11, 5:30–1, 10:39–42; 1 Peter 1:21, 2:7, 2:24, 3:22).

(4) These messianic events will shortly reach their fulfilment in the return of Christ in glory and the judgment of the living and the dead (Acts 3:19–23, 10:42; 1 Peter 1:5, 1:7, 1:13, 4:5, 4:13, 4:17–18, 5:1, 5:4).

(5) These facts are made the grounds for an appeal for repentance, and the offer of forgiveness and of the Holy Spirit, and the promise of eternal life (Acts 2:38–9, 3:19, 5:31, 10:43; 1 Peter 1:13–25, 2:1–3, 4:1–5).

These declarations are the five main building blocks in the structure of early Christian preaching, as recorded for us in the sermons of Peter in the early chapters of Acts. They are also the dominant ideas in 1 Peter. The correspondence is so close and so consistent that we are almost certainly looking at the same hand and mind in both.

Quotations from the Fathers

We may add another point to our evidence that 1 Peter is an early work. Very early on, the fathers and preachers of the Church begin to quote it. The first person to quote 1 Peter by name is Irenaeus, who lived from AD 130 until well into the next century. He twice quotes 1 Peter 1:8: 'Although you have not seen him, you love him; and even though you do not see him now, you believe in him and rejoice with an indescribable and glorious joy.' And he once quotes 1 Peter 2:16, with its command not to use liberty as a pretext for evil. But, even before this, the fathers of the Church are quoting Peter without mentioning his name. Clement of Rome, writing about AD 95, speaks of 'the precious blood of Christ', an unusual phrase which may well come from Peter's statement that we are redeemed by the precious blood of Christ (1:19). Polycarp, who was martyred in AD 155, repeatedly quotes Peter without using his name. We may select three passages to show how closely he gives Peter's words.

> Wherefore, girding up your loins, serve God in fear . . . believing on him who raised up our Lord Jesus Christ from the dead, and gave him glory (Polycarp, *To the Philippians*, 2:1).

> Therefore, gird up your minds . . . through him you have confidence in God, who raised him from the dead and gave him glory (1 Peter 1:13, 1:21).

> Christ Jesus who bore our sins in his own body on the tree, who did no sin, neither was guile found in his mouth (Polycarp, *To the Philippians*, 8:1).

> He committed no sin; no guile was found on his life . . . He himself bore our sins in his body on the tree (1 Peter 2:22, 2:24).

> Having your conversation blameless among the Gentiles (Polycarp, *To the Philippians*, 10:2).

> Maintain good conduct among the Gentiles (1 Peter 2:12).

There can be no doubt that Polycarp is quoting Peter, although he does not name him. It takes some time for a book to acquire such an authority and familiarity that it can be quoted almost unconsciously, its language woven into the language of the Church. Once again, we see that 1 Peter must be a very early book.

The Excellence of the Greek

If, however, we are defending the Petrine authorship of this letter, there is one problem we must face – and that is the excellence of the Greek. It seems impossible that it could be the work of a Galilaean fisherman. New Testament scholars are at one in praising the Greek of this letter. F. W. Beare writes: 'The epistle is quite obviously the work of a man of letters, skilled in all the devices of rhetoric, and able to draw on an extensive, and even learned, vocabulary. He is a stylist of no ordinary capacity, and he writes some of the best Greek in the whole New Testament, far smoother and more literary than that of the highly-trained Paul.' James Moffatt speaks of this letter's 'plastic language and love of metaphor'. J. B. Mayor says that 1 Peter has no equal in the New Testament for 'sustained stateliness of rhythm'. Charles Bigg has likened certain of 1 Peter's phrases to the writing of the Greek historian Thucydides. In his commentary, E. G. Selwyn has spoken of 1 Peter's 'Euripidean tenderness' and of its ability to coin compound words as the poet and dramatist Aeschylus might have done. The Greek of 1 Peter is not entirely unworthy to be set beside that of the masters of the language. It is difficult, if not impossible, to imagine Peter using the Greek language like that.

The letter itself supplies the solution to this problem. In the concluding short section, Peter himself says: 'Through Silvanus . . . I have written this short letter' (1 Peter 5:12). *Through Silvanus – dia Silouanou* – is an unusual phrase. The Greek means that Silvanus was Peter's agent in the writing of the letter; it means that he was more than merely Peter's secretary, taking down word for word what Peter said.

Let us approach this from two angles. First, let us inquire what we know about Silvanus. (The evidence is set out more fully in our study section on 1 Peter 5:12.) In all probability, he is the same person as the Silvanus of Paul's letters and the Silas of Acts, Silas being a shortened and more familiar form of Silvanus. When we examine these passages, we find that Silas or Silvanus was no ordinary person but a leading figure in the life and counsels of the early Church.

He was a prophet (Acts 15:32); he was one of the 'leaders among the brothers' at the Council of Jerusalem and one of the two chosen to deliver the decisions of the Council to the church at Antioch (Acts 15:22, 15:27). He was Paul's chosen companion in the second missionary journey, and was with Paul both in Philippi and in Corinth (Acts 15:37–40, 16:19, 16:25, 16:29, 18.5, 2 Corinthians 1:19). He was associated with Paul in the initial greetings of 1 and 2 Thessalonians (1 Thessalonians 1:1; 2 Thessalonians 1:1). He was a Roman citizen (Acts 16:37).

Silvanus, then, was a notable man in the early Church; he was not so much the assistant as the colleague of Paul; and, since he was a Roman citizen, there is at least a possibility that he was a man who had an education and culture such as Peter could never have enjoyed.

Now let us add our second line of thought. In a missionary situation, when missionaries can speak a language well enough but cannot write it very well, it is quite common for them to do one of two things in order to send a message to the people. They either write it out in as good a style as they can, and then get a native speaker of the language to correct mistakes and to polish the style; or, if they have a reliable native-speaking colleague, they explain what they want to say, leave the colleague to put the message into written form and then vet the result.

We can well imagine that this was the part Silvanus played in the writing of 1 Peter. Either he corrected and polished Peter's inevitably inadequate Greek, or he wrote in his own words what Peter wanted said, with Peter vetting the final product and adding the last personal paragraph to it.

The thought is that of Peter, but the style is that of Silvanus. And so, although the Greek is excellent, there is no need to deny that the letter comes from Peter himself.

The Recipients of the Letter

The recipients of the letter are the exiles (a Christian is always a temporary resident on the earth) scattered throughout Pontus, Galatia, Cappadocia, Asia and Bithynia.

Almost all of these words had a double significance. They stood for ancient kingdoms, and they stood for Roman provinces to which the ancient names had been given; and the ancient kingdoms and the new provinces did not always cover the same territory. Pontus was never a province. It had originally been the kingdom of Mithradates, and part of it was incorporated in Bithynia and part of it in Galatia. Galatia had originally been the kingdom of the Gauls in the area of the three cities Ancyra, Pessinus and Tavium, but the Romans had expanded it into a much larger unit of administration, including sections of Phrygia, Pisidia, Lycaonia and Isauria. The kingdom of Cappadocia had become a Roman province in AD 17 in practically its original form. Asia was not the continent of Asia as we use the term. It had been an independent kingdom, whose last king, Attalus III, had bequeathed it as a gift to Rome in 133 BC. It included the centre of Asia Minor and was bounded on the north by Bithynia, on the south by Lycia, and on the east by Phrygia and Galatia. In popular language, it was that part of Asia Minor which lay along the shores of the Aegean Sea.

We do not know why these particular districts were picked out, but this much is certain – they covered a large area with a very large population, and the fact that they are all mentioned is one of the greatest proofs of the immense missionary activity of the early Church, quite apart from the missionary activities of Paul.

All these districts lie in the north-east corner of Asia Minor. Why they are named as a group and why they are named in this particular order, we do not know. But a glance at the map will show that, if the bearer of this letter – who may well have been Silvanus – sailed from Italy and landed at Sinope in north-east Asia Minor, a journey through these provinces would be a circular tour which would take him back to Sinope. From Sinope in Bithynia, he would go south to Galatia, further south to Cappadocia, west to Asia, north again to Bithynia, and then east to arrive back in Sinope.

It is clear from the letter itself that its recipients were mainly Gentiles. There is no mention of any question of the law, a question which always arose when there was a Jewish background. Their previous condition had been one of physical passions (1:14, 4:3–4) which fits Gentiles far better than Jews. At one time, they were not a people – Gentiles outside the covenant – but now they are the people of God (2:9–10).

The form of his name which Peter uses also shows that this letter was intended for Gentiles, for Peter is a Greek name. Paul calls him Cephas (1 Corinthians 1:12, 3:22, 9:5, 15:5; Galatians 1:18, 2:9, 2:11, 2:14); among his fellow Jews, he was known as Simeon (Acts 15:14), which is the name by which he is called in 2 Peter (1:1). Since he uses his Greek name here, it is likely that he was writing to Greek people.

The Circumstances behind the Letter

That this letter was written in a time when persecution threatened is abundantly clear. They are going through various trials (1:6). They are likely to be falsely accused as evildoers (3:16). A fiery ordeal is going to try them (4:12). When they suffer, they are to commit themselves to God (4:19). They may well have to suffer for doing what is right (3:14). They are sharing in the afflictions which Christians throughout the world are called upon to endure (5:9). Behind this letter lie fiery trial, a campaign of slander and suffering for the sake of Christ. Can we identify this situation?

There was a time when the Christians had little to fear from the Roman government. In Acts, it is repeatedly the Roman magistrates and the Roman soldiers and officials who save Paul from the fury of Jews and Gentiles alike. As the author of *The Decline and Fall of the Roman Empire*, Edward Gibbon, had it, the tribunal of the Roman magistrate proved the most assured refuge against the fury of the synagogue. The reason was that in the early days the Roman government was not able to distinguish between Jews and Christians. Within the empire, Judaism was what was called a *religio licita*, a permitted religion, and Jews were completely free to worship in their own way. It was not that the Jews did not try to enlighten the Romans as to the true facts of the situation; they did so in Corinth, for example (Acts 18:12–17). But, for some time, the Romans simply regarded the Christians as a Jewish sect and, therefore, did not molest them.

The change came in the days of Nero, and we can trace almost every detail of the story. On 19th July, AD 64, the great fire of Rome broke out. Rome, a city of narrow streets and high wooden tenements, was in real danger of being wiped out. The fire burned for three days and three nights, was halted, and then broke out again with redoubled violence. The Roman populace had no doubt who was responsible, and put the blame on the emperor. Nero had a passion for building, and they believed that he had deliberately taken steps to obliterate Rome so that he could rebuild it. Nero's responsibility must remain forever in doubt; but it is certain that he watched the raging inferno from the tower of Maecenas and expressed himself as charmed with the flower and loveliness of the flames. It was freely said that those who tried to extinguish the fire were deliberately hindered and that men were seen to rekindle it again when it was likely to subside. The people were overwhelmed. The ancient landmarks and the ancestral shrines had vanished; the Temple of Luna, the Ara Maxima, the great altar, the Temple of Jupiter Stator, the shrine of Vesta, their very household gods were gone. They were homeless; and, in the phrase of the Dean of Canterbury, F. W. Farrar, there was 'a hopeless brotherhood of wretchedness'.

The resentment of the people was bitter. Nero had to divert suspicion from himself; a scapegoat had to be found. The Christians were made the scapegoat. Tacitus, the Roman historian, tells the story (*Annals*, 15:44):

> Neither human assistance in the shape of imperial gifts, nor attempts to appease the gods, could remove the sinister report that the fire was due to Nero's own orders. And, so, in the hope of dissipating the rumour, he falsely diverted the charge on to a set of people to whom the vulgar gave the name of Chrestians, and who were detested for the abominations they perpetrated. The founder of the sect, one Christus by name, had been executed by Pontius Pilate in the reign of Tiberius; and the dangerous superstition, though put down for the moment, broke out again, not only in Judaea, the original home of the pest, but even in Rome, where everything shameful and horrible collects and is practised.

Clearly, Tacitus had no doubt that the Christians were not to blame for the fire and that Nero was simply choosing them to be the scapegoats for his own crime.

Why did Nero pick on the Christians, and how was it possible even to suggest that they were responsible for the fire of Rome? There are two possible answers.

(1) The Christians were already the victims of certain slanders.

(a) In popular opinion, they were connected with the Jews. Anti-semitism is no new thing, and it was easy for the Roman mob to attach any crime to the Jews and, therefore, to the Christians.

(b) The Lord's Supper was secret, at least in a sense. It was open only to the members of the Church. And certain phrases connected with it were fruitful sources of slanders. There were phrases about eating someone's body and drinking someone's blood. That was enough to produce a rumour that the Christians were cannibals. In time, the rumour grew until it became a story that the Christians killed and ate a Gentile, or a newly born child. At the Lord's table, the Christians gave each other the kiss of peace (1 Peter 5:14). Their meeting was called the *Agape*, the Love Feast. That was enough for stories to spread that the Christian meetings were orgies of vice.

(c) It was always a charge against the Christians that they 'tampered with family relationships'. There was some truth in such a charge, for Christianity did indeed become a sword to split families, when some members of a family became Christian and some did not. A religion which split homes was bound to be unpopular.

(d) It was the case that the Christians spoke of a coming day when the world would dissolve in flames. Many Christian preachers must have been heard preaching of the second coming and the fiery dissolution of all things (Acts 2:19–20). It would not be difficult to put the blame for the fire on people who spoke like that.

There was abundant material which could be distorted into false charges against the Christians by anyone maliciously disposed to victimize them.

(2) The Jewish faith had always appealed especially to women because of its moral standards in a world where

chastity did not exist. There were, therefore, many women of the aristocracy who had embraced Judaism. The Jews did not hesitate to work upon these women to influence their husbands against the Christians. We get a definite example of that in what happened to Paul and his company in Antioch of Pisidia. There, it was through such women that the Jews stirred up action against Paul (Acts 13:50). Two of Nero's court favourites were Jewish converts. There was Aliturus, his favourite actor, and there was Poppaea, his mistress. It is very likely that through them the Jews influenced Nero to take action against the Christians.

In any event, the blame for the fire was attached to the Christians, and a savage outbreak of persecution occurred. Nor was it simply persecution by legal means. What the Roman historian Tacitus called an *ingens multitudo*, a huge multitude, of Christians perished in the most sadistic ways. Nero rolled the Christians in pitch, set light to them and used them as living torches to light his gardens. He sewed them up in the skins of wild animals and set his hunting dogs on them, to tear them limb from limb while they were still alive.

Tacitus writes (*Annals*, 15:44):

> Mockery of every sort was added to their deaths. Covered with the skins of beasts, they were torn by dogs and perished, or were nailed to crosses, or were doomed to the flames and burned, to serve as a nightly illumination, when daylight had expired. Nero offered his gardens for the spectacle and was exhibiting a show in the circus, while he mingled with the people in the dress of a charioteer or stood aloft on a car. Hence, even for criminals who deserve extreme and exemplary punishment, there arose a feeling of compassion; for it was not, as it seemed, for the public good, but to glut one man's cruelty that they were being destroyed.

The same terrible story is told by the later Christian historian, Sulpicius Severus, in his *Chronicle*:

> In the meantime, the number of Christians being now very large, it happened that Rome was destroyed by fire, while Nero was stationed at Antium. But the opinion of all cast the odium of causing the fire upon the emperor, and he was believed in this way to have sought for the glory of building a new city. And, in fact, Nero could not, by any means he tried, escape from the charge that the fire had been caused by his orders. He, therefore, turned the accusation against the Christians and the most cruel tortures were accordingly inflicted upon the innocent. Nay, even new kinds of death were invented so that, being covered in the skins of wild beasts, they perished by being devoured by dogs, while many were crucified, or slain by fire, and not a few were set apart for this purpose, that, when the day came to a close, they should be consumed to serve for light during the night. In this way, cruelty first began to be manifested against the Christians. Afterwards, too, their religion was prohibited by laws which were enacted; and by edicts openly set forth it was proclaimed unlawful to be a Christian.

It is true that this persecution was confined originally to Rome; but the gateway to persecution had been opened, and in every place they were ready victims for the mob.

The New Testament scholar James Moffatt writes:

> After the Neronic wave had passed over the capital, the wash of it was felt on the far shores of the provinces; the dramatic publicity of the punishment must have spread the name of Christian *urbi et orbi*, far and wide, over the entire empire; the provincials would soon hear of it, and when they desired a similar outburst at the

expense of the loyal Christians, all that they needed was
a proconsul to gratify their wishes and some outstanding
disciple to serve as a victim.

Forever after, the Christians were to live under threat. The
mobs of the Roman cities knew what had happened in Rome,
and the slanderous stories against the Christians persisted.
There were times when the mob loved blood, and there were
many governors ready to pander to their blood lust. It was
not Roman law but lynch law which threatened the Christians.

From now on, Christians were in peril of their lives. For
years, nothing might happen; then some spark might set off
the explosion, and the terror would break out. That is what
lies behind 1 Peter; and it is confronted by that situation that
Peter calls his people to hope and to courage and to that lovely
Christian living which alone can give the lie to the slanders
with which they are attacked and which are the grounds for
taking measures against them. First Peter was not written to
meet theological heresy; it was written to strengthen men
and women who were in danger of losing their lives.

The Doubts

We have set out in full the arguments which go to prove that
Peter is really the author of the first letter which bears his
name. But, as we have said, a number of first-class scholars
have felt that it cannot have been his work. We ourselves
accept the view that Peter is the author of the letter; but in
fairness we set out the other side, largely as it is presented in
the chapter on 1 Peter in *The Primitive Church* by B. H.
Streeter.

Strange Silences

Charles Bigg writes in the introduction to his commentary:
'There is no book in the New Testament which has earlier,

better, or stronger attestation [than 1 Peter].' It is true that Eusebius, the great fourth-century scholar and historian of the Church, classes 1 Peter among the books universally accepted in the early Church as part of Scripture (Eusebius, *Ecclesiastical History*, 3:25:2). But certain things are to be noted.

(a) Eusebius cites certain quotations from earlier writers to prove his contention that 1 Peter was universally accepted. This he never does in connection with the gospels or the letters of Paul; and the very fact that he feels called upon to produce his evidence in the case of 1 Peter might be held to indicate that in it he felt the need to prove his point, a need which did not exist in connection with the other books. Was there a doubt in Eusebius' own mind? Or were there people who had to be convinced? Was the universal acceptance of 1 Peter not so unanimous after all?

(b) In his book, *The Canon of the New Testament*, B. F. Westcott noted that, although no one in the early Church questions the right of 1 Peter to be part of the New Testament, surprisingly few of the early fathers quote it and, still more surprising, very few of the early fathers in the west and in Rome quote it. Tertullian is a frequent quoter of Scripture. In his writings, there are 7,258 quotations from the New Testament, but only two of them are from 1 Peter. If Peter wrote this letter and wrote it in Rome, we would expect it to be well known and largely used in the Church of the west.

(c) The earliest known official list of New Testament books is the Muratorian Canon, so called after Cardinal Muratori who discovered it. It is the official list of New Testament books as accepted in the church at Rome about the year AD 170. It is an extraordinary fact that 1 Peter does not appear at all. It can be fairly argued that the Muratorian Canon, as we possess it, is defective and that it may originally have contained a reference to 1 Peter. But that argument is seriously weakened by the next consideration.

(d) It is a fact that 1 Peter was still not in the New Testament of the Syrian church as late as AD 373. It did not get in until the Syriac version of the New Testament known as the Peshitto was made about AD 400. We know that it was the Christian scholar Tatian who brought the New Testament books to the Syriac-speaking church, and he brought them to Syria from Rome when he went to Edessa and founded the church there in AD 172. It could, therefore, be argued that the Muratorian Canon is correct as we possess it and that 1 Peter was not part of the Roman church's New Testament as late as AD 170. This would be a very surprising fact if Peter wrote it – and actually wrote it at Rome.

When all these facts are put together, it does seem that there are some strange silences in regard to 1 Peter and that the evidence supporting it may not be as strong as is usually assumed.

First Peter and Ephesians

Further, there is definitely some connection between 1 Peter and Ephesians. There are many close parallels of thought and expression between the two, and we select the following specimens of this similarity.

Blessed be the God and Father of our Lord Jesus Christ! By his great mercy he has given us a new birth into a living hope through the resurrection of Jesus Christ from the dead (1 Peter 1:3).

Blessed be the God and Father of our Lord Jesus Christ, who has blessed us in Christ with every spiritual blessing in the heavenly places (Ephesians 1:3).

> Therefore prepare your minds for action; discipline yourselves; set all your hope on the grace that Jesus Christ will bring you when he is revealed (1 Peter 1:13).

> Stand, therefore, and fasten the belt of truth around your waist (Ephesians 6:14).

> He was destined before the foundation of the world, but was revealed at the end of the ages for your sake (1 Peter 1:20).

> Just as he chose us in Christ, before the foundation of the world (Ephesians 1:4).

> Jesus Christ, who has gone into heaven and is at the right hand of God, with angels, authorities, and powers made subject to him (1 Peter 3:21–2).

> God . . . seated him at his right hand in the heavenly places, far above all rule and authority and power and dominion (Ephesians 1:20–1).

In addition, the instructions to slaves, husbands and wives in 1 Peter and Ephesians are very similar.

The argument is put forward that 1 Peter is quoting Ephesians. Although Ephesians must have been written somewhere about AD 64, Paul's letters were not collected and edited until about AD 90, If, then, Peter was also writing in AD 64, how could he know Ephesians?

This is an argument to which there is more than one reply. (a) The instructions to slaves, husbands and wives are part of the standardized ethical teaching given to all converts in all churches. Peter was not borrowing from Paul; both were using common material. (b) All the similarities quoted can well be explained from the fact that certain phrases and lines of thought were universal in the early Church. For instance, 'Blessed be the God and Father of our Lord Jesus Christ' was part of the universal devotional language of the early

Church, which both Peter and Paul would know and use without any borrowing from each other. (c) Even if there was mutual borrowing, it is by no means certain that 1 Peter borrowed from Ephesians; the borrowing might well have been the other way round and probably was, for 1 Peter is much simpler than Ephesians. (d) Last, even if 1 Peter borrowed from Ephesians, if Peter and Paul were in Rome at the same time, it is perfectly possible that Peter could have seen a copy of Ephesians before it was sent to Asia Minor, and he might well have discussed its ideas with Paul.

The argument that 1 Peter must be late because it quotes from Ephesians seems to us very uncertain and insecure, and probably mistaken.

As an Elder Myself

It is objected that Peter could not well have written the sentence: 'Now as an elder myself . . . I exhort the elders among you' (1 Peter 5:1). It is maintained that Peter could not have called himself an elder. He was an apostle whose function was quite different from that of an elder. The apostle was characteristically someone whose work and authority were not confined to any one congregation, but whose remit ran throughout the whole Church; whereas the elder was the governing official of the local congregation.

That is perfectly true. But it must be remembered that among the Jews there was no office more universally honoured than that of elder. Elders had the respect of the whole community, and the community looked to them for guidance in its problems and justice in its disputes. Peter, as a Jew, would feel nothing out of place in calling himself an elder, and in so doing he would avoid the conscious claim of authority that the title of apostle might have implied, and graciously and courteously identify himself with the people to whom he spoke.

A Witness of the Sufferings of Christ

It is objected that Peter could not honestly have called himself a witness of Christ's sufferings, for after the arrest in the garden all the disciples forsook Jesus and fled (Matthew 26:56), and, apart from the beloved disciple, none was a witness of the cross (John 19:26–7). Peter could call himself a witness of the *resurrection*, and indeed to be such a witness was the function of an apostle (Acts 1:22); but a witness of the cross he was not. In a sense, that is undeniable. And yet Peter is here claiming not to be a witness of the crucifixion but to be a witness of the sufferings of Christ. He did see Christ suffer, in his continual rejection by the people, in the poignant moments of the Last Supper, in the agony in the garden and in that moment when, after he had denied him, Jesus turned and looked on him (Luke 22:61). It is an insensitive and unimaginative criticism which denies to Peter the right to say that he had been a witness of the sufferings of Christ.

Persecution for the Name

The main argument for a late date for 1 Peter is drawn from its references to persecution. It is argued that 1 Peter implies that it was already a crime to be a Christian and that Christians were brought before the courts, not for any crime but for the bare fact of their faith. First Peter speaks about being reproached for the name of Christ (4:14); it speaks of suffering as a Christian (4:16). It is argued that this stage of persecution was not reached until after AD 100, and that prior to that date their persecution was on the charge of alleged evildoing, as in the time of Nero.

There is no doubt that this was the law by AD 112. At that time, Pliny was governor of Bithynia. He was a personal friend of the Emperor Trajan, and he had a way of referring all his difficulties to Trajan for solution. He wrote to the emperor to tell how he dealt with the Christians. Pliny was well aware that they were law-abiding citizens to whose practices no crimes were attached. They told him that 'they had been accustomed to assemble on a fixed day before daylight, and sing by turns a hymn to Christ as God; that they had bound themselves with an oath, not for any crime, but to commit neither theft, nor robbery, nor adultery, nor to break their word, and not to deny a deposit when demanded'. Pliny accepted all this; but, when they were brought before him, he asked only one question. 'I have asked them whether they were Christians. Those who confessed I asked a second and a third time, threatening punishment. Those who persisted I ordered to be led away to execution.' Their sole crime was that of being Christians.

Trajan replied that this was the correct way to go about things and that anyone who denied being a Christian and proved it by sacrificing to the gods was immediately to be set free. From the letters, it is clear that there was a good deal of information being laid against the Christians, and Trajan laid it down that no anonymous letters of information were to be accepted or acted upon (Pliny, *Letters* 96 and 97).

It is argued that this stage of persecution did not emerge until the time of Trajan, and that 1 Peter therefore implies a situation which must be as late as Trajan's time.

The only way in which we can settle this is to sketch the progress of persecution and the reason for it in the Roman Empire. We may do so by setting out one basic fact and three developments from it.

(1) Under the Roman system, religions were divided into two kinds. There were those which were *religiones licitae*, permitted religions; these were recognized by the state, and

it was open to anyone to practise them. There were *religiones illicitae*; these were forbidden by the state, and it was illegal for anyone to practise them on pain of automatic prosecution as a criminal. It is to be noted that Roman toleration was very wide, and that any religion which did not affect public morality and civil order was certain to be permitted.

(2) Judaism was a *religio licita*, and in the very early days the Romans, not unnaturally, did not know the difference between Judaism and Christianity. Christianity, as far as they were concerned, was merely a sect of Judaism, and any tension and hostility between the two was a private quarrel which was no concern of the Roman government. Because of that, in the very early days Christianity was under no danger of persecution. It enjoyed the same freedom of worship as Judaism enjoyed because it was assumed to be a *religio licita*.

(3) The action of Nero changed the situation. However it came about, and most likely it was by the deliberate action of the Jews, the Roman government discovered that Judaism and Christianity were different. It is true that Nero first persecuted the Christians, not for being Christians but for burning Rome. But the fact remains that the government had discovered that Christianity was a separate religion.

(4) The consequence was immediate and inevitable. Christianity became at once a prohibited religion, and immediately every Christian by definition automatically became an outlaw. In the writings of the Roman historian Suetonius, we have direct evidence that this was precisely what happened. He gives a kind of list of the legislative reforms initiated by Nero:

> During his reign, many abuses were severely punished and put down, and not a few new laws were made; a limit was set to expenditures; the public banquets were confined to a distribution of food; the sale of any kind

of cooked viands in the taverns was forbidden, with the exception of pulse and vegetables, whereas, before, every kind of dainty was exposed for sale. Punishment was inflicted on the Christians, a class of men given to a new and mischievous superstition. He put an end to the diversions of the chariot-drivers, who from immunity of long standing claimed the right of ranging at large and amusing themselves by cheating and robbing the people. The pantomimic actors and their partisans were banished from the city.

We have quoted that passage in full because it is proof that by the time of Nero the punishment of Christians had become an ordinary police affair. It is abundantly clear that we do not need to wait until the time of Trajan for the mere fact of being a Christian to be a crime. Any time after Nero, Christians were liable to punishment and death simply for the name they bore.

This does not mean that persecution was constant and consistent, but it does mean that any Christian was liable to execution at any time, purely as a police matter. In one area, a Christian might live a whole lifetime at peace; in another, there might be outbreaks of persecution every few months. It depended very largely on two things. It depended on the governor himself, who might either leave the Christians alone or equally set the processes of the law in action against them. It depended on informers. The governor might not want to act against the Christians, but if information was laid against a Christian he had to; and there were times when the mob was out for blood, information was presented and Christians were butchered as entertainment for a Roman holiday.

To compare small things with great, the legal position of the Christians and the attitude of the Roman law can be paralleled in Britain today. There are certain actions which are illegal – to take a very small example, parking a car in a restricted area – but which for a while may be permitted. But if the authorities decide to institute a drive against such an action, or if it develops into too blatant a breaking of the law, or if someone lodges a complaint and produces evidence, the law will go into action, and due penalty and punishment will be exacted. That was the position of the Christians in the empire. Technically they were outlaws; in actual fact no action might be taken against them, but a kind of sword of Damocles was always there, suspended over them. They never knew when information would be produced against them, or when a governor would take action. They never knew when they might have to die. And that was the situation consistently after the action of Nero. Up to that time, the Roman authorities had not realized that Christianity was a new religion, but from then on Christians were automatically outlaws.

Let us, then, look at the situation as depicted in 1 Peter. Peter's people are undergoing various trials (1:6). Their faith is liable to be tried as metal is tested with fire (1:7). Clearly, they are undergoing a campaign of slander in which ignorant charges with no foundation are being maliciously directed against them (2:12, 2:15, 3:16, 4:4). At this very moment, they are in the middle of an outbreak of persecution because they are Christians (4:12, 4:14, 4:16, 5:9). Such suffering is only to be expected, and they must not be surprised at it (4:12). In any event, it gives them the happiness of suffering for what is right (3:14, 3:17), and of being sharers in the sufferings of Christ (4:13). There is no need to come down to the time of Trajan for this situation. It is one in which Christians in every part of the empire found themselves every day at any time after their true status had been disclosed by the action of Nero. The persecution situation in 1 Peter does not in any way compel us to date it after the lifetime of Peter.

Honour the King

But we must proceed with the arguments of those who cannot support the Petrine authorship. It is argued that, in the situation which existed in the time of Nero, Peter could never have written: 'For the Lord's sake accept the authority of every human institution, whether of the emperor as supreme, or of governors, as sent by him to punish those who do wrong and to praise those who do right . . . Fear God. Honour the emperor' (2:13–17). The fact is, however, that this is precisely the point of view expressed in Romans 13:1–7. The whole teaching of the New Testament, except only in the Book of Revelation in which Rome is damned, is that Christians must be loyal citizens and must demonstrate the falsity of the charges made against them by the excellence of their behaviour (1 Peter 2:15). Even in times of persecution, Christians fully acknowledged their obligation to be good citizens; and their only defence against persecution was to show by the excellence of their citizenship that they did not deserve such treatment. It is by no means impossible that Peter could have written like that.

A Sermon and a Pastoral Letter

What is the view of those who cannot believe that 1 Peter is the work of Peter himself?

First of all, it is suggested that the initial address (1:1–2) and the closing greetings and salutations (5:12–14) are later additions and no part of the original letter.

It is then suggested that 1 Peter as it stands is composed of two separate and quite different works. In 4:11, we find a doxology, a hymn of praise. The natural place for a doxology is at the end, and it is suggested that 1:3–4:11 is the first of the two works of which the letter is composed. It is further suggested that this part of 1 Peter was originally a baptismal sermon. There is indeed in it a reference to the baptism which saves us (3:21); and the advice to slaves, wives and husbands (2:18–3:7) would be entirely relevant to those who were entering the Christian Church from worship of the ancient Greek and Roman gods and setting out on the newness of the Christian life.

It is suggested that the second part of the letter, 4:12–5:11, contains the substance of a pastoral letter, written to strengthen and comfort during a time of persecution (4:12–19). At such a time, the elders were very important; the resistance power of the Church depended on them. The writer of this pastoral letter fears that greed and arrogance are creeping in (5:1–3), and he urges them faithfully to perform their important task (5:4).

On this view, 1 Peter is composed of two separate works – a baptismal sermon and a pastoral letter written in time of persecution, and neither has anything to do with Peter.

Asia Minor, not Rome

If 1 Peter is a baptismal sermon and a pastoral letter in time of persecution, where is its place of origin? If the letter is not Peter's, there is no need to connect it with Rome, and in any event it appears that the Roman church did not know or use 1 Peter. Let us put together certain facts.

(1) Pontus, Galatia, Cappadocia, Asia and Bithynia (1:1) are all in Asia Minor and all centred in Sinope.

(2) The first person to quote extensively from 1 Peter is Polycarp, Bishop of Smyrna – and Smyrna is in Asia Minor.

(3) Certain phrases in 1 Peter immediately turn our thoughts to parallel phrases in other parts of the New Testament. In 1 Peter 5:13, the church is called 'your sister church . . . chosen together with you', and in 2 John 13 the

church is described as an 'elect sister'. First Peter 1:8 speaks of Jesus Christ: 'Although you have not seen him, you love him; and even though you do not see him now, you believe in him and rejoice with an indescribable and glorious joy.' This turns our thoughts very naturally to Jesus' saying to Thomas in the Fourth Gospel: 'Blessed are those who have not seen and yet have come to believe' (John 20:29). First Peter urges the elders to tend, that is, to shepherd, the flock of God (1 Peter 5:2). That turns our thoughts to Jesus' instruction to Peter to feed his lambs and his sheep (John 21:15–17), and to Paul's farewell instruction to the elders of Ephesus to keep watch over the flock over which the Holy Spirit has made them guardians (Acts 20:28). All this is to say that the memories which 1 Peter awakens are of the Fourth Gospel, the Letters of John and of Paul at Ephesus. The Fourth Gospel and the Letters of John were most probably written at Ephesus – and Ephesus is in Asia Minor.

It seems that, in the case of 1 Peter, all roads lead to Asia Minor.

The Occasion of the Publication of 1 Peter

Assuming that 1 Peter has its origin in Asia Minor, can we suggest an occasion for its writing? It was written at a time of persecution. We know from Pliny's letters that in Bithynia about AD 112 there was a serious persecution of the Christians, and Bithynia is one of the provinces named in the address. We may well conjecture that it was to give courage to the Christians that 1 Peter was issued. It may be that at that time someone in a church in Asia Minor came upon these two documents and sent them out under the name of Peter. This would not be looked upon as forgery. Both in Jewish and in Greek practice, it was the regular custom to attach books to the name of the great writers of the past.

The Author of 1 Peter

If Peter did not write 1 Peter, is it possible to guess at the author? Let us reconstruct some of his essential qualifications. On our previous assumption, he must come from Asia Minor. On the basis of 1 Peter itself, he must be an *elder* and an *eyewitness* of the sufferings of Christ (1 Peter 5:1). Is there anyone who fits these requirements? Papias, Bishop of Hierapolis in about AD 170, who spent his life collecting all the information he could about the early days of the Church, tells of his methods and his sources: 'Nor shall I hesitate, along with my own interpretations, to set down for thee whatsoever I learned with care and remembered with care from the elders, guaranteeing its truth . . . Furthermore, if anyone chanced to arrive who had been really a follower of the elders, I would enquire as to the sayings of the elders – as to what Andrew or Peter said, or Philip, or Thomas or James, or John or Matthew, or any other of the Lord's disciples, also as to what Aristion or the Presbyter John, the Lord's disciples say. For I supposed that things out of books would not be of such use to me as the utterances of a living voice which was still with us.' Here, we have an elder called Aristion, who was a disciple of the Lord and, therefore, a witness of his sufferings. Is there anything to connect him with 1 Peter?

Aristion of Smyrna

When we turn to the *Apostolic Constitutions*, we find that one of the first bishops of Smyrna was called Ariston – which is the same name as Aristion. Now who is the one who quotes so often from 1 Peter? None other than Polycarp, a later Bishop of Smyrna. What more natural than that Polycarp should quote what might well have been the devotional classic of his own church?

Let us turn to the letters to the seven churches in the Book of Revelation and read the letter to Smyrna: 'Do not fear what you are about to suffer. Beware, the devil is about to throw some of you into prison so that you may be tested, and for ten days you will have affliction. Be faithful until death, and I will give you the crown of life' (Revelation 2:10). Can this be the very same persecution as that which originally lay behind 1 Peter? And was it for this persecution that Aristion, the Bishop of Smyrna, first wrote the pastoral letter which was afterwards to become a part of 1 Peter?

Such is the suggestion of B. H. Streeter. He thinks that 1 Peter is composed of a baptismal sermon and a pastoral letter written by Aristion, Bishop of Smyrna. Originally the pastoral letter was written to comfort and strengthen the people of Smyrna in AD 90 when the persecution mentioned in the Book of Revelation threatened the church. These writings of Aristion became the devotional classics and the cherished possessions of the church at Smyrna. Rather more than twenty years later, a much wider and more far-reaching persecution broke out in Bithynia and spread throughout northern Asia Minor. Someone remembered the letter and the sermon of Aristion, felt that they were the very thing the Church needed in its time of trial, and sent them out under the name of Peter, the great apostle.

An Apostle's Letter

We have stated in full both views of the origin, date and authorship of 1 Peter. There is no doubt about the ingenuity of the theory which B. H. Streeter has produced, nor that those who favour a later date have produced arguments which have to be considered. For our own part, however, we see no reason to doubt that the letter is the work of Peter himself, and that it was written not long after the great fire of Rome

and the first persecution of the Christians with the object of
encouraging the Christians of Asia Minor to stand fast when
the onrushing tide of persecution sought to engulf them and
take their faith away.

1 PETER

THE GREAT INHERITANCE

1 Peter 1:1–2

> Peter, an apostle of Jesus Christ, to God's chosen people,
> who are scattered as exiles throughout Pontus, Galatia,
> Cappadocia, Asia and Bithynia. I am an apostle, and
> you are chosen, according to the foreknowledge of God,
> through the consecration of the Spirit, for obedience and
> to be sprinkled by the blood of Jesus Christ. May grace
> and peace be multiplied to you.

IT happens again and again in the New Testament that the
true greatness of a passage lies not only on the surface and in
what is actually said, but in the ideas and the convictions which
lie behind it. That is particularly so here.

It is clear that this letter was written to people who were
Gentiles. They have been released from the futile way of life
which they had learned from their ancestors (1:18). Those
who were at one time not a people had become nothing less
than the people of God (2:10). In previous times, they had
followed the ways, the will and the lusts of the Gentiles (4:3).
But the outstanding thing about this passage is that it takes
words and conceptions which had originally applied only to
the Jews, the chosen nation, and applies them to the Gentiles,
who had once been believed to be outside the mercy of God.

Once, it had been said that 'God created the Gentiles to be fuel for the fires of hell.' Once, it had been said that, just as the best of the snakes must be crushed, so even the best of the Gentiles must be destroyed. Once, it had been said that God loved only Israel of all nations upon the earth. But now the mercy, the privileges and the grace of God have gone out to all the earth and to all people, even to those who could never have expected them.

(1) Peter calls the people to whom he writes *the elect, God's chosen people*. Once, that had been a title which belonged to Israel alone: 'For you are a people holy to the Lord your God; the Lord your God has chosen you out of all the peoples on earth to be his people, his treasured possession' (Deuteronomy 7:6; cf. 14:2). The prophet speaks of 'Israel my chosen' (Isaiah 45:4). The psalmist speaks of 'children of Jacob, his chosen ones' (Psalm 105:6, 43).

But the nation of Israel failed in the purposes of God, for, when he sent his Son into the world, they rejected and crucified him. When Jesus told the parable of the wicked tenants, he said that the inheritance of Israel was to be taken from them and given to others (Matthew 21:41; Mark 12:9; Luke 20:16). That is the basis of the great New Testament idea of the Christian Church as the true Israel, the new Israel, the Israel of God (cf. Galatians 6:16). All the privileges which had once belonged to Israel now belonged to the Christian Church. The mercy of God has gone out to the ends of the earth, and all nations have seen the glory and experienced the grace of God.

(2) There is another word here which once belonged exclusively to Israel. The address literally reads: 'To the elect strangers of the Diaspora throughout Pontus, Galatia, Cappadocia, Asia and Bithynia.' *Diaspora*, literally the *dispersion*, was the technical name for the Jews scattered in exile in all the countries outside the bounds of Palestine.

Sometimes in their troubled history, the Jews had been forcibly
deported from their native land; sometimes they had gone of
their own free will to work, and often to prosper, in other
lands. Those exiled Jews were called the *Diaspora*. But now
the real Diaspora is not the Jewish nation; it is the Christian
Church scattered abroad throughout the provinces of the
Roman Empire and the nations of the world. Once, the people
who had been different from others were the Jews; now the
people who are different are the Christians. They are the people
whose King is God, whose home is eternity, and who are
exiles in the world.

THE CHOSEN OF GOD
AND THE EXILES OF ETERNITY

I Peter I:I–2 (*contd*)

WHAT we have just been saying means that the two great titles
of which we have been thinking belong to us who are
Christians.

(I) We are *the chosen people of God*. There is something
uplifting here. Surely there can be no greater compliment and
privilege in all the world than to be chosen by God. The word
eklektos can describe anything that is specially chosen; it can
describe specially chosen fruit, articles specially chosen
because they are so outstandingly well made, hand-picked
troops specially chosen for some great mission. We have the
honour of being specially chosen by God. But there is also
challenge and *responsibility* here. God always chooses for
service. The honour which he gives to us is that of being used
for his purposes.

(2) We are *the exiles of eternity*. This is never to say that
we must withdraw from the world, but that in a very real sense

we must be at the same time both in the world and not of it. It has been wisely said that Christians must be *apart* from the world but never *aloof* from it. Wherever the exiled Jews settled, their eyes were always towards Jerusalem. In foreign countries, the synagogues were so built that, when the worshippers entered, they were facing towards Jerusalem. However useful as citizens of their adopted country the Jews were, their greatest loyalty was to Jerusalem.

The Greek word for such a resident in a strange land is *paroikos*. A *paroikos* was someone who was in a strange land and whose thoughts always turned to home. This kind of temporary residence was called a *paroikia*, and *paroikia* is the direct derivation of the English word *parish*. The Christians in any place are a group of people whose eyes are turned to God and whose loyalty is beyond. 'Here', said the writer to the Hebrews, 'we have no lasting city, but we are looking for the city that is to come' (Hebrews 13:14).

We must repeat that this does not mean withdrawal from the world, but it does mean that Christians see all things in the light of eternity and life as a journey towards God. It is this which decides the importance which they attach to anything; it is this which dictates their conduct. It is the measure and the driving force of their lives.

There is a famous unwritten saying of Jesus: 'The world is a bridge. The wise man will pass over it, but he will not build his house upon it.' This is the thought which is behind the famous passage in *The Epistle to Diognetus*, one of the best-known works of the post-apostolic age: 'Christians are not marked out from the rest of mankind by their country or their speech or their customs . . . They dwell in cities both Greek and barbarian, each as his lot is cast, following the customs of the region in clothing and in food and in the outward things of life generally; yet they manifest the wonderful and openly paradoxical character of their own state. They inhabit the lands of their birth, but as temporary residents thereof; they take their share of all responsibilities as citizens, and endure all disabilities as aliens. Every foreign land is their native land, and every native land a foreign land . . . They pass their days upon earth, but their citizenship is in heaven.'

It would be wrong to think that this makes Christians bad citizens of the land in which they live. It is because they see all things in the light of eternity that they are the best of all citizens, for it is only in the light of eternity that the true values of things can be seen.

We, as Christians, are the chosen people of God; we are the exiles of eternity. Therein lie both our priceless privilege and our inescapable responsibility.

THE THREE GREAT FACTS OF
THE CHRISTIAN LIFE

1 Peter 1:1-2 (contd)

IN verse 2, we are confronted with the three great facts of the Christian life.

(1) The Christian is *chosen according to the foreknowledge of God*. The New Testament scholar C. E. B. Cranfield has a fine comment on this phrase: 'If all our attention is concentrated on the hostility or indifference of the world or the exiguousness of our own progress in the Christian life, we may well be discouraged. At such times we need to be reminded that our election is *according to the foreknowledge of God the Father*. The Church is not just a human organization – though, of course, it is that. Its origin lies, not in the will of the flesh, in the idealism of men, in human aspirations and plans, but in the eternal purpose of God.' When we are

discouraged, we may well remind ourselves that the Christian Church came into being according to the purpose and plan of God – and, if it is true to him, it can never ultimately fail.

(2) The Christian is chosen *to be consecrated by the Spirit*. The reformer Martin Luther said: 'I believe that I cannot by my own reason or strength believe in Jesus Christ my Lord, or come to him.' For Christians, the Holy Spirit is essential to every part of the Christian life and every step in it. It is the Holy Spirit who awakens within us the first faint longings for God and goodness. It is the Holy Spirit who convicts us of our sin and leads us to the cross where that sin is forgiven. It is the Holy Spirit who enables us to be freed from the sins which have us in their grip and to gain the virtues which are the fruit of the Spirit. It is the Holy Spirit who gives us the assurance that our sins are forgiven and that Jesus Christ is Lord. The beginning, the middle and the end of the Christian life are the work of the Holy Spirit.

(3) The Christian is chosen *for obedience and for sprinkling by the blood of Jesus Christ*. In the Old Testament, there are three occasions when sprinkling with blood is mentioned. It may well be that all three were in Peter's mind and that all three have something to contribute to the thinking behind these words.

(a) When a leper had been healed, he was sprinkled with the blood of a bird (Leviticus 14:1–7). Sprinkling with blood is, therefore, the symbol of *cleansing*. By the sacrifice of Christ, Christians are cleansed from sin.

(b) Sprinkling with blood was part of the ritual of the setting apart of Aaron and the priests (Exodus 29:20–1; Leviticus 8:30). It was the sign of *setting apart* for the service of God. Christians are specially set apart for the service of God, not only within the Temple, but also within the world.

(c) The great picture of the sprinkling comes from the covenant relationship between Israel and God. In the covenant, God, of his own gracious will, approached Israel that they might be his people and that he might be their God. But that relationship depended on the Israelites accepting the conditions of the covenant and obeying the law. Obedience was a necessary condition of the covenant, and failure in obedience meant failure of the covenant relationship between God and Israel. So the book of the covenant was read to Israel, and the people pledged themselves: 'All the words which the Lord has spoken we will do.' As a token of this relationship of obedience between the people and God, Moses took half the blood of the sacrifice and sprinkled it on the altar, and half the blood of the sacrifice and sprinkled it on the people (Exodus 24:1–8). Sprinkling was for *obedience*.

Through the sacrifice of Jesus Christ, Christians are called into a new relationship with God, in which the sins of the past are forgiven and they are pledged to obedience in the time to come.

It is in the purpose of God that Christians are called. It is by the work of the Holy Spirit that their lives are consecrated to God. It is by the sprinkling of the blood of Christ that they are cleansed from past sin and dedicated to future obedience to God.

THE REBIRTH OF CHRISTIANS

1 Peter 1:3–5

> Blessed be the God and Father of our Lord Jesus Christ,
> who, according to his great mercy, has brought about in
> us that rebirth which leads to a living hope through the

resurrection of Jesus Christ from the dead, an inheritance imperishable, undefilable and unfading, kept safe in heaven for us, who are protected by the power of God through faith, until there comes that deliverance which is ready to be revealed at the last time.

It will take us a long time fully to take in and understand the riches of this passage, for there are few passages in the New Testament where more of the great fundamental Christian ideas come together.

It begins with a doxology, a hymn of praise, to God – but a doxology with a difference. For a Jew, the most common of all beginnings to prayer was: 'Blessed are you, O God.' Christians take over that prayer – but with a difference. Their prayer begins: 'Blessed be the God and Father of our Lord Jesus Christ.' They are not praying to a distant, unknown God; they are praying to the God who is like Jesus and to whom, through Jesus Christ, they may come with childlike confidence.

This passage begins with the idea of *rebirth*; Christians are men and women who have been reborn; they have been given new birth by God to a new kind of life. Whatever else this means, it means that, when people become Christians, there comes into their lives a change so radical that the only thing that can be said is that life has begun all over again for them. This idea of rebirth runs all through the New Testament. Let us try to collect what it says about it.

(1) Christian rebirth happens by the will and by the act of God (John 1:13; James 1:18). It is not something which we achieve any more than we achieve our physical birth.

(2) Another way to put that is to say that this rebirth is the work of the Spirit (John 3:1–15). It happens to people, not by their own effort, but when they give themselves up to be possessed and re-created by the Spirit within them.

(3) It happens by the word of truth (James 1:18; 1 Peter 1:23). In the beginning, it was the word of God which created heaven and earth and all that is in them. God spoke and the chaos became a world, and the world was equipped with and for life. It is the creative word of God in Jesus Christ which brings about this rebirth in our lives.

(4) The result of this rebirth is that those who are reborn become the first fruits of a new creation (James 1:18). It lifts them out of this world of space and time, of change and decay, of sin and defeat, and brings them here and now into touch with eternity and eternal life.

(5) When we are reborn, it is to a living hope (1 Peter 1:3). Paul describes the world without Christ as being without hope (Ephesians 2:12). Sophocles wrote: 'Not to be born at all – that is by far the best fortune; the second best is as soon as one is born with all speed to return thither whence one has come.' To the Gentiles, the world was a place where all things faded and decayed; it might be pleasant enough in itself, but it was leading out into nothing but an endless dark. To the ancient world, the Christian characteristic was hope. That hope came from two things. (a) Christians felt that they had been born not of perishable but of imperishable seed (1 Peter 1:23). They had something of the very seed of God in them and, therefore, had in them a life which neither time nor eternity could destroy. (b) It came from the resurrection of Jesus Christ (1 Peter 1:3). Christians had always beside them – even more, were one with – this Jesus Christ who had conquered even death, and therefore there was nothing of which they needed to be afraid.

(6) The rebirth of Christians is a rebirth to righteousness (1 John 2:29, 3:9, 5:18). In this rebirth, they are cleansed from themselves, the sins which shackle them and the habits which bind them; and they are given a power which enables them to

walk in righteousness. That is not to say that those who are reborn will never sin, but it is to say that every time they fall, they will be given the power and the grace to rise again.

(7) The rebirth of Christians is a rebirth to love (1 John 4:7). Because the life of God is in them, they are cleansed from the essential unforgiving bitterness of the self-centred life, and there is in them something of the forgiving and sacrificial love of God.

(8) Finally, the rebirth of Christians is rebirth to victory (1 John 5:4). Life ceases to be defeat and begins to be victory, over self and sin and circumstances. Because the life of God is in them, Christians have learned the secret of victorious living.

THE GREAT INHERITANCE

1 Peter 1:3–5 (*contd*)

FURTHER, Christians have entered into a great *inheritance* (*klēronomia*). Here is a word with a history; for it is the word which is regularly used in the Greek Old Testament for the inheritance of Canaan, the Promised Land. Again and again, the Old Testament speaks of the land which God had given his people *for an inheritance to possess* (cf. Deuteronomy 15:4, 19:10). To us, *inheritance* tends to mean something which we shall possess in the future; but as the Bible uses the word, it means a secure possession. To the Jews, the great settled possession was the Promised Land.

But the Christian inheritance is even greater. Peter uses three words with three pictures behind them to describe it. It is *imperishable* (*aphthartos*). The word does mean *imperishable*, but it can also mean *unravaged by any invading army*. Time after time, Palestine had been ravaged by the armies of other nations; it had been fought over and destroyed. But

Christians possess a peace and a joy, which no invading army can ravage and destroy. It is *undefilable*. The word is *amiantos*; and the verb *miainein*, from which this adjective comes, means to *pollute* with an impurity that is unholy. Time after time, Palestine had been rendered impure by false worship of false gods (Jeremiah 2:7, 2:23, 3:2; Ezekiel 20:43). The defiling things had often left their touch and their mark even on the Promised Land; but Christians have a purity which the sin of the world cannot infect. It is *unfading* (*amarantos*). In the promised land, as in any land, even the loveliest flower fades and the loveliest blossom dies. But Christians are lifted into a world where there is no change and decay, and where their peace and joy are untouched by the chances and the changes of life.

What, then, is this wonderful inheritance which reborn Christians possess? There may be many secondary answers to that question, but there is only one primary answer – the inheritance of Christians is God himself. The psalmist said: 'The Lord is my chosen portion . . . I have a goodly heritage' (Psalm 16:5–6). God is his portion forever (Psalm 73:23–6). 'The Lord', said the prophet, 'is my portion . . . therefore I will hope in him' (Lamentations 3:24).

It is because Christians possess God and are possessed by God that they have the inheritance which is imperishable and undefilable and which can never fade away.

PROTECTED IN TIME AND SAFE IN ETERNITY

1 Peter 1:3–5 (*contd*)

THE inheritance of Christians, the full joy of God, is waiting for them in heaven; and of that Peter has two great things to say.

(1) On our journey through this world to eternity, we are protected by the power of God through faith. The word which Peter uses for *protect* (*phrourein*) is a military word. It means that our life is garrisoned by God and that he stands sentry over us all our days. Those who have faith never doubt that God is standing within the shadows keeping watch over his own even when they cannot see him. It is not that God saves us from the troubles and the sorrows and the problems of life, but he enables us to conquer them and move on.

(2) The final salvation will be revealed at the last time. Here we have two concepts which are at the very basis of New Testament thought.

The New Testament frequently speaks of the last day or days, or the last time. Behind this is the way the Jews divided all time into two ages – the present age, which is wholly under the domination of evil, and the age to come, which will be the golden age of God. In between came the day of the Lord during which the world would be destroyed and remade and judgment would come. It is this in-between time which is the last days or the last time, that time when the world as we know it will come to an end.

It is not given to us to know when that time will come nor what will happen then. But we can gather together what the New Testament says about these last days.

(1) The Christians believed that they were already living in the last days. 'It is the last hour', says John to his people (1 John 2:18). The writer to the Hebrews speaks of the fullness of the revelation which has come in Christ in these last days (Hebrews 1:2). As the first Christians saw it, God had already invaded time, and the end was hastening on.

(2) The last times were to be times of the pouring out of God's Spirit upon all people (Acts 2:17). The early Christians

saw that being fulfilled in Pentecost and in the Spirit-filled Church.

(3) It was the conviction of the early Christians that, before the end, the powers of evil would make a final assault and that all kinds of false teachers would arise (2 Timothy 3:1; I John 2:18; Jude 18).

(4) The dead would be raised. It is Jesus' promise that at the last time he will raise up his own (John 6:39–40, 6:44, 6:54, 11:24).

(5) Inevitably, it would be a time of judgment when God's justice would be exercised and his enemies would find their just condemnation and punishment (John 12:48; James 5:3).

Such are the ideas which are in the minds of the New Testament writers when they use this phrase *the last times or the last days*.

Clearly, for many, such a time will be a time of terror; but for Christians there is not terror but deliverance. The word *sōzein* means *to save* in far more than a theological sense. It is the word meaning *to rescue from danger* and *to heal in sickness*. In his commentary, Charles Bigg points out that in the New Testament *sōzein*, to save, and *sōtēria*, salvation, have four different but closely related spheres of meaning. (a) They describe deliverance from danger (Matthew 8:25). (b) They describe deliverance from disease (Matthew 9:21). (c) They describe deliverance from the condemnation of God (Matthew 10:22, 24:13). (d) They describe deliverance from the disease and power of sin (Matthew 1:21). Salvation is a many-sided thing. In it there is deliverance from danger, deliverance from disease, deliverance from condemnation and deliverance from sin. And it is that, and nothing less than that, to which Christians can look forward at the end.

THE SECRET OF ENDURANCE

I Peter 1:6–7

> Herein you rejoice, even if it is at present necessary that
> for a brief time you should be grieved by all kinds of
> trials, for the object of these trials is that your tried and
> tested faith, more precious than gold which perishes
> though it is tested by the fire, may win praise and glory
> and honour when Jesus Christ shall appear.

PETER comes to the actual situation in life in which his readers
found themselves. Their Christianity had always made them
unpopular, but now they were facing almost certain persecution. Soon the storm was going to break and life was going
to be an agonizing experience. Faced with that threatening
situation, Peter, in effect, reminds them of three reasons why
they can stand anything that may come upon them.

(1) They can stand anything because of what they are able
to look forward to. At the end, there is for them the magnificent
inheritance, life with God. In fact, this is how the scholar
B. F. Westcott understands the phrase *in the last time* (*en
kairō eschatō*). We have taken it to mean *in the time when
the world as we know it will come to an end*, but the Greek
can mean *when the worst comes to the worst*. It is then, says
Westcott, when things have reached their limit, that the saving
power of Christ will be displayed.

In any event, the ultimate meaning is the same. For
Christians, persecution and trouble are not the end; beyond
lies the glory, and in the hope of that glory they can endure
anything that life brings to them. It sometimes happens that
people have to undergo a painful operation or course of
treatment, but they gladly accept the pain and the discomfort
because of the renewed health and strength which lie beyond.
It is one of the basic facts of life that we can endure anything

as long as we have something to look forward to – and Christians can look forward to the ultimate joy.

(2) They can stand anything that comes if they remember that every trial is, in fact, a test. Before gold is pure, it has to be tested in the fire. The trials which come to us test our faith, and out of them that faith can emerge stronger than ever it was before. The rigours which athletes have to undergo are meant not to make them collapse but to make them able to develop more strength and staying power. In this world, trials are meant not to take the strength out of us but to put the strength into us.

In this connection, there is something more to be found in the language Peter uses. He says that Christians for the moment may well have to undergo *various* trials. The Greek is *poikilos*, which literally means *many-coloured*. Peter uses that word only on one other occasion, and it is to describe the grace of God (1 Peter 4:10). Our troubles may be many-coloured, but so is the grace of God; there is no colour in the human situation which that grace cannot match. There is a grace to match every trial, and there is no trial without its grace.

(3) They can stand anything, because at the end of it, when Jesus Christ appears, they will receive from him praise and glory and honour. Again and again in this life, we make our biggest efforts and do our best work not for pay or profit but in order to see the light in someone's eyes and to hear a word of praise. These things mean more than anything else in the world. Christians know that, if they endure, they will in the end hear the Master's 'Well done!'

Here is the recipe for endurance when life is hard and faith is difficult. We can stand up to things because of the greatness to which we can look forward, because every trial is another test to strengthen and to purify our faith, and because at the end of it Jesus Christ is waiting to say 'Well done!' to all his faithful servants.

UNSEEN BUT NOT UNKNOWN

1 Peter 1:8–9

> Although you never knew him, you love him; although you do not see him, you believe in him. And you rejoice with unspeakable and glorious joy because you are receiving that which faith must end in – the salvation of your souls.

PETER is drawing an implicit contrast between himself and his readers. It was his great privilege to have known Jesus in his days on earth. His readers had not had that joy, but, although they never knew Jesus on earth, they love him; and, although they do not actually see him, they believe. And that belief brings to them a glorious joy beyond words, for even here and now it makes them certain of the ultimate welfare of their souls.

E. G. Selwyn in his commentary distinguishes four stages in our understanding and knowledge of Christ.

(1) The first is the stage of hope and desire, the stage of those who throughout the ages dreamed of the coming of the King. As Jesus himself said to his disciples, 'Many prophets and kings desired to see what you see, but did not see it' (Luke 10:24). There were the days of longings and expectations which were never fully brought to fruition.

(2) The second stage came to those who knew Christ on earth. That is what Peter is thinking about here. That is what he was thinking about when he said to Cornelius: 'We are witnesses to all that he did both in Judaea and in Jerusalem' (Acts 10:39). There were those who walked with Jesus and

on whose witness our knowledge of his life and his words depends.

(3) There are those in every nation and time who see Jesus with the eye of faith. Jesus said to Thomas: 'Have you believed because you have seen me? Blessed are those who have not seen and yet have come to believe' (John 20:29). This way of seeing Jesus is possible only because he is not someone who lived and died and exists now only as a figure in a book. He is someone who lived and died and is alive for evermore. It has been said that 'no apostle ever *remembered* Jesus'. That is to say, Jesus is not only a memory; he is a person whom we can meet.

(4) There is the heavenly vision. It was John's confidence that we shall see him as he is (1 John 3:2). 'Now', said Paul, 'we see in a mirror, dimly, but then we will see face to face' (1 Corinthians 13:12). If the eye of faith endures, the day will come when it will be the eye of sight, and we shall see face to face and know even as we are known. As the hymn has it:

> Jesus, these eyes have never seen
> That radiant form of thine;
> The veil of sense hangs dark between
> Thy blessed face and mine.
>
> I see thee not, I hear thee not,
> Yet art thou oft with me;
> And earth hath ne'er so dear a spot
> As where I meet with thee.
>
> Yet, though I have not seen, and still
> Must rest in faith alone,
> I love thee, dearest Lord, and will,
> Unseen but not unknown.
>
> When death these mortal eyes shall seal,
> And still this throbbing heart,
> The rending veil shall thee reveal
> All glorious as thou art.

THE FORETELLING OF THE GLORY

1 Peter 1:10–12

> Prophets, who prophesied about the grace which was to come to you, inquired and searched concerning that salvation, seeking to find out when and how the Spirit of Christ within them, testifying in advance to the sufferings destined for Christ and to the glories which must follow them, was telling them that it would come. It was revealed to them that the ministry which they were exercising in these things was not for themselves but for you, things which have now been proclaimed to you through those who preached the gospel to you through the power of the Holy Spirit sent down from heaven, things of which the angels long to catch a glimpse.

HERE again we have a rich passage. The wonder of the salvation which was to come to men and women in Christ was such that the prophets searched and inquired about it; and even the angels were eager to catch a glimpse of it. Few passages have more to tell us about how the prophets wrote and about how they were inspired.

(1) We are told two things about the prophets. First, they searched and inquired about the salvation which was to come. Second, the Spirit of Christ told them about Christ. Here we have the great truth that inspiration depends on two things – the searching human mind and the revealing Spirit of God. It used sometimes to be said that those who wrote Scripture were pens in the hands of God or flutes into which his Spirit breathed or lyres across which his Spirit moved. That is to say, they were held to be nothing more than almost unconscious instruments in God's hands. But this passage tells us that God's truth comes only to those who search for it. In

inspiration, there is an element which is human and an element which is divine; it is the product at one and the same time of the search of the human mind and the revelation of God's Spirit.

Further, this passage tells us that the Holy Spirit, the Spirit of Christ, was always at work in this world. Wherever people have glimpsed beauty, wherever they have laid hold on truth, wherever they have had longings for God, the Spirit of Christ was there. Never has there been any time in any nation when the Spirit of Christ was not moving men and women to seek God and guiding them to find him. Sometimes they have been blind and deaf, sometimes they have misinterpreted that guidance, sometimes they have grasped only fragments of it – but always that revealing Spirit has been there to guide the searching mind.

(2) This passage tells us that the prophets spoke of the sufferings and the glory of Christ. Such passages as Psalm 22 and Isaiah 52:13–53:12 found their consummation and fulfilment in the sufferings of Christ. Such passages as Psalm 2, Psalm 16:8–11 and Psalm 110 found their fulfilment in the glory and the triumph of Christ. We need not think that the prophets foresaw the actual man Jesus. What they did foresee was that some day there would come one in whom their dreams and visions would all be fulfilled.

(3) This passage tells us for whom the prophets spoke. It was the message of the glorious deliverance of God that they brought to the people. That was a deliverance which they themselves never experienced. Sometimes God gives someone a vision, but says to that person: 'Not yet!' He took Moses to Pisgah and showed him the promised land and said to him: 'I have let you see it with your eyes, but you shall not cross over there' (Deuteronomy 34:4). A vivid image from the past tells of someone watching a blind lamp-lighter lighting the

lamps one night at dusk. He tapped his way from lamp-post to lamp-post bringing to others a light which he himself would never see. As the prophets knew, it is a great gift to receive the vision, even if the fulfilment of the vision is for others still to come.

THE MESSAGE OF THE PREACHER

1 Peter 1:10–12 (*contd*)

THIS passage tells us not only of the visions of the prophets but also of the message of the preacher. It was the preachers who brought the message of salvation to the readers of Peter's letter.

(1) It tells us that preaching is the announcement of salvation. Preaching may at different times have many notes and many aspects, but fundamentally it is the proclamation of the gospel, the good news. Preachers may at times have to warn, threaten and condemn; they may have to remind people of the judgment and the wrath of God; but basically, beyond all else, their message is the announcement of salvation.

(2) It tells us that preaching is through the Holy Spirit sent down from heaven. The preachers' message is not their own; it is given to them. They do not bring their own opinions and even prejudices; they bring the truth as given to them by the Holy Spirit. Like the prophets, they will have to search and to inquire; they will have to study and to learn; but they must then wait for the guidance of the Spirit to come to them.

(3) It tells us that the preachers' message is of things of which the angels long to catch a glimpse. There is no excuse for triviality in preaching. There is no excuse for an earthbound and unlovely message without interest or thrill. The salvation of God is a tremendous thing.

It is with the message of salvation and the inspiration of the Spirit of Christ that preachers must always appear before others.

THE NECESSARY STRENGTH AND POWER OF THE CHRISTIAN FAITH

1 Peter 1:13

> So, then, gird up the loins of your mind; be sober; come to a final decision to place your hope on the grace which is going to be brought to you at the revealing of Jesus Christ.

PETER has been talking about the greatness and the glory to which Christians may look forward; but Christians can never be lost in dreams of the future; they must always be strong and powerful in the battle of the present. So Peter sends out three challenges to his people.

(1) He tells them to *gird up the loins of their mind*. This is a deliberately vivid phrase. In the middle east, men wore long flowing robes which hindered fast progress or strenuous action. Round the waist, they wore a broad belt or girdle; and when strenuous action was necessary they shortened the long robe by pulling it up within the belt in order to give themselves freedom of movement. The English equivalent of the phrase would be to roll up one's sleeves or to take off one's jacket. Peter is telling his people that they must be ready for the most strenuous mental endeavour. They must never be content with a flabby and unexamined faith; they must set to and think things out and think them through. It may be that they will have to discard some things. It may be that they will make mistakes. But what they are left with will be theirs in such a way that nothing and nobody can ever take it away from them.

(2) He tells them to *be sober*. The Greek word, like the English, can have two meanings. It can mean that they must refrain from drunkenness in the literal sense of the term, and it can also mean that they must be steady in their minds. They must become intoxicated neither with intoxicating liquor nor with intoxicating thoughts; they must preserve a balanced judgment. It is easy for Christians to be carried away with this, that or the next sudden enthusiasm and quickly to become completely under the influence of the latest fashion and the newest craze. Peter is appealing to them to maintain the essential steadiness of the men and women who know what they believe.

(3) He tells them to *set their hope on the grace which is going to be given to them when Jesus Christ comes*. It is the great characteristic of Christians that they live in hope, and because they live in hope they can endure the trials of the present. We can all endure struggle and effort and toil, if we are certain that it is all leading somewhere. That is why athletes accept their training and students their study. For Christians, the best is always still to come. They can live with gratitude for all the mercies of the past, with resolution to meet the challenge of the present and with the certain hope that in Christ the best is yet to come.

THE CHRISTLESS LIFE
AND THE CHRIST-FILLED LIFE

1 Peter 1:14–25

Be obedient children. Do not continue to live a life which matches the desires of the days of your former ignorance, but show yourselves holy in all your conduct of life as he who called you is holy, because it stands written:

'You must be holy, because I am holy.' If you address
as Father him who judges each man according to his
work with complete impartiality, conduct yourselves
with reverence throughout the time of your sojourn in
this world; for you know that it was not by perishable
things, by silver or gold, that you were rescued from the
futile way of life which you learned from your fathers,
but it was by the precious blood of Christ, as of a lamb
without blemish and without spot. It was before the
creation of the world that he was predestined to his work;
it is at the end of the ages that he has appeared, for the
sake of you who through him believe in God, who raised
him from the dead and gave him glory, so that your faith
and hope might be in God. Now that you have purified
your souls by obedience to the truth – a purification that
must issue in a brotherly love that is sincere – love each
other heartily and steadfastly, for you have been reborn,
not of mortal but of immortal seed, through the living
and abiding word of God, for 'All flesh is grass, and its
beauty is like the flower of the field. The grass withers,
the flower fades; but the word of our God will stand
forever.' And that is the word, the good news of which
was brought to you.

THERE are three great lines of approach in this passage, and
we look at them one by one.

1. JESUS CHRIST REDEEMER AND LORD

It has great things to say about Jesus Christ as Redeemer and
Lord.

(1) Jesus Christ is the liberator, through whom men and
women are delivered from the bondage of sin and death; he is
the lamb without blemish and without spot (verse 19). When
Peter spoke like that about Jesus, his mind was going back to
two Old Testament pictures – to Isaiah 53, with its picture of

the Suffering Servant, through whose suffering the people were saved and healed, and above all to the picture of the Passover lamb (Exodus 12:5). On the memorable night when they left the slavery of Egypt, the children of Israel were told to take a lamb and kill it and mark their doorposts with its blood; and, when the angel of death went through the land slaying the first-born sons of the Egyptians, he passed over every house marked in that way. In that picture of the Passover lamb, there are the twin thoughts of freedom from slavery and deliverance from death. No matter how we interpret it, it cost the life and death of Jesus Christ to free us from our bondage to sin and to death.

(2) Jesus Christ is the eternal purpose of God. It was before the creation of the world that he was predestined for the work which was given to him to do (verse 20). Here is a great thought. Sometimes we tend to think of God as first Creator and then Redeemer, as having created the world and then, when things went wrong, finding a way to rescue it through Jesus Christ. But here we have the vision of a God who was Redeemer *before* he was Creator. His redeeming purpose was not an emergency measure to which he was compelled when things went wrong. It goes back before creation.

(3) Peter has a connection of thought which is universal in the New Testament. Jesus Christ is not only the lamb who was slain; he is the resurrected and triumphant one to whom God gave glory. The New Testament thinkers seldom separate the cross and the resurrection; they seldom think of the *sacrifice* of Christ without thinking of his *triumph*. The Methodist, Edward Rogers, in *That they might have Life*, tells us that on one occasion he went carefully through the whole story of the passion and the resurrection in order to find a way to represent it dramatically, and goes on: 'I began to feel

that there was something subtly and tragically wrong in any emphasis on the agony of the Cross which dimmed the brightness of the Resurrection, any suggestion that it was endured pain rather than overcoming love which secured man's salvation.' He asks where the eyes of Christians turn at the beginning of Lent. What above all else do we see? 'Is it the darkness that covered the earth at noon, swirling round the pain and anguish of the Cross? Or is it the dazzling, mysterious early-morning brightness that shone from an empty tomb?' He continues: 'There are forms of most earnest and devoted evangelical preaching and theological writing which convey the impression that somehow the Crucifixion has overshadowed the Resurrection and that the whole purpose of God in Christ was completed on Calvary. The truth, which is obscured only at grave spiritual peril, is that the Crucifixion cannot be interpreted and understood save in the light of the Resurrection.'

Through his death, Jesus freed men and women from their bondage to slavery and death, but through his resurrection he gives them a life which is as glorious and indestructible as his own. Through this triumphant resurrection, we have faith and hope in God (verse 21).

In this passage, we see Jesus the great liberator at the cost of Calvary; we see Jesus the eternal redeeming purpose of God; we see Jesus the triumphant victor over death and the glorious Lord of life, the giver of life which death cannot touch and the bringer of hope which nothing can take away.

2. THE CHRISTLESS LIFE

Peter picks out three characteristics of the Christless life.

(1) It is the life of *ignorance* (verse 14). The Gentile world was always haunted by the unknowability of God; at best, people could only feel their way towards his mystery. 'It is

hard', said Plato, 'to investigate and to find the framer and the father of the universe; and, if one did find him, it would be impossible to express him in terms which all could understand.' Even for philosophers, to find God is difficult; and for the ordinary man or woman, to understand him fully is impossible. Aristotle spoke of God as the supreme cause, dreamed of by all and known by none. The ancient world did not doubt that there was a God or gods, but it believed that such gods as did exist were quite unknowable and totally uninterested in human beings and the universe. In a world without Christ, God was mystery and power but never love; there was no one to whom people could raise their hands for help or their eyes for hope.

(2) It is the life *dominated by desire* (verse 14). As we read the records of that world into which Christianity came, we cannot but be appalled at the sheer sensuality of life within it. There was desperate poverty at the lower end of the social scale, but at the top we read of fabulously expensive banquets, where peacocks' brains and nightingales' tongues were served and where the Emperor Vitellius set on the table at one banquet 2,000 fish and 7,000 birds. Chastity was forgotten. The Roman poet Martial speaks of a woman who had reached her tenth husband; Juvenal, the lawyer and satirist, speaks of a woman who had eight husbands in five years; and the biblical scholar Jerome tells us that in Rome there was one woman who was married to her twenty-third husband, she herself being his twenty-first wife. Both in Greece and in Rome, homosexual practices were common and viewed as completely natural. It was a world ruled by desire, whose aim was to find newer and wilder ways of gratifying its lusts.

(3) It was a life characterized by *futility*. Its basic trouble was that it was not going anywhere. The Roman poet Catullus writes to his Lesbia pleading for the delights of love. He pleads

with her to seize the moment with its fleeting joys. 'Suns can rise and set again; but once our brief light is dead, there is nothing left but one long night from which we never shall awake.' If people were to die like dogs, why should they not live like dogs? Life was a futile business with a few brief years in the light of the sun and then an eternal nothingness. There was nothing to live for and nothing to die for. Life is always futile when there is nothing on the other side of death.

3. THE CHRIST-FILLED LIFE

Peter finds three characteristics of the Christ-filled life, and for each he finds compelling reasons.

(1) The Christ-filled life is the life of *obedience and of holiness* (verses 14–16). To be chosen by God is to enter not only into great privilege but also into great responsibility. Peter remembers the ancient command at the very heart of all Hebrew religion. It was God's insistence to his people that they must be holy because he was holy (Leviticus 11:44, 19:2, 20:7, 20:26). The word for *holy* is *hagios*, whose root meaning is *different*. The Temple is *hagios* because it is different from other buildings; the Sabbath is *hagios* because it is different from other days; the Christian is *hagios* because he or she is different from others. Christians are God's people by God's choice. They are chosen for a task in the world and for a destiny in eternity. They are chosen to live for God in time and with him in eternity. In the world, they must obey his law and reproduce his life. There is laid on Christians the task of being different.

(2) The Christ-filled life is the life of *reverence* (verses 17–21). Reverence is the attitude of mind of those who are always aware that they are in the presence of God. In these five verses, Peter picks out three reasons for this Christian

reverence. (a) Christians are temporary dwellers in this world. Life for them is lived in the shadow of eternity; they think all the time, not only of where they are but also of where they are going. (b) They are going to God; true, they can call God Father, but that very God whom they call Father is also the one who judges everyone with strict impartiality. Christians are people for whom there is a day of reckoning. They are people with a destiny to win or to lose. Life in this world becomes of tremendous importance because it is leading to the life beyond. (c) Christians must live life in reverence because it cost so much – nothing less than the life and death of Jesus Christ. Since, then, life is of such supreme value, it cannot be wasted or thrown away. No honourable person squanders what is of infinite human worth.

(3) The Christ-filled life is the life of *mutual love*. It must be visible in a love for others which is sincere and heartfelt and steadfast. Christians are men and women who are reborn, not of mortal but of immortal seed. That may mean either of two things. It may mean that the remaking of Christians is due not to human agency but to the agency of God, another way of saying what John said when he spoke of those 'who were born, not of blood or of the will of the flesh . . . but of God' (John 1:13). More probably, it means that Christians are remade by the entry into them of the seed of the word; and the picture is that of the parable of the sower (Matthew 13:1–9). The quotation which Peter uses is from Isaiah 40:6–8, and the second interpretation fits that better. However we take it, the meaning is that Christians are remade. Because they are reborn, the life of God is in them. The great characteristic of the life of God is love, and so Christians must show that divine love for all people.

Christians are people who live the Christ-filled life, the life that is different, that never forgets the endless nature of its obligation, and is made beautiful by the love of the God who gave it birth.

WHAT TO LOSE AND WHAT TO YEARN FOR

1 Peter 2:1-3

> Strip off, therefore, all the evil of the heathen world and all deceitfulness, acts of hypocrisy and feelings of envy, and all gossiping disparagements of other people, and, like newly-born babes, yearn for the unadulterated milk of the word, so that by it you may grow up until you reach salvation. You are bound to do this if you have tasted that the Lord is kind.

CHRISTIANS cannot stay the way they are; and Peter urges his people to have done with evil things and to set their hearts on that which alone can nourish life.

There are things which must be *stripped off. Apothesthai* is the word for *stripping off* one's clothes. There are things of which Christians must divest themselves as they would strip off a soiled garment.

They must strip off *all the evil of the heathen world.* The word for *evil* is *kakia*; it is the most general word for wickedness, and includes all the wicked ways of the Christless world. The other words are illustrations and manifestations of this *kakia*; and it is to be noted that they are all faults of character which hurt the great Christian virtue of mutual love. There can be no mutual love as long as these evil things exist.

There is *deceitfulness* (*dolos*). *Dolos* is the trickery of those who are out to deceive others to achieve their own ends, the vice of people whose motives are never pure.

There is *hypocrisy* (*hupokrisis*). *Hupokritēs* (*hypocrite*) is a word with a curious history. It is the noun from the verb *hupokrinesthai*, which means *to answer*; a *hupokritēs* begins by being an *answerer*. Then, it comes to mean an *actor*, the one who takes part in the question-and-answer of the stage. Next, it comes to mean a *hypocrite*, someone who all the time is acting a part and whose real motives are concealed. Hypocrites are people whose professed allegiance to Christianity is for their own profit and prestige and not for the service and glory of Christ,

There is *envy* (*phthonos*). It may well be said that envy is the last sin to die. It reared its ugly head even in the company of the apostles. The other ten were envious of James and John, when they seemed to steal a march upon them in the matter of precedence in the coming kingdom (Mark 10:41). Even at the Last Supper, the disciples were arguing about who should occupy the seats of greatest honour (Luke 22:24). As long as self remains active within someone's heart, there will be envy in that person's life. If we look at the commentaries, E. G. Selwyn calls envy 'the constant plague of all voluntary organisations, not least religious organisations'. C. E. B. Cranfield says that 'we do not have to be engaged in what is called "church work" very long to discover what a perennial source of trouble envy is'.

There is *gossiping disparagement* (*katalalia*). *Katalalia* is a word with a definite flavour. It means *evil-speaking*; it is almost always the fruit of envy in the heart; and it usually takes place when its victim is not there to offer a defence. Few things are so attractive as hearing or repeating spicy gossip. Disparaging gossip is something which everyone admits to be wrong and which at the same time almost everyone enjoys; and yet there is nothing more likely to produce heartbreak and nothing is so destructive of mutual love and Christian unity.

These, then, are the things which those who are reborn must strip off – for, if they continue to allow them to have a grip upon their lives, the unity of the church community will inevitably be injured.

THAT ON WHICH TO SET THE HEART

1 Peter 2:1–3 (contd)

BUT there is something on which Christians must set their hearts. They must yearn for *the unadulterated milk of the word*. This is a phrase about whose meaning there is some difficulty. The difficulty is with the word *logikos*, which with the Authorized Version we have translated as *of the word*. The Revised Version translates it as *spiritual*, and in the margin gives the alternative translation *reasonable*. James Moffatt has *spiritual*, as has the Revised Standard Version.

Logikos is the adjective from the noun *logos*, and the difficulty is that it has three perfectly possible translations.

(1) *Logos* is the great Stoic word for the reason which guides the universe; *logikos* is a favourite Stoic word which describes what has to do with this divine reason which is the governor of all things. If this is what lies behind the word, clearly *spiritual* is the meaning.

(2) *Logos* is the normal Greek word for *mind* or *reason*; therefore, *logikos* often means *reasonable* or *intelligent*. It is in that way that the Authorized Version translates it in Romans 12:1, where it speaks of our *reasonable* service.

(3) *Logos* is the Greek for *word*, and *logikos* means *belonging to the word*. This is the sense in which the Authorized Version takes it, and we think it is correct. Peter has just been talking about the word of God which abides forever (1 Peter 1:23–5). It is the word of God which is in his

mind; and we think that what he means here is that Christians must desire with their whole heart the nourishment which comes from the word of God, for by that nourishment they can grow until they reach salvation itself. In face of all the evil of the Gentile world, Christians must strengthen their souls with the pure food of the word of God.

This food of the word is *unadulterated* (*adolos*). That is to say, there is not the slightest element of anything evil in it. *Adolos* is used in a technical sense to describe corn that is entirely free from chaff or dust or useless or harmful matter. In all human wisdom, there is some element of what is either useless or harmful; the word of God alone is altogether good.

Christians are to yearn for this milk of the word; *yearn* is *epipothein*, which is a strong word. It is the word which is used for the deer longing for the flowing streams (Psalm 42:1), and for the psalmist *longing* for the salvation of the Lord (Psalm 119:174). For sincere Christians, to study God's word is not a labour but a delight, for they know that there the heart will find the nourishment for which it longs.

The metaphor of Christians as babies and the word of God as the milk with which they are nourished is common in the New Testament. Paul thinks of himself as the nurse who cares for the infant Christians of Thessalonica (1 Thessalonians 2:7). He thinks of himself as feeding the Corinthians with milk, for they are not yet at the stage of meat (1 Corinthians 3:2); and the writer of the Letter to the Hebrews blames his people for being still at the stage of milk when they should have gone on to maturity (Hebrews 5:12, 6:2). To symbolize the rebirth of baptism in the early Church, the newly baptized Christians were clothed in white robes, and sometimes they were fed with milk as if they were little children. It is this nourishment with the milk of the word which makes Christians grow up and grow on until they reach salvation.

Peter finishes this introduction with an allusion to Psalm 34:8. 'You are bound to do this', he writes, 'if you have tasted the kindness of God.' Here is something of the greatest significance. The fact that God is gracious is not an excuse for us to do as we like, depending on him to overlook it; it lays on us an obligation to work towards deserving his graciousness and love. The kindness of God is not an excuse for laziness in the Christian life; it is the greatest of all incentives to effort.

THE NATURE AND FUNCTION OF THE CHURCH

1 Peter 2:4–10

> Come to him, the living stone, rejected by men but chosen and precious with God, and be yourselves, like living stones, built into a spiritual house until you become a holy priesthood to offer spiritual sacrifices, which are well-pleasing to God through Jesus Christ; for there is a passage in Scripture which says: 'Behold, I place in Zion a stone, chosen, a cornerstone, precious, and he who believes in him shall not be put to shame.' So, then, there is preciousness in that stone to you who believe; but, to those who disbelieve, the stone which the builders rejected has become the headstone of the corner, and a stone over which they will stumble, and a rock over which they will trip. They stumble because they disobey the word – a fate for which they were appointed. But you are a chosen race, a royal priesthood, a people dedicated to God, a nation for him specially to possess that you might tell forth the excellencies of him who called you out of darkness into his glorious light, you, who were once not a people and are now the people of the Lord, you who were once without mercy and have now found mercy.

PETER sets before us the nature and the function of the Church. There is so much in the passage that we divide it into four sections.

1. THE STONE WHICH THE BUILDERS REJECTED

Much is made of the idea of the *stone*. Three Old Testament passages are used symbolically; let us look at them one by one.

(1) The beginning of the whole matter goes back to the words of Jesus himself. One of the most illuminating parables he ever told was the parable of the wicked tenants. In it, he told how the wicked tenants killed servant after servant and in the end even murdered the son. He was showing how the nation of Israel had again and again refused to listen to the prophets and had persecuted them, and how this refusal was to reach its climax with his own death. But beyond the death he saw the triumph, and he told of that triumph in words taken from the Psalms: 'The stone that the builders rejected has become the cornerstone; this was the Lord's doing, and it is amazing in our eyes' (Matthew 21:42; Mark 12:10; Luke 20:17).

That is a quotation from Psalm 118:22. In the original, it is a reference to the nation of Israel. The Old Testament scholar, A. F. Kirkpatrick, writes of it: 'Israel is "the head cornerstone". The powers of the world flung it aside as useless, but God destined it for the most honourable and important place in the building of his kingdom in the world. The words express Israel's consciousness of its mission and destiny in the purpose of God.' Jesus took these words and applied them to himself. It looked as if he had been utterly rejected, but in the purpose of God he was the cornerstone of the structure of the kingdom, honoured above all.

(2) In the Old Testament, there are other references to this symbolic stone, and the early Christian writers used them for

their purposes. The first is in Isaiah 28:16: 'Therefore thus says the Lord God. See, I am laying in Zion a foundation stone, a tested stone, a precious cornerstone, a sure foundation: "One who trusts will not panic."' Again the reference is to Israel. The sure and precious stone is God's unfailing relationship to his people, a relationship which was to culminate in the coming of the Messiah. Once again, the early Christian writers took this passage and applied it to Jesus Christ as the precious and immovable foundation stone of God.

(3) The second of these other passages is also from Isaiah: 'But the Lord of hosts, him you shall regard as holy; let him be your fear, and let him be your dread. He will become a sanctuary, a stone one strikes against; for both houses of Israel he will become a rock one stumbles over – a trap and a snare for the inhabitants of Jerusalem' (Isaiah 8:13–14). Its meaning is that God is offering his lordship to the people of Israel, that to those who accept him he will become a sanctuary and a salvation, but to those who reject him he will become a terror and a destruction. Again the early Christian writers took this passage and applied it to Jesus. To those who accept him, Jesus is Saviour and Friend; to those who reject him, he is judgment and condemnation.

(4) For the understanding of this passage, we have to include a New Testament reference alongside these Old Testament ones. It is hardly possible that Peter could speak of Jesus as the cornerstone and of Christians as being built into a spiritual house, united in him, without thinking of Jesus' own words to himself. When he made his great confession of faith at Caesarea Philippi, Jesus said to him: 'You are Peter, and on this rock I will build my church' (Matthew 16:18). It is on the faith of the loyal believer that the Church is built.

These are the origins of the pictures in this passage.

2. THE NATURE OF THE CHURCH

From this passage, we learn three things about the very nature of the Church.

(1) Christians are likened to living stones and the Church to a living house into which they are built (verse 5). Clearly, that means that *Christianity is community*; individual Christians find their true place only when they are built into that structure. 'Solitary religion' is ruled out as an impossibility. The biblical scholar C. E. B. Cranfield writes: 'The free-lance Christian, who would be a Christian but is too superior to belong to the visible Church upon earth in one of its forms, is simply a contradiction in terms.'

There is a famous story from Sparta. A Spartan king boasted to a visiting monarch about the walls of Sparta. The visiting monarch looked around and could see no walls. He said to the Spartan king: 'Where are these walls about which you boast so much?' His host pointed at his bodyguard of magnificent troops. 'These', he said, 'are the walls of Sparta, every man a brick.'

The point is clear. As long as a brick lies by itself, it is useless; it becomes of use only when it is incorporated into a building. So it is with individual Christians. To achieve their destiny, they must not remain alone but must be built into the fabric of the Church.

Suppose that in time of war someone says: 'I want to serve my country and to defend it from its enemies.' If that person tries to carry out that resolution alone, nothing can be accomplished. An individual can be effective in that purpose only by standing shoulder to shoulder with others of like mind. It is so with the Church. Individualistic Christianity is an absurdity; Christianity is community within the fellowship of the Church.

(2) Christians are a holy priesthood (verse 5). There are two great characteristics of the priest.

(a) The priest is the person who has access to God and whose task it is to bring others to him. In the ancient world, this access to God was the privilege of the professional priests, and in particular of the high priest, who alone could enter into the Holy of Holies. Through Jesus Christ, the new and living way, access to God becomes the privilege of all Christians. Further, the Latin word for priest is *pontifex*, which means *bridge-builder*; the priest is someone who builds a bridge for others to come to God; and Christians have the duty and the privilege of bringing others to that Saviour whom they themselves have found and love.

(b) The priest is the person who brings an offering to God. Christians must also constantly bring their offerings to God. Under the old religious system, the offerings brought were animal sacrifices; but the sacrifices of Christians are *spiritual* sacrifices. Christians make their *work* an offering to God. Everything is done for God; and so even the most insignificant or menial task shines with glory. Christians make their *worship* an offering to God; and so the worship of God's house becomes not a burden but a joy. Christians make *themselves* an offering to God. 'Present your bodies', said Paul, 'as a living sacrifice . . . to God' (Romans 12:1). What God desires most of all is the love of our hearts and the service of our lives. That is the perfect sacrifice which every Christian must make.

(3) The function of the Church is *to tell forth the excellencies* of God. That is to say, it is to witness to others concerning the mighty acts of God. By their very lives, even more than by their words, Christians are to be witnesses of what God in Christ has done for them.

3. THE GLORY OF THE CHURCH

In verse 9, we read of the things to which Christians are witnesses.

(1) God has called Christians out of darkness into his glorious light. *Christians are called out of darkness into light.* When we come to know Jesus Christ, we come to know *God*. We no longer need to guess and to feel our way. 'Whoever has seen me', said Jesus, 'has seen the Father' (John 14:9). In Jesus is the light of the knowledge of God. When we come to know Jesus, we come to know *goodness*. In Christ, we have a standard by which all actions and motives may be tested. When we come to know Jesus Christ, we come to know the *way*. Life is no longer a trackless road without a star to guide. In Christ, the way becomes clear. When we come to know Jesus Christ, we come to know *power*. It would be little use to know God without the power to serve him. It would be little use to know goodness and yet be helpless to attain it. It would be little use to see the right way and be quite unable to take it. In Jesus Christ, there is both the vision *and* the power.

(2) God has made those who were not a people into the people of God. Here, Peter is quoting from Hosea 1:6, 1:9–10, 2:1, 2:23). This means that *Christians are called out of insignificance into significance*. It continually happens in this world that greatness lies not in the self but in what an individual has been given to do. The greatness for Christians lies in the fact that God has chosen them to be his people and to do his work in the world. Christians can never be ordinary, for they are people of God.

(3) *Christians are called out of no mercy into mercy.* The characteristic of non-Christian religion is the fear of God. Christians have discovered the love of God and know that

they need no longer fear him, because all is well with their souls.

4. THE FUNCTION OF THE CHURCH

In verse 9, Peter uses a whole series of phrases which are a summary of the functions of the Church. He calls Christians 'a chosen race, a royal priesthood, a people dedicated to God, a nation for him specially to possess'. Peter is steeped in the Old Testament, and these phrases are all great descriptions of the people of Israel.

They come from two main sources. In Isaiah 43:21, Isaiah hears God say: 'The people whom I formed for myself.' But even more in Exodus 19:5–6 the voice of God is heard: 'Now therefore, if you will obey my voice and keep my covenant, you shall be my treasured possession out of all the peoples. Indeed, the whole earth is mine, but you shall be for me a priestly kingdom and a holy nation.' The great promises which God made to his people Israel are being fulfilled to the Church, the new Israel. Every one of these titles is full of meaning.

(1) Christians are *a chosen people*. Here, we are back to the covenant idea. Exodus 19:5–6 is from the passage which describes how God entered into his covenant with Israel. In the covenant, he offered a special relationship with himself to Israel, but it depended on the people of Israel accepting the conditions of the covenant and keeping the law. That relationship would hold only 'if you will obey my voice and keep my covenant' (Exodus 19:5).

From this, we learn that Christians are chosen for three things. (a) They are chosen for *privilege*. In Jesus Christ, a new and intimate fellowship with God is offered to them. God has become their friend, and they have become God's friends. (b) They are chosen for *obedience*. Privilege brings with it responsibility. Christians are chosen in order that they may become the obedient children of God. They are chosen not to do as they like but to do as God likes. (c) They are chosen for *service*. Their honour is that they are the servants of God. Their privilege is that they will be used for the purposes of God. But they can be so used only when they bring to God the obedience he desires. Chosen for privilege, chosen for obedience, chosen for service – these three great facts go hand in hand.

(2) Christians are *a royal priesthood*. We have already seen that this means that all Christians have the right of access to God, and that they must offer their work, their worship and themselves to God.

(3) Christians are what the Revised Standard Version calls *a holy nation*. We have already seen that the basic meaning of *hagios* (holy) is *different*. Christians have been chosen in order that they may be different from other people. That difference lies in the fact that they are dedicated to God's will and to God's service. Other people may follow the standards of the world, but for Christians the only standards are God's. People need not even start on the Christian way unless they realize that it will compel them to be different from others.

(4) Christians are *a people for God specially to possess*. It frequently happens that the value of a thing lies in the fact that someone has possessed it. A very ordinary thing acquires a new value if it has been possessed by some famous person. In any museum, we find quite ordinary things – clothes, a walking-stick, a pen, books, pieces of furniture – which are of value only because they were once possessed by some great person. It is the same with Christians. Christians may be very ordinary people, but they acquire a new value because they belong to God.

REASONS FOR RIGHT LIVING

1 Peter 2:11–12

> Beloved, I urge you, as strangers and sojourners, to
> abstain from the fleshly desires which carry on their
> campaign against the soul. Make your conduct among
> the Gentiles fine, so that in every matter in which they
> slander you as evildoers, they may see from your fine
> deeds what you are really like and glorify God on the
> day when he will visit the earth.

THE basic commandment in this passage is that Christians
should *abstain from fleshly desires*. It is of the greatest
importance that we should see what Peter means by this.
The phrases *sins of the flesh* and *fleshly desires* have acquired
a much narrower meaning in modern usage. For us, they
usually mean sexual sin; but in the New Testament sins
of the flesh are understood in a much wider sense than
that. Paul's list of the sins of the flesh in Galatians 5:19–21
includes 'fornication, impurity, licentiousness, idolatry,
sorcery, enmities, strife, jealousy, anger, quarrels, dissensions,
envy, drunkenness, carousing, and things like these'. There
are far more than *bodily* sins here.

In the New Testament, *flesh* stands for far more than our
physical nature. It stands for *human nature apart from God*;
it means unredeemed human nature; it means life lived without
the standards, the help, the grace and the influence of Christ.
Fleshly desires and *sins of the flesh*, therefore, include not
only sexual sins but all that is characteristic of fallen human
nature. From these sins and desires, Christians must abstain.
As Peter sees it, there are two reasons for this abstinence.

(1) Christians must abstain from these sins because they
are strangers and pilgrims. The words are *paroikos* and
parepidēmos. They are quite common Greek words, and they

describe someone who is only temporarily resident in a place and whose home is somewhere else. They are used to describe the patriarchs in their wanderings, and especially Abraham, who went out not knowing where he was to go and whose search was for the city whose maker and builder is God (Hebrews 11:9, 11:13). They are used to describe the children of Israel when they were slaves and strangers in the land of Egypt before they entered into the promised land (Acts 7:6).

These words give us two great truths about Christians. (a) There is a real sense in which they are strangers in the world; and, because of that, they cannot accept the world's laws and ways and standards. Others may accept them; but Christians are citizens of the kingdom of God, and it is by the laws of that kingdom that they must direct their lives. They must take their full share of responsibility for living upon earth; but their citizenship is in heaven, and the laws of heaven have supreme importance for them. (b) Christians are not permanent residents upon earth; they are on the way to the country which is beyond. They must, therefore, do nothing which would keep them from reaching their ultimate goal. They must never become so entangled in the world that they cannot escape from its grip; they must never so soil themselves as to be unfit to enter the presence of the holy God to whom they are going.

THE GREATEST ANSWER AND DEFENCE

1 Peter 2:11–12 (contd)

(2) But there was for Peter another and even more practical reason why Christians had to abstain from fleshly desires. The early Church was under fire. Slanderous charges were

continually being made against them, and the only effective way to refute these charges was to live lives so lovely that the charges would be seen to be obviously untrue.

To modern ears, the Authorized Version can be a little misleading. It speaks about 'having your conversation honest among the Gentiles'. That sounds to us as if it meant that Christians must always speak the truth; but the word translated as *conversation* is *anastrophē*, which means a person's *whole conduct*, not simply talk. That is, in fact, what *conversation* did mean in the seventeenth century. The word translated as *honest* is *kalos*. In Greek, there are two words for *good*. There is *agathos*, which simply means good in quality, and there is *kalos*, which means not only *good* but also *lovely* – fine, attractive, pleasing. That is what *honestus* means in Latin. So, what Peter is saying is that Christians must make their whole way of life so lovely and so good to look upon that the slanders of their non-Christian enemies may be demonstrated to be false.

Here is timeless truth. Whether we like it or not, all Christians are an advertisement for Christianity; by their lives, they either commend it to others or make them think less of it. The strongest missionary force in the world is the Christian life.

In the early Church, this demonstration of the loveliness of the Christian life was necessary above all because of the slanders that were deliberately circulated about the Christian Church. Let us see what some of these slanders were.

(1) In the beginning, Christianity was closely connected with the Jews. By race, Jesus was a Jew; Paul was a Jew; Christianity was born and nurtured within Judaism; and inevitably many of its early converts were Jews. For a time, Christianity was regarded merely as a sect of Judaism. Anti-semitism is not new. Ludwig Friedländer gives a selection of

the slanders which were repeated against the Jews in his *Roman Life and Manners under the Early Empire*. 'According to Tacitus they [the Jews] taught their proselytes above all to despise the gods, to renounce their fatherland, to disregard parents, children, brothers and sisters. According to Juvenal, Moses taught the Jews not to show anyone the way, nor to guide thirsty travellers to the spring, except if they were also Jews. Apion declares that, in the reign of Antiochus Epiphanes, the Jews every year fattened a Greek, and having solemnly offered him up as a sacrifice on a fixed day in a certain forest, ate his entrails and swore eternal hostility to the Greeks.' These were the things which Roman society had persuaded itself were true about the Jews, and inevitably the Christians were included in that view and shared in the widespread dislike suffered by Jews.

(2) Apart from these slanders attached to the Jews, there were slanders directed particularly against the Christians themselves. They were accused of cannibalism. This accusation arose out of a distortion of the words of the Last Supper, 'This is my body.' 'This cup is the new covenant in my blood.' The Christians were accused of killing and eating a child at their feasts.

They were also accused of immorality and even of incest. This accusation arose from the fact that they called their meeting the *Agape*, the Love Feast. That name was distorted to mean that the Christian feasts were sensual orgies at which shameless deeds were done.

The Christians were accused of damaging trade. That was the charge of the silversmiths of Ephesus (Acts 19:21–41).

They were accused of 'tampering with family relationships' because often homes were, in fact, broken up when some members of the family became Christians and others did not.

They were accused of turning slaves against their masters, and indeed Christianity did give to everyone a new sense of worth and dignity.

They were accused of 'hatred for the world', and indeed Christians did speak as if the world and the Church were entirely opposed to each other.

Above all, they were accused of disloyalty to Caesar, for no Christian would worship the emperor's godhead and burn a pinch of incense and declare that Caesar was Lord. For Christians, Jesus Christ and no other was Lord.

Such were the charges which were directed against Christians. To Peter, there was only one way to refute them, and that was to live in such a way that their Christian life demonstrated that the charges were unfounded. When Plato was told that a certain man had been making slanderous charges against him, his answer was: 'I will live in such a way that no one will believe what he says.' That was Peter's solution.

Jesus himself had said – and doubtless the saying was in Peter's mind: 'Let your light shine before others, so that they may see your good works and give glory to your Father in heaven' (Matthew 5:16). This was a line of thought which the Jews knew well. In one of the books written between the Old and the New Testaments, it says: 'If you work that which is good, my children, both men and angels shall bless you; and God shall be glorified among the Gentiles through you, and the devil shall flee from you' (The Testament of Naphtali 8:4).

The striking fact of history is that by their lives the Christians actually did defeat the slanders of the Gentile world. In the early part of the third century, Celsus made the most famous and the most systematic attack of all upon the Christians, in which he accused them of ignorance and foolishness and superstition and all kinds of things – *but never of immorality*. In the first half of the fourth century, Eusebius, the great church historian, could write: 'But the splendour of the catholic and only true Church, which is always the same, grew in magnitude and power, and reflected its piety and simplicity and freedom, and the modesty and purity of its inspired life and philosophy to every nation both of Greeks and barbarians. At the same time the slanderous accusations which had been brought against the whole Church also vanished, and there remained our teaching alone, which has prevailed over all, and which is acknowledged to be superior to all in dignity and temperance, and in divine and philosophical doctrines. So that none of them now ventures to affix a base calumny upon our faith, or any such slander as our ancient enemies formerly delighted to utter' (*The Ecclesiastical History*, 4:7:15). It is true that the terrors of persecution were not even then ended, for the Christians would never admit that Caesar was Lord; but the excellence of their lives had silenced the malicious accusations against the Church.

Here is our challenge and our inspiration. It is by the loveliness of our daily life and conduct that we must commend Christianity to those who do not believe.

THE DUTY OF CHRISTIANS

1 Peter 2:13–15

> Submit to every human institution for the Lord's sake, whether it be to the king, who has the first place, or to governors as sent by him for the punishment of those whose deeds are evil and the praise of those whose deeds are good, for it is the will of God that by so doing you should muzzle the ignorance of foolish men.

1. As Citizens

PETER looks at the duty of Christians within the different spheres of life; and he begins with their duty as citizens of the country in which they happen to live.

Nothing is further from the thought of the New Testament than any kind of anarchy. Jesus had said: 'Give therefore to the emperor the things that are the emperor's, and to God the things that are God's' (Matthew 22:21). Paul was certain that those who governed the nation were sent by God and held their responsibility from him, and were therefore no terror to anyone who lived an honourable life (Romans 13:1–7). In the Pastoral Epistles, Christians are instructed to pray for kings and all in authority (1 Timothy 2:2). The instruction of the New Testament is that Christians must be good and useful citizens of the country in which their lives are set.

It has been said that fear built the cities and that people huddled behind a wall in order to be safe. People join themselves together and agree to live under certain laws, so that the good may have peace to do their work and go about their business, and the evil people may be restrained and kept from their evildoing. According to the New Testament, life is meant by God to be an ordered business, and the state is divinely appointed to provide and to maintain that order.

The New Testament view is perfectly logical and just. It holds that no one can accept the privileges which the state provides without also accepting the responsibilities and the duties which it demands. No one can in honour and decency take everything and give nothing.

How are we to translate this into modern terms? C. E. B. Cranfield has pointed out that there is a fundamental difference between the state in New Testament times and the state as we know it today. In New Testament times, the state was *authoritarian*. The ruler was an absolute ruler; and the sole duty of the citizen was to render absolute obedience and to pay taxes (Romans 13:6–7). Under these conditions, the keynote was bound to be *subjection to the state*. But we live in a *democracy*, and in a democracy something far more than unquestioning subjection becomes necessary. Government is not only government *of* the people; it is also *for* the people and *by* the people. The demand of the New Testament is that Christians should fulfil their responsibilities to the state. In the authoritarian state, that consisted solely in submission. But what is that obligation in the very different circumstances of a democracy?

In any state, there must be a certain subjection. As Cranfield puts it, there must be 'a voluntary subordination of oneself to others, putting the interest and welfare of others above one's own, preferring to give rather than to get, to serve rather than to be served'. But, in a democratic state, the keynote must be not *subjection* but *co-operation*, for the duty of all citizens is not only to submit to be ruled but to take a necessary share in ruling. Hence, if Christians are to fulfil their duty to the state, they must take their part in its government. They must also take their part in local government and in the life of the trade union or association connected with their trade, craft or profession. It is tragic that so few Christians really fulfil their obligation to the state and the society in which they live.

It remains to say that Christians have a higher obligation than even their obligation to the state. While, as the Revised Standard Version puts it, they must render to Caesar the things which are Caesar's, they must also render to God the things which are God's. They must on occasion make it quite clear that they have to listen to God rather than to any secular authority (Acts 4:19, 5:29). There may be times, therefore, when Christians will fulfil their highest duty to the state by refusing to obey it and by insisting on obeying God. By so doing, at least they will witness to the truth, and at best they may lead the state to take the Christian way.

1 Peter 2:16

> You must live as free men, yet not using your freedom as a cloak for evil, but as the slaves of God.

2. IN SOCIETY

ANY great Christian doctrine can be distorted into an excuse for evil. The doctrine of grace can be distorted into an excuse for sinning to one's heart's content. The doctrine of the love of God can be sentimentalized into an excuse for breaking God's law. The doctrine of the life to come can be distorted into an excuse for neglecting life in this world. And there is no doctrine so easy to distort as that of Christian freedom.

There are hints in the New Testament that it was indeed frequently distorted. Paul tells the Galatians that they have been called to liberty but they must not use that liberty as an occasion for self-indulgence (Galatians 5:13). In 2 Peter, we read of those who promise others liberty and are themselves the slaves of corruption (2 Peter 2:19). Even the great Greek and Roman thinkers saw quite clearly that perfect freedom is, in fact, the product of perfect obedience. Seneca said: 'No one is free who is the slave of his body', and 'Liberty consists in obeying God.' Cicero said: 'We are the servants of the laws that we may be able to be free.' Plutarch insisted that every bad man is a slave; and Epictetus declared that no bad man can ever be free.

We may put it this way. Christian freedom is always conditioned by Christian responsibility. Christian responsibility is always conditioned by Christian love. Christian love is the reflection of God's love. And, therefore, Christian liberty can rightly be summed up in St Augustine's memorable phrase: 'Love God, and do what you like.'

Christians are free because they are the slaves of God. Christian freedom does not mean being free to do as we like; it means being free to do as we ought.

In this matter, we have to return to the great central truth which we have already seen. *Christianity is community*. The Christian is not an isolated unit; a Christian is a member of a community, and within that community individual freedom operates. Christian freedom, therefore, is the freedom to serve. Only in Christ are individuals so freed from self and sin that they can become as good as they ought to be. Freedom comes when people receive Christ as king of their hearts and Lord of their lives.

A SUMMARY OF CHRISTIAN DUTY

1 Peter 2:17

> Honour all men; love the brotherhood; fear God; honour
> the king.

HERE is what we might call a four-point summary of Christian duty.

(1) *Honour all men*. To us, this may seem hardly needing to be said, but when Peter wrote this letter it was something quite new. There were 60,000,000 slaves in the Roman Empire, every one of whom was considered in law to be not a person but a thing, with no rights whatever. In effect, Peter is saying: 'Remember the rights of human personality and the dignity of every individual.' It is still possible to treat people as things. An employer may treat employees as so many human machines for producing so much work. Even in a

welfare state, where the aim is to do so much for their physical welfare, there is a very real danger that people may be regarded as numbers on a form or as cards in a filing system.

John Lawrence, in his book *Hard Facts: A Christian Looks at the World*, says that one of the greatest needs in the welfare state is 'to see through the files and forms in triplicate to God's creatures who are at the other end of the chain of organization'. The danger is that we fail to see men and women as persons. This matter comes nearer home. When we regard people as existing solely to minister to our comfort or to further our plans, we are in effect regarding them not as persons but as things. The most tragic danger of all is that we may come to regard those who are nearest and dearest to us as existing for our convenience – and that is to treat them as things.

(2) *Love the brotherhood.* Within the Christian community, this respect for every individual turns to something warmer and closer; it turns to love. The dominant atmosphere of the Church must always be love. One of the truest definitions of the Church is that it is 'the extension of the family'. The Church is the larger family of God, and its bond must be love. As the psalmist had it (Psalm 133:1 from the *Metrical Psalter*):

> Behold, how good a thing it is,
> And how becoming well,
> Together such as brethren are
> In unity to dwell!

(3) *Fear God.* The writer of the proverbs has it: 'The fear of the Lord is the beginning of knowledge' (Proverbs 1:7). It may well be that the translation should not be that the fear of the Lord is the *beginning* of knowledge but that the fear of the Lord is *the principal part*, the very *foundation* of knowledge. *Fear* here does not mean terror; it means awe

and reverence. It is the simple fact of life that we will never honour one another until we honour God. It is only when God is given his proper place in the centre that all other things take their proper place.

(4) *Honour the king.* Of the four instructions of this verse, this is the most amazing – for, if it was really Peter who wrote this letter, the king in question is none other than Nero. It is the teaching of the New Testament that the ruler is sent by God to preserve order in society and must be respected, even when that ruler is a Nero.

THE DUTY OF CHRISTIANS AS SERVANTS

Peter 2:18–25

> Servants, be subject to your masters with all respect, not only to those who are good and equitable, but also to those who are perverse, for it is a real sign of grace when a man bears pains in unjust suffering because of his consciousness of God. It is to live like this that you were called, because Christ too suffered for us, leaving behind him an example that we should follow in his steps. He did no sin, nor was any guile found in his mouth. When he was insulted, he did not return insult for insult. When he suffered, he uttered no threats, but he committed himself to him who judges justly. He himself bore our sins in his body on the tree, that we might depart from sins and live to righteousness. With his stripes you have been healed, for you were straying away like sheep but now you have turned to the Shepherd and Watchman of your souls.

HERE is the passage which would be relevant to by far the greatest number of the readers of this letter, for Peter writes to servants and slaves, and they formed by far the greatest part of the early Church. The word Peter uses for *servants* is not *douloi*, which is the most common word for *slaves*, but *oiketai*, the word for the household and domestic slaves.

To understand the real meaning of what Peter is saying, we must understand something of the nature of slavery in the time of the early Church. In the Roman Empire, there were as many as 60,000,000 slaves. Slavery began with Roman conquests, slaves being originally mainly prisoners taken in war; and in very early times Rome had few slaves, but by New Testament times slaves were counted by the million.

It was by no means only menial tasks which were performed by slaves. Doctors, teachers, musicians, actors, secretaries and stewards were slaves. In fact, all the work of Rome was done by slaves. The Roman attitude was that there was no point in being rulers of the world and doing one's own work. Let the slaves do that, and let the citizens live in pampered idleness. The supply of slaves would never run out.

Slaves were not allowed to marry; but they cohabited, and the children born of such a partnership were the property of the master, not of the parents, just as the lambs born to the sheep belonged to the owner of the flock, and not to the sheep.

It would be wrong to think that the situation of slaves was always wretched and unhappy, and that they were always treated with cruelty. Many slaves were loved and trusted members of the family; but one great inescapable fact dominated the whole situation. In Roman law, a slave was not a person but a thing and had absolutely no legal rights whatsoever. For that reason, there could be no such thing as justice where a slave was concerned. Aristotle writes: ' There can be no friendship nor justice towards inanimate things; indeed, not even towards a horse or an ox, nor yet towards a slave as a slave. For master and slave have nothing in common; a slave is a living tool, just as a tool is an inanimate slave.'

Varro, the Roman writer on agriculture, divides the instruments of agriculture into three classes – the articulate, the inarticulate and the mute, 'the articulate comprising the slaves, the inarticulate comprising the cattle, and the mute comprising the vehicles'. The only difference between a slave and an animal or a farmyard cart was that a slave happened to be able to speak. The fifth-century Archbishop of Ravenna, Peter Chrysologus, sums the matter up: 'Whatever a master does to a slave, undeservedly, in anger, willingly, unwillingly, in forgetfulness, after careful thought, knowingly, unknowingly, is judgment, justice and law.' In regard to a slave, the master's will, and even the master's whim, was the only law.

The dominant fact in the lives of slaves was that, even if they were well treated, they were still only things. They did not possess even the elementary rights of a person, and for them justice did not even exist.

THE PERIL OF THE NEW SITUATION

1 Peter 2:18–25 (*contd*)

INTO this situation came Christianity with its message that everyone was precious in the sight of God. The result was that, within the Church, the social barriers were broken down. Callistus, one of the earliest bishops of Rome, was a slave; and Perpetua, the aristocrat, and Felicitas, the slave girl, met martyrdom hand in hand. The great majority of the early Christians were humble men and women, and many of them were slaves. It was quite possible in the early days that the slave might be the president of the congregation and the master a member of it. This was a new and revolutionary situation. It had its glory and it had its dangers. In this passage, Peter is urging the slave to be a good slave and a faithful worker, for he sees two dangers.

(1) Suppose both master and servant became Christians; there arose the danger that the slave might presume upon the new relationship and make an excuse for shirking his work, assuming that since he and his master were both Christians, he could get away with anything. That situation is by no means at an end. There are still people who trade on the goodwill of a Christian employer and think that the fact that both they and their employers are Christians gives them a right to do away with discipline and punishment. But Peter is quite clear. The relationship between Christians does not abolish the relationship between people as individuals. Christians must, indeed, be better workers than anyone else. Their Christianity is not a reason for claiming exemption from discipline; it should bring them under self-discipline and make them more conscientious than anyone else.

(2) There was the danger that the new dignity which Christianity brought them would make slaves rebel and seek to abolish slavery altogether. Some students are puzzled that no New Testament writer ever pleads for the abolition of slavery or even says in so many words that it is wrong. The reason was simple. To have encouraged the slaves to rise against their masters would have been the way to speedy disaster. There had been such revolts before, and they had always been quickly and savagely crushed. In any event, such teaching would merely have gained for Christianity the reputation of being a subversive religion. There are some things which cannot happen quickly; there are some situations in which the leaven has to work and in which haste is the surest way to delay the desired end. The leaven of Christianity had to work in the world for many generations before the abolition of slavery became a practical possibility. Peter was concerned

that Christian slaves should demonstrate to the world that their Christianity did not make them disgruntled rebels but rather workers who had found a new inspiration to do an honest day's work. It will still often happen that, when some situation cannot at the time be changed, the Christian duty is to be Christian within that situation and to accept what cannot be changed until the leaven has worked.

THE NEW ATTITUDE TO WORK

1 Peter 2:18–25 (*contd*)

BUT Christianity did not leave the matter in that merely negative form. It introduced three great new principles into an individual's attitude as a servant and as a worker.

(1) Christianity introduced a new relationship between master and servant. When Paul sent the runaway slave Onesimus back to Philemon, he did not for a moment suggest that Philemon should set Onesimus free. He did not suggest that Philemon should cease to be the master and that Onesimus should cease to be the slave. What he did say was that Philemon must receive Onesimus not now as a servant, but as a beloved brother (Philemon 16). Christianity did not abolish social differences, but it introduced a new relationship in which these other differences were left behind and transformed. Where there is real community, it does not matter if some are in positions of authority and others offer service. There is between them a bond which transforms the necessary differences which the circumstances of life make necessary. The solution of the world's problems lies in the new relationship between individuals.

(2) Christianity introduced a new attitude to work. It is the conviction of the New Testament that all work must be

done for Jesus Christ. Paul writes: 'And whatever you do, in word or deed, do everything in the name of the Lord Jesus' (Colossians 3:17). 'So, whether you eat or drink, or whatever you do, do everything for the glory of God' (1 Corinthians 10:31). In the Christian ideal, work is not done for personal prestige or to make so much money; it is done for God. It is, of course, true that people must work in order to earn a living, and often they must work to satisfy an employer; but beyond that there is for Christians the conviction that their work must be done well enough to be able to show it to God without shame.

(3) But when these great ideals were set against the situation in the early Church – and the situation does not entirely change – one great question arose. Suppose someone has the Christian attitude to other people and to work and is treated with injustice, insult and injury – what then? Peter's answer is that this is exactly what happened to Jesus. He was none other than the *Suffering Servant*. Verses 21–5 are full of reminiscences and quotations from Isaiah 53, the supreme picture of the Suffering Servant of God, which came to life in Jesus. He was without sin, and yet he was insulted and he suffered; but he accepted the insults and the suffering with serene love and bore them for the sins of the world.

In so doing, he left us an example that we should follow in his steps (verse 21). The word Peter uses for *example* is very vivid. It is *hupogrammos*, a word which comes from the way in which children were taught to write in the ancient world. *Hupogrammos* can mean two things – an *outline sketch* which the learner had to fill in, or the *copyhead of clear and regular handwriting* in a writing-exercise book which the child had to copy out on the lines below. Jesus gave us the pattern which we have to follow. If we have to suffer insult and injustice and injury, we are only going through what he has already gone through. It may be that at the back of Peter's mind there was a glimpse of a tremendous truth. That suffering of Jesus was for the sake of human sin; he suffered in order to bring men and women back to God. And it may be that, when Christians suffer insult and injury with uncomplaining steadfastness and unfailing love, they present such a fine example of how to live that it will lead others to God.

TWO PRECIOUS NAMES FOR GOD

1. The Shepherd of our Souls

1 Peter 2:18–25 (*contd*)

In the last verse of this chapter, we come upon two of the great names for God – the Shepherd and Bishop of our souls, as the Authorized Version has it.

(1) God is *the Shepherd of our souls*. The Greek is *poimēn*, and *shepherd* is one of the oldest descriptions of God. The psalmist has it in the best-loved of all the Psalms: 'The Lord is my shepherd' (Psalm 23:1). Isaiah has it: 'He will feed his flock like a shepherd; he will gather the lambs in his arms, and carry them in his bosom, and gently lead the mother sheep' (Isaiah 40:11).

The great king whom God was going to send to Israel would be the shepherd of his people. Ezekiel hears the promise of God: 'I will set up over them one shepherd, my servant David, and he shall feed them: he shall feed them and be their shepherd' (Ezekiel 34:23, 37:24).

This was the title which Jesus took to himself when he called himself the good shepherd and when he said that the good shepherd lays down his life for the sheep (John 10:1–18). To Jesus, the men and women who did not know God

248

and who were waiting for what he could give them were like sheep without a shepherd (Mark 6:34). The great privilege given to the servant and the minister of Christ is to shepherd the flock of God (John 21:16; 1 Peter 5:2).

It may be difficult for those of us who live in an industrial civilization to grasp the greatness of this picture; but, in the middle east the picture would be very vivid, particularly in Judaea, where there was a narrow central plateau which held danger on either side. It was on this narrow tableland that the sheep grazed. Grass was sparse; there were no protecting walls; and the sheep wandered. The shepherd, therefore, had to be ceaselessly and sleeplessly on the watch in case any harm should come to his flock.

In *The Historical Geography of the Holy Land*, George Adam Smith describes the shepherd of Judaea. 'With us, sheep are often left to themselves; but I do not remember ever to have seen in the East a flock of sheep without a shepherd. In such a landscape as Judaea, where a day's pasture is thinly scattered over an unfenced tract of country, covered with delusive paths, still frequented by wild beasts, and rolling off into the desert, the man and his character are indispensable. On some high moor, across which at night the hyenas howl, when you meet him, sleepless, far-sighted, weather-beaten, armed, leaning upon his staff, and looking out over his scattered sheep, every one of them on his heart, you understand why the shepherd of Judaea sprang to the front in his people's history; why they gave his name to their king, and made him the symbol of providence; why Christ took him as the type of self-sacrifice.'

This word *shepherd* tells us most vividly of the ceaseless vigilance and the self-sacrificing love of God for us who are his flock. 'We are his people, and the sheep of his pasture' (Psalm 100:3).

2. THE GUARDIAN OF OUR SOULS

1 Peter 2:18–25 (*contd*)

(2) The Authorized Version speaks of God as the Shepherd and *Bishop* of our souls, but nowadays *Bishop* is an inadequate and misleading translation of the Greek (*episkopos*).

Episkopos is a word with a great history. In Homer's *Iliad*, Hector, the great champion of the Trojans, is called the *episkopos* who, during his lifetime, guarded the city of Troy and kept safe its noble wives and infants. *Episkopos* is used of the gods who are the guardians of the treaties which people make and of the agreements to which they come, and who are the protectors of house and home. Justice, for instance, is the *episkopos*, who sees to it that individuals shall pay the price for the wrong that they have done.

In Plato's *Laws*, the Guardians of the state are those whose duty it is to oversee the games, the feeding and the education of the children that 'they may be sound of hand and foot, and may in no wise, if possible, get their natures warped by their habits'. The people whom Plato calls market-stewards are the *episkopoi* who 'supervise personal conduct, keeping an eye on intemperate and outrageous behaviour, so as to punish him who needs punishment'.

In Athenian law and administration, the *episkopoi* were governors and administrators and inspectors sent out to subject states to see that law and order and loyalty were observed. In Rhodes, the main magistrates were five *episkopoi* who presided over the good government and the law and order of the state.

Episkopos is, therefore, a many-sided but always a noble word. It means the protector of public safety; the guardian of honour and honesty; the overseer of right education and of public morals; the administrator of public law and order.

So, to call God the *episkopos* of our souls is to call him our Guardian, our Protector, our Guide, and our Director.

God is the Shepherd and the Guardian of our souls. In his love he cares for us; in his power he protects us; and in his wisdom he guides us in the right way.

THE SILENT PREACHING OF
A LOVELY LIFE

1 Peter 3:1-2

> Likewise, you wives, be submissive to your husbands, so that, if there are any who refuse to believe the word, they may be won for Christ without a word because they have seen your pure and reverent behaviour.

PETER turns to the domestic problems which Christianity inevitably produced. It was inevitable that one marriage partner might be won for Christ while the other remained untouched by the appeal of the gospel – and such a situation inevitably had difficulties.

It may seem strange that Peter's advice to wives is six times as long as that offered to husbands. This is because the wife's position was far more difficult than that of the husband. If a husband became a Christian, he would automatically bring his wife with him into the Church and there would be no problem. But if a wife became a Christian while her husband did not, she was taking a step which was unprecedented and which produced the most acute problems.

In every sphere of ancient civilization, women had no rights at all. Under Jewish law, a woman was a thing; she was owned by her husband in exactly the same way as he owned his sheep and his goats; on no account could she leave him, although he could dismiss her at any moment. For a wife to change her religion while her husband did not was unthinkable.

In Greek civilization, the duty of the woman was 'to remain indoors and to be obedient to her husband'. It was the sign of a good woman that she must see as little, hear as little and ask as little as possible. She had no kind of independent existence and no kind of mind of her own, and her husband could divorce her almost at a whim, as long as he returned her dowry.

Under Roman law, a woman had no rights. In law, she remained forever a child. When she remained with her father she was under the *patria potestas*, the father's power, which gave the father the right even of life and death over her; and when she married, she passed equally into the power of her husband. She was entirely subject to her husband and completely at his mercy. Cato the Censor, the typical ancient Roman, wrote: 'If you were to catch your wife in an act of infidelity, you can kill her with impunity without a trial.' Roman wives were prohibited from drinking wine, and Egnatius beat his wife to death when he found her doing so. Sulpicius Gallus dismissed his wife because she had once appeared in the streets without a veil. Antistius Vetus divorced his wife because he saw her secretly speaking to a freed woman in public. Publius Sempronius Sophus divorced his wife because once she went to the public games. The whole attitude of ancient civilization was that no woman could dare take any decision for herself.

What, then, must have been the problems of the wife who became a Christian while her husband remained faithful to the ancestral gods? It is almost impossible for us to realize what life must have been like for the wife who was brave enough to become a Christian.

What, then, is Peter's advice in such a case? We must first note what he does *not* advise.

He does not advise the wife to leave her husband. In this, he takes exactly the same attitude as Paul takes (1 Corinthians 7:13–16). Both Paul and Peter are quite sure that the Christian wife must remain with the non-Christian husband as long as he does not send her away. Peter does not tell the wife to preach or to argue. He does not tell her to insist that there is no difference between slave and free, Gentile and Jew, male and female, but that all are the same in the presence of the Christ whom she has come to know (cf. Galatians 3:28).

He tells her something very simple – nothing else than to be a good wife. It is by the silent preaching of the loveliness of her life that she must break down the barriers of prejudice and hostility, and win her husband for her new Master.

She must be *submissive*. It is not a spineless submission that is meant, but rather what has been described as a 'voluntary selflessness'. It is the submission which is based on the death of pride and the desire to serve. It is the submission not of fear but of perfect love.

She must be *pure*. There must be in her life a lovely chastity and faithfulness founded on love.

She must be *reverent*. She must live in the conviction that the whole world is the Temple of God and that all life is lived in the presence of Christ.

THE TRUE ADORNMENT

1 Peter 3:3–6

> Let not your adornment be an outward thing of braided hair and ornaments of gold and wearing of robes, but let it be an adornment of the inward personality of the heart, wrought by the unfading loveliness of a gentle and quiet spirit, which is very precious in the sight of God. For it was thus in days of old the holy women,

who placed their hopes in God, adorned themselves in
submission to their husbands. It was thus that Sara
obeyed Abraham, calling him 'Lord'. And you have
become her children, if you do good, and if you do not
become a prey to fluttering fears.

JOHANNES Bengel, the eighteenth-century New Testament
scholar, speaks of 'the labour bestowed on dress which
consumes much time'. Such labour, as we find in our own
times, is not something new. We have already seen that in the
ancient world women had no part in public life whatsoever;
they had nothing to pass their time; for that reason, it was
sometimes argued that they must be allowed an interest in
dress and adornment. The Roman statesman Cato the Censor
insisted on simplicity; Lucius Valerius answered: 'Why should
men grudge women their ornaments and their dress? Women
cannot hold public offices, or priesthoods, or gain triumphs;
they have no public occupations. What, then, can they do but
devote their time to adornment and to dress?' Undue interest
in self-adornment was then, as it still is, a sign that the person
who indulged in it had nothing better with which to occupy
her mind.

The ancient moralists condemned undue luxury as much
as the Christian teachers did. Quintilian, the Roman master
of oratory, wrote: 'A tasteful and magnificent dress, as the
Greek poet tells us, lends added dignity to the wearer: but
effeminate and luxurious apparel fails to adorn the body, and
only reveals the sordidness of the mind.' Epictetus, the
philosopher, thinking of the narrow life to which women were
condemned in the ancient world, said: 'Immediately after they
are fourteen, women are called "ladies" by men. And so, when
they see that they have nothing else than to be bedfellows of
men, they begin to beautify themselves and put all their hopes
on that. It is, therefore, worthwhile for us to take pains to

make them understand that they are honoured for nothing else but only for appearing modest and self-respecting.' Epictetus and Peter agree.

There is at least one passage in the Old Testament which lists the various items of female adornment and threatens the day of judgment in which they will be destroyed. The passage is Isaiah 3:18–24. It speaks of the 'finery of the anklets, the headbands, and the crescents; the pendants, the bracelets, and the scarves; the headdresses, the armlets, the sashes, the perfume boxes, and the amulets; the signet rings and nose-rings; the festal robes, the mantles, the cloaks, and the hand-bags; the garments of gauze, the linen garments, the turbans, and the veils'.

In the world of the Greeks and the Romans, it is interesting to collect the references to personal adornments. There were as many ways of dressing the hair as there were bees in Hybla, the legendary city famed for its honey. Hair was waved and dyed, sometimes black, more often auburn. Wigs were worn, especially blonde wigs, which are found even in the Christian catacombs; and hair to manufacture them was imported from Germany, and even from as far away as India. Hairbands, pins and combs were made of ivory, and boxwood, and tortoiseshell; and sometimes of gold, studded with gems.

Purple was the favourite colour for clothes. One pound weight of the best Tyrian purple wool, strained through twice, cost 1,000 denarii – that is, more than three years' wages for a working man. A Tyrian cloak of the best purple cost more than twice that amount. In one year, huge quantities of silks, pearls, scents and jewellery were imported from India. Similar imports of luxury came from Arabia.

Diamonds, emeralds, topazes, opals and the sardonyx were favourite stones. Pearls were loved most of all. Earrings were made of pearls, and Seneca spoke of women with two or three fortunes in their ears. Slippers were encrusted with them; Nero had a room whose walls were covered with them; and, according to Pliny, Caligula's wife, Lollia Paulina, had a dress decorated entirely with pearls and emeralds.

Christianity came into a world of luxury and decadence. Confronted by all this, Peter pleads for the graces which adorn the heart, which are precious in the sight of God. These were the jewels which adorned the holy women of the past. Isaiah had called Sara the mother of God's faithful people (Isaiah 51:2); and, if Christian wives are adorned with the same graces of modesty, humility and chastity, they too will be her daughters and will be within the family of the faithful people of God.

A Christian wife of those times lived in a society where she would be tempted to senseless extravagance and where she might well go in fear of her non-Christian husband's whims; but she must live in selfless service, in goodness and in serene trust. That would be the best sermon she could preach to win her husband for Christ. There are few passages where the value of a lovely Christian life is so vividly stressed.

THE HUSBAND'S OBLIGATION

1 Peter 3:7

> Likewise, you husbands, live understandingly with your wives, remembering that women are the weaker sex and assigning honour to them as fellow heirs of the grace of life, so that there may be no barrier to your prayers.

SHORT as this passage is, it has in it much of the very essence of the Christian ethic. That ethic is what may be called a *reciprocal* ethic. It never places all the responsibility on one side. If it speaks of the duties of slaves, it speaks also of the obligations of masters. If it speaks of the duty of children, it speaks also of the obligations of parents (cf. Ephesians 6:1–9; Colossians 3:20–4:1). Peter has just laid down the duty of wives; now he lays down the duty of husbands. A marriage must be based on mutual obligation. A marriage in which all the privileges are on one side and all the obligations on the other is bound to be imperfect with every chance of failure. This was a new concept in the ancient world. We have already noted the woman's total lack of rights then, and quoted Cato's statement of the rights of the husband. But we did not finish that quotation, and we do so now: 'If you were to catch your wife in an act of infidelity, you can kill her with impunity without a trial; but, if she were to catch you, she would not venture to touch you with her finger and, indeed, she has no right.' In the Roman moral code, all the obligation was on the wife and all the privilege with the husband. The Christian ethic never grants a privilege without a corresponding obligation.

What are the obligations of the husband?

(1) He must be *understanding*. He must be considerate and sensitive to the feelings of his wife. The novelist Somerset Maugham's mother was a very beautiful woman with the world at her feet, but his father was not handsome. Someone once asked her: 'Why do you remain faithful to that ugly little man you married?' Her answer was: 'Because he never hurts me.' Understanding and considerateness had forged an unbreakable bond. The cruelty that is hardest to bear is often not deliberate but the product of sheer thoughtlessness.

(2) He must be *considerate*. He must remember that women are the weaker sex and treat them with courtesy. In the ancient world, consideration for women was practically unknown. It was, and still is, no uncommon sight in the middle east to see the man riding on a donkey while the woman

trudged by his side. It was Christianity which introduced mutual care and consideration into the relationship between men and women.

(3) He must remember that the woman has *equal spiritual rights*. She is a fellow heir of the grace of life. Women did not share in the worship of the Greeks and the Romans. Even in the Jewish synagogue, they had no share in the service, and in orthodox synagogues this is still the case. When they were admitted to the synagogue at all, they were segregated from the men and hidden behind a screen. Here in Christianity emerged the revolutionary principle that women had equal spiritual rights – and, with that, the relationship between the sexes was changed.

(4) Unless a man fulfils these obligations, there is a barrier between his prayers and God. As Charles Bigg puts it in his commentary: 'The sighs of the injured wife come between the husband's prayers and God's hearing.' Here is a great truth. Our relationships with God can never be right if our relationships with one another are wrong. It is when we are at one with each other that we are at one with God.

THE MARKS OF THE CHRISTIAN LIFE (1)

I Peter 3:8–12

> Finally, you must all be of one mind; you must have sympathy with each other and you must live in brotherly love; you must be compassionate and humble; you must not return evil for evil, nor insult for insult; on the contrary, you must return blessing; for it was to give and to inherit blessing that you were called.

> He that would love life,
>   And see good days,

Let him keep his tongue from evil,
  And his lips from speaking guile:
Let him turn away from evil and do right;
  Let him seek peace, and pursue it,
For the eyes of the Lord are upon the righteous,
  And his ears are open to their prayer;
But the face of the Lord is against those that do evil.

HERE, Peter gathers together what might be described as the great qualities of the Christian life.

(1) Right in the forefront, he sets *Christian unity*. It is worth while to collect together the great New Testament passages about unity in order to see how great a place it occupies in New Testament thought. The basis of the whole matter is in the words of Jesus, who prayed for his people that they might all be one, as he and his Father were one (John 17:21–3). In the thrilling early days of the Church, this prayer was fulfilled, for they were all of one heart and one soul (Acts 4:32). Over and over again, Paul exhorts men and women to this unity and prays for it. He reminds the Christians of Rome that, though they are many, they are one body, and he pleads with them to be of one mind (Romans 12:4, 12:16). In writing to the Christians of Corinth, he uses the same picture of the Christians as members of one body in spite of all their differing qualities and gifts (1 Corinthians 12:12–31). He pleads with the quarrelling Corinthians that there should be no divisions among them and that they should be perfectly joined together in the same mind (1 Corinthians 1:10). He tells them that strifes and divisions are things of the flesh, marks that they are living on purely human standards, without the mind of Christ (1 Corinthians 3:3). Because they have shared the one bread, they must be one body (1 Corinthians 10:17). He tells them that they must be of one mind and must live in peace (2 Corinthians 13:11). In Christ Jesus, the dividing walls are

down, and Jew and Greek are united into one (Ephesians 2:13–14). Christians must maintain the unity of the Spirit in the bond of peace, remembering that there is one Lord, one faith, one baptism, one God and Father of all (Ephesians 4:3–6). The Philippians must stand fast in one spirit, striving together with one mind for the faith of the gospel; they will make Paul's happiness complete, if they have the same love and have one accord and one mind; the quarrelling Euodias and Syntyche are urged to be of one mind in the Lord (Philippians 1:27, 2:2, 4:2).

All through the New Testament rings the plea for Christian unity. It is more than a plea; it is an announcement that people cannot live the Christian life unless in their personal relationships they are at unity with one another, and that the Church cannot be truly Christian if there are divisions within it. It is tragic to realize how far we are from achieving this unity in our personal lives and how far the Church is from achieving it within itself. The New Testament scholar C. E. B. Cranfield writes so well of this that we cannot do other than quote his whole comment in full, lengthy though it is: 'The New Testament never treats this agreeing in Christ as an unnecessary though highly desirable spiritual luxury, but as something essential to the true being of the Church. Divisions, whether disagreements between individual members or the existence of factions and parties and – how much more! – our present-day denominations, constitute a calling in question of the Gospel itself and a sign that those who are involved are carnal. The more seriously we take the New Testament, the more urgent and painful becomes our sense of the sinfulness of the divisions, and the more earnest our prayers and strivings after the peace and unity of the Church on earth. That does not mean that the like-mindedness we are to strive for is to be a drab uniformity of the sort beloved of bureaucrats.

Rather is it to be a unity in which powerful tensions are held together by an over-mastering loyalty, and strong antipathies of race and colour, temperament and taste, social position and economic interest, are overcome in common worship and common obedience. Such unity will only come when Christians are humble and bold enough to lay hold on the unity already given in Christ and to take it more seriously than their own self-importance and sin, and to make of these deep differences of doctrine, which originate in our imperfect understanding of the Gospel and which we dare not belittle, not an excuse for letting go of one another or staying apart, but rather an incentive for a more earnest seeking in fellowship together to hear and obey the voice of Christ.' There speaks the prophetic voice to our modern condition.

THE MARKS OF THE CHRISTIAN LIFE (2)

1 Peter 3:8–12 (*contd*)

(2) Second, Peter sets *sympathy*. Here again, the whole New Testament urges this duty upon us. We are to rejoice with those who rejoice and to weep with those who weep (Romans 12:15). When one member of the body suffers, all the other members suffer with it; and when one member is honoured, all the members rejoice with it (1 Corinthians 12:26); and it must be the same with Christians, who are the body of Christ. One thing is clear: sympathy and selfishness cannot co-exist. As long as the self is the most important thing in the world, there can be no such thing as sympathy; sympathy depends on the willingness to forget self and to identify oneself with the pains and sorrows of others. Sympathy comes to the heart when Christ reigns there.

(3) Third, Peter sets what is literally translated as *brotherly love*, the love of Christians for one another and for others. Again the matter goes back to the words of Jesus. 'I give you a new commandment, that you love one another . . . By this everyone will know that you are my disciples, if you have love for one another' (John 13:34–5). Here, the New Testament speaks with unmistakable definiteness and with almost frightening directness. 'We know that we have passed from death to life because we love one another. Whoever does not love abides in death. All who hate a brother or sister are murderers' (1 John 3:14–15). 'Those who say "I love God", and hate their brothers or sisters, are liars' (1 John 4:20). The simple fact is that love of God and love of others go hand in hand; the one cannot exist without the other. The simplest test of the reality of the Christianity of an individual or a church is whether or not it makes them love their neighbours.

(4) Fourth, Peter sets *compassion*. There is a sense in which compassion is in danger of becoming a lost virtue. The conditions of our own time tend to blunt our sensitivity or feelings of sympathy. As C. E. B. Cranfield puts it: 'We got used to hearing on the radio of a thousand-bomber raid as we ate our breakfast. We have got used to the idea of millions of people becoming refugees.' We can read of the thousands of casualties on the roads with no reaction within our hearts, forgetting that each means a broken body or a broken heart for someone. It is easy to lose the sense of pity and still easier to be satisfied with a sentimentalism which feels a moment's comfortable sorrow and does nothing. Pity is of the very essence of God, and compassion of the very being of Jesus Christ – a pity so great that God sent his only Son to die for us, a compassion so intense that it took Christ to the cross. There can be no Christianity without compassion.

(5) Fifth, Peter sets *humility*. Christian humility comes from two things. It comes, first, from the sense of creatureliness. Christians are humble because they are constantly aware of their utter dependence on God and that they can do nothing without God. It comes, second, from the fact that Christians have a new standard of comparison. It may well be that, when they compare themselves with others, they have nothing to fear from the comparison. But the standard of comparison for Christians is Christ, and, compared with his sinless perfection, we can never fully measure up. When Christians remember their dependence on God and hold themselves up to the standard of Christ, they must remain humble.

(6) Last, and as a climax, Peter sets *forgiveness*. It is to receive forgiveness from God and to give forgiveness to others that Christians are called. The one cannot exist without the other; it is only when we forgive others their sins against us that we are forgiven our sins against God (Matthew 6:12, 6:14–15). The mark of Christians is that they forgive others as God has forgiven them (Ephesians 4:32).

As was natural for him, Peter sums the matter up by quoting Psalm 34, with its picture of the righteous, whom God receives, and those who do evil, whom God rejects.

THE CHRISTIAN'S SECURITY IN A THREATENING WORLD

1 Peter 3:13–15a

> Who will hurt you, if you are ardent lovers of goodness? Even if you do have to suffer for the sake of righteousness, you are blessed. Have no fear of them; do not be troubled; but in your hearts give Christ a unique place.

In this passage, we can see how Peter was steeped in the Old Testament; there are two Old Testament foundations for it. It is not so much that he actually quotes them, as that he could not have written the passage at all unless the Old Testament had been in his mind. The very first sentence is a reminiscence of Isaiah 50:9: 'It is the Lord God who helps me; who will declare me guilty?' Again, when Peter is talking about the banishing of fear, he is thinking of Isaiah 8:13: 'But the Lord of hosts, him you shall regard as holy; let him be your fear, and let him be your dread.'

There are three important ideas in this passage.

(1) Peter begins by insisting on a passionate love of goodness. People may have more than one attitude to goodness. It may be to them a burden or a bore or something which they vaguely want to achieve, but the price of which they are not willing to pay in terms of effort, The word we have translated as *ardent lover* is *zēlōtēs*, which is often translated as *Zealot*. The Zealots were fanatical patriots, who were pledged to liberate their native land by every possible means. They were prepared to take their lives in their hands, to sacrifice rest and comfort, home and loved ones, in their passionate love for their country. What Peter is saying is: 'Love goodness with that passionate intensity with which the most fanatical patriots love their country.' The nineteenth-century historian Sir John Seeley said: 'No heart is pure that is not passionate; no virtue safe which is not enthusiastic.' It is only when people fall in love with goodness that wrong things lose their fascination and their power.

(2) Peter goes on to speak about the Christian attitude to suffering. It has been rightly pointed out that we are involved in two kinds of suffering. There is the suffering in which we are involved because of our *humanity*. Because we are human, we experience physical suffering, death, sorrow, mental

distress and physical weariness and pain. But there is also the suffering in which we may be involved because of our *Christianity*. There may be unpopularity, persecution, sacrifice for the sake of principle and the deliberate choosing of the difficult way, the necessary discipline and toil of the Christian life. Yet the Christian life has a certain blessedness which runs through it all. What is the reason for it?

(3) Peter's answer is this. Christians are people for whom God and Jesus Christ are of prime importance in life; their relationship to God in Christ is life's greatest value. If people's hearts are set on earthly things, possessions, happiness, pleasure, an easy life and comfort, they are of all people most vulnerable. For, in the nature of things, they may lose these things at any moment. Such people are desperately easily hurt. On the other hand, if they give to Jesus Christ the unique place in their lives, the most precious thing for them is their relationship to God, and nothing can take that from them. Therefore, they are completely secure.

So, even in suffering, Christians are still blessed. When the suffering is for Christ, they are demonstrating their loyalty to Christ and are sharing his sufferings. When the suffering is part of the human situation, it still cannot rob them of the most precious things in life. No one escapes suffering; but, for Christians, suffering cannot touch the things which matter most of all.

THE CHRISTIAN ARGUMENT FOR CHRIST

1 Peter 3:15b–16

> Always be prepared to make your defence to anyone who calls you to account concerning the hope that is in you; but do so with gentleness and reverence. Keep your

> conscience clear, so that, when you are abused, those
> who revile your good behaviour in Christ may be put to
> shame.

In a hostile and suspicious world, it was inevitable that
Christians would be called upon to defend the faith they held
and the hope by which they lived. Here, Peter has certain
things to say about this Christian defence.

(1) It must be *reasonable*. It is a *logos* that Christians must
give, and a *logos* is a reasonable and intelligent statement of
someone's position. An educated Greek believed that it was
the mark of an intelligent person to be able to give and to
receive a *logos* concerning actions and beliefs. As Charles
Bigg puts it, such a person was expected 'intelligently and
temperately to discuss matters of conduct'. To do so, we must
know what we believe; we must have thought it out; we
must be able to state it intelligently and intelligibly. Our
faith must be a first-hand discovery and not a second-hand
story. It is one of the tragedies of the modern situation that
there are so many church members who, if they were asked
what they believe, could not tell, and who, if they were asked
why they believe it, would be equally helpless. Christians
must go through the mental and spiritual effort of thinking
out their faith, so that they can explain what they believe and
why.

(2) Their defence must be given *with gentleness*. There
are many people who state their beliefs with a kind of arrogant
belligerence. Their attitude is that anyone who does not
agree with them is either stupid or unreliable, and they seek
to ram their beliefs down other people's throats. The case for
Christianity must be presented in an attractive manner and
with love, and with that wise tolerance which realizes that it
is not given to anyone to possess the whole truth. 'There are
as many ways to the stars as there are men to climb them.'

People may be wooed into the Christian faith when they cannot be bullied into it.

(3) Their defence must be given *with reverence*. That is to say, any argument in which Christians are involved must be carried on in a tone which God can hear with joy. No debates have been so acrimonious as theological debates; no differences have caused such bitterness as religious differences. In any presentation of the Christian case and in any argument for the Christian faith, the tone should be the tone of love.

(4) The only compelling argument is the argument of the Christian life. Let people act in such a way that their consciences are clear. Let them meet criticism with lives which are beyond reproach. Such conduct will silence slander and disarm criticism. 'A saint', as has been said, 'is someone whose life makes it easier to believe in God.'

THE SAVING WORK OF CHRIST

I Peter 3:17–4:6

> For it is better to suffer for doing right, if that should be the will of God, than to suffer for doing wrong. For Christ also died once and for all for our sins, the just for the unjust, that he might bring us to God. He was put to death in the flesh, but he was raised to life in the Spirit, in which also he went and preached to the spirits who are in prison, the spirits who were once upon a time disobedient, in the time when the patience of God waited in the days of Noah, while the ark was being built, in which some few – that is, eight souls – were brought in safety through the water. And water now saves you, who were symbolically represented in Noah and his company, I mean the water of baptism; and baptism is not merely the removal of dirt from the body, but the pledge to God

of a good conscience, through the resurrection of Jesus Christ, who is at the right hand of God, because he went to heaven, after angels and authorities and powers had been made subject to him.

Since, then, Christ suffered in the flesh, you too must arm yourselves with the same conviction, that he who has suffered in the flesh has ceased from sin, and as a result of this the aim of such a man now is to spend the time that remains to him of life in the flesh no longer in obedience to human passions, but in obedience to the will of God. For the time that is past is sufficient to have done what the Gentiles will to do, to have lived a life of licentiousness, lust, drunkenness, revellings, carousings and abominable idolatry. They think it strange when you do not rush to join them in the same flood of profligacy, and they abuse you for not doing so. They will give account to him who is ready to judge the living and the dead. For this is why the gospel was preached even to the dead, so that, although they have already been judged in the flesh like men, they might live in the Spirit like God.

THIS is not only one of the most difficult passages in Peter's letter, it is one of the most difficult in the whole New Testament; and it is also the basis of one of the most difficult articles in the creed, 'He descended into hell.' It is, therefore, better first of all to read it as a whole and then to study it in its various sections.

THE EXAMPLE OF THE WORK OF CHRIST

1 Peter 3:17–18a

For it is better to suffer for doing right, if that should be the will of God, than to suffer for doing wrong. For Christ

also died once and for all for our sins, the just for the
unjust, that he might bring us to God.

ALTHOUGH this passage is one of the most difficult in the New
Testament, it begins with something which anyone can understand. The point that Peter is making is that, even if Christians
are compelled to suffer unjustly for their faith, they are only
walking the way that their Lord and Saviour has already
walked. Suffering Christians must always remember that they
have a suffering Lord. In the space of these two short verses,
Peter has the greatest and the deepest things to say about the
work of Christ.

(1) He lays it down that the work of Christ was *unique*
and need never be repeated. Christ died *once and for all* for
sins. The New Testament says this same thing often. When
Christ died, he died once and for all (Romans 6:10). The
priestly sacrifices in the Temple have to be repeated daily,
but Christ made the perfect sacrifice once and for all when he
offered himself up (Hebrews 7:27). Christ was once and for
all offered to bear the sin of many (Hebrews 9:28). We are
sanctified through the offering of the body of Christ once
and for all (Hebrews 10:10). The New Testament is completely
sure that on the cross something happened which never needs
to happen again and that in that happening sin is finally
defeated. On the cross, God dealt with human sin in a way
which is adequate for all sin, for all people, for all time.

(2) He lays it down that that sacrifice was *for sin*. Christ
died once and for all *for sins*. This, again, is frequently said
in the New Testament. Christ died for our sins according to
the Scriptures (1 Corinthians 15:3). Christ gave himself for
our sins (Galatians 1:4). The function of the high priest, and
Jesus Christ is the perfect high priest, is to offer sacrifice for
sins (Hebrews 5:1, 5:3). He is the atoning sacrifice for our
sins (1 John 2:2).

The Greek for *for sins* is either *huper* or *peri hamartiōn*. It so happens that, in the Greek version of the Old Testament, the usual phrase for a *sin offering* is *peri hamartias* (*hamartias* is the singular of *hamartiōn*), as, for instance, in Leviticus 5:7 and 6:30. That is to say, Peter is laying it down that the death of Christ is the sacrifice which atones for the sin of all.

We may put it this way. Sin is that which interrupts the relationship which should exist between God and all humanity. The object of sacrifice is to restore that lost relationship. The death of Christ upon the cross, however we explain it, restores the lost relationship between God and human beings. As Charles Wesley put it in verse, in the hymn 'And Can it Be?':

> No condemnation now I dread:
>   Jesus, and all in him, is mine!
> Alive in him, my living Head,
>   And clothed in righteousness divine,
> Bold I approach the eternal throne,
> And claim the crown, through Christ my own.

It may be that we will never agree in our theories of what exactly happened on the cross – for, indeed, as Charles Wesley said in that same hymn: ''Tis mystery all!' But on one thing we can agree – through what happened there, we may enter into a new relationship with God.

(3) He lays it down that that sacrifice was *vicarious*, that is, it was on behalf of others. Christ died once and for all for sins, *the just for the unjust*. That the just should suffer for the unjust is an extraordinary thing. At first sight, it looks like injustice. As the Baptist writer Edwin H. Robertson put it: 'Only forgiveness without reason can match sin without excuse.' The suffering of Christ was for us; and the mystery is that he who deserved no suffering bore that suffering for us

who deserved to suffer. He sacrificed himself to restore our lost relationship with God.

(4) He lays it down that the work of Christ was *to bring us to God*. Christ died once and for all for sins, the just for the unjust, *that he might bring us to God*. The word for *to bring* is *prosagein*. Its background has two vivid strands.

(a) It has a Jewish background. It is used in the Old Testament of bringing to God those who are to be priests. It is God's instruction: 'You shall bring Aaron and his sons to the entrance of the tent of meeting' (Exodus 29:4). The point is this – as the Jews saw it, only the priests had the right of close access to God. In the Temple, the ordinary worshippers might come so far; they could pass through the Court of the Gentiles, the Court of the Women, the Court of the Israelites – but there they must stop. Into the Court of the Priests, into the nearer presence of God, they could not go; and, of the priests, only the high priest could enter into the Holy of Holies. But Jesus Christ brings *us* to God; he opens the way for *all* men and women to come into his nearer presence.

(b) It has a Greek background. In the New Testament, the corresponding noun *prosagōgē* is used three times. *Prosagein* means *to bring in*; *prosagōgē* means the right of *access*, the result of the bringing in. Through Christ, we have *access* to grace (Romans 5:2). Through him, we have *access* to God the Father (Ephesians 2:18). Through him, we have boldness and *access* and confidence to come to God (Ephesians 3:12). In Greek, this had a specialized meaning. At the court of kings, there was an official called the *prosagōgeus*, the *introducer*, the *giver of access*, and it was his function to decide who should be admitted to the king's presence and who should be kept out. He, as it were, held the keys of access. It is Jesus Christ, through what he did, who gives us access to God.

(5) When we go beyond these two verses, further into the passage, we can add two more great truths to Peter's view of the work of Christ. In 3:19, he says that Jesus preached to the spirits in prison, and in 4:6 he says that the gospel was preached to the dead. As we shall go on to see, this most probably means that in the time between his death and his resurrection Jesus actually preached the gospel in the realm of the dead – that is to say, to those who in their lifetime had never had the opportunity to hear it. Here is a tremendous thought. It means that the work of Christ is infinite in its range. It means that no one who ever lived is outside the grace of God.

(6) Peter sees the work of Christ in terms of *complete triumph*. He says that, after his resurrection, Jesus went into heaven and is at the right hand of God, angels and authorities and powers having been made subject to him (3:22). The meaning is that there is nothing in earth and heaven outside the empire of Christ. To all people, he brought the new relationship between human beings and God; in his death, he even brought the good news to the dead; in his resurrection, he conquered death; even the angelic and the demonic powers are subject to him; and he shares the very power and throne of God. Christ the sufferer has become Christ the victor; Christ the crucified has become Christ the crowned.

THE DESCENT INTO HELL (1)

1 Peter 3:18b–20, 4:6

> He was put to death in the flesh, but he was raised to life in the Spirit, in which also he went and preached to the spirits who are in prison, the spirits who were once upon a time disobedient, in the time when the patience of God

waited in the days of Noah, while the ark was being
built . . . For this is why the gospel was preached even
to the dead, so that, although they have already been
judged in the flesh like men, they might live in the Spirit
like God.

WE have already said that we are here faced with one of the
most difficult passages not only in Peter's letter but in the
whole New Testament; and, if we are to grasp what it means,
we must follow Peter's own advice and mentally 'gird up our
loins' – prepare our minds to study it.

This passage has found a place in the creed in the phrase:
'He descended into hell.' We must first note that this phrase
is very misleading. The idea of the New Testament is not that
Jesus descended into *hell* but that he descended into *Hades*.
Acts 2:27, as all the newer translations correctly show, should
be translated not as 'Thou wilt not leave my soul in hell', as
the Authorized Version has it, but as 'You will not abandon
my soul to Hades.' The difference is that hell is the place of
the punishment of the wicked; Hades was the place where all
the dead went.

The Jews had a very shadowy picture of life beyond the
grave. They thought in terms not of heaven and of hell but of
a shadowy world, where the spirits of men and women moved
like grey ghosts in an everlasting twilight and where there
was neither strength nor joy. Such was Hades, into which the
spirits of all people went after death. Isaiah writes: 'For Sheol
cannot thank you, death cannot praise you; those who go down
to the Pit cannot hope for your faithfulness' (Isaiah 38:18).
The psalmist wrote: 'In death there is no remembrance of
you; in Sheol who can give you praise?' (Psalm 6:5). 'What
profit is there in my death if I go down to the Pit? Will the
dust praise you? Will it tell of your faithfulness?' (Psalm 30:9).
'Do you work wonders for the dead? Do the shades rise up to

praise you? Is your steadfast love declared in the grave, or your faithfulness in Abaddon? Are your wonders known in the darkness, or your saving help in the land of forgetfulness?' (Psalm 88:10–12). 'The dead do not praise the Lord, nor do any that go down into silence' (Psalm 115:17). 'Whatever your hand finds to do, do with your might; for there is no work or thought or knowledge or wisdom in Sheol, to which you are going' (Ecclesiastes 9:10). The Jewish idea of the world after death was of this grey world of shadows and forgetfulness, in which the dead were separated from life and light and God.

As time went on, there emerged the idea of stages and divisions in this shadow land. For some, it was to last forever; but for others it was a kind of prison house in which they were held until the final judgment of God's wrath should destroy them (Isaiah 24:21–2; 2 Peter 2:4; Revelation 20:1–7). So, it must first of all be remembered that this whole matter is to be thought of not in terms of hell, as we understand the word, but in terms of Christ's going to the dead in their shadowy world.

THE DESCENT INTO HELL (2)

1 Peter 3:18b–20, 4:6 (*contd*)

THIS doctrine of the descent into Hades, as we must now call it, is based on two phrases in our present passage. It says that Jesus went and preached to the spirits who are in prison (3:19); and it speaks of the gospel being preached to the dead (4:6). There have always been differing viewpoints towards this doctrine.

(1) There is the viewpoint of *elimination*. Some wish to eliminate it altogether, and attempt to do so along two lines.

(a) Peter says that in the Spirit Christ preached to the spirits in prison, who were disobedient in the time when the patience of God waited in the days of Noah, when the ark was being built. It is argued that what this means is that it was *in the time of Noah himself* that Christ did this preaching; that in the Spirit, long ages before this, he made his appeal to the wicked of Noah's day. This would completely do away with the idea of the descent into Hades. Many scholars have accepted that view; but we do not think it is the view which comes naturally from Peter's words.

(b) If we look at James Moffatt's translation, we find something quite different. He translates: 'In the flesh he [Christ] was put to death, but he came to life in the Spirit. It was in the Spirit that Enoch also went and preached to the imprisoned spirits who had disobeyed at the time when God's patience held out during the construction of the ark in the days of Noah.' How does Moffatt arrive at this translation?

The name of Enoch does not appear in any Greek manuscript. But, in the consideration of the text of any Greek author, scholars sometimes use a process called *emendation*. They think that there is something wrong with the text as it stands, that some scribe has perhaps copied it wrongly, and they therefore suggest that some word should be changed or added. In this passage, the biblical scholar Rendel Harris suggested that the word *Enoch* was missed out in the copying of Peter's writing and should be put back in.

Although it involves the use of Greek, some readers may be interested to see how Rendel Harris arrived at this famous emendation. In the top line in italic print, we have set down the Greek of the passage in English lettering and beneath each Greek word its English translation:

thanatōtheis	*men sarki*
having been put to death	in the flesh
zōopoiētheis	*de pneumati*
having been raised to life	in the spirit

en	*hō*	*kai*	*tois*	*en*	*phulakē*	*pneumasi*
in	which	also	to the	in	prison	spirits

poreutheis	*ekēruxen*
having gone	he preached.

(*Men* and *de* are what are called particles; they are not translated but merely mark the contrast between *sarki* and *pneumati*.) It was Rendel Harris's suggestion that between *kai* and *tois* the word *Enōch* had dropped out. His explanation was that, since most manuscript copying was done to dictation, scribes were very liable to miss out words which followed each other, if they sounded very similar. In this passage,

en hō kai   and   *Enōch*

sound very much alike, and Rendel Harris thought it very likely that *Enōch* had for that reason been mistakenly omitted.

What reason is there for bringing *Enoch* into this passage at all? He has always been a fascinating and mysterious person. 'Enoch walked with God; then he was no more, because God took him' (Genesis 5:24). In between the Old and New Testaments, many legends sprang up about Enoch, and famous and important books were written under his name. One of the legends was that Enoch, though a man, acted as 'God's envoy' to the angels who sinned by coming to earth and lustfully seducing mortal women (Genesis 6:2). In the Book of Enoch, it is said that he was sent down from heaven to announce to these angels their final doom (1 Enoch

12:1) and that he proclaimed that for them, because of their sin, there was neither peace nor forgiveness ever (1 Enoch 12–13).

So, according to Jewish legend, Enoch did go to Hades and preach doom to the fallen angels. And Rendel Harris thought that this passage referred not to Jesus but to Enoch, and Moffatt so far agreed with him as to put Enoch into his translation. That is an extremely interesting and ingenious suggestion, but without doubt it must be rejected. There is no evidence for it at all; and it is not natural to bring in Enoch, for the whole picture is of the work of Christ.

THE DESCENT INTO HELL (3)

1 Peter 3:18b–20, 4:6 (contd)

WE have seen that the attempt at the *elimination* of this passage fails.

(2) The second viewpoint is *limitation*. This position – and it is that of some very great New Testament interpreters – believes that Peter is indeed saying that Jesus went to Hades and preached, but that he by no means preached to all the inhabitants of Hades. Different interpreters limit that preaching in different ways.

(a) It is argued that Jesus preached in Hades *only* to the spirits of those who were disobedient in the days of Noah. Scholars who hold this view often go on to argue that, since these sinners were desperately disobedient, so much so that God sent the flood and destroyed them (Genesis 6:12–13), we may believe that no one is outside the mercy of God. They were the worst of all sinners, and yet they were given another chance of repentance; therefore, the worst people of all still have a chance in Christ.

(b) It is argued that Jesus preached to the fallen angels, and preached not salvation but final and awful doom. We have already mentioned these angels. Their story is told in Genesis 6:1–8. They were tempted by the beauty of mortal women; they came to earth, seduced them and fathered children; and because of their action, it is implied, human wickedness was great and human thoughts were always evil. Second Peter 2:4 speaks of these sinning angels as being imprisoned in hell, awaiting judgment. It was to them that Enoch did, in fact, preach; and there are those who think that what this passage means is not that Christ preached mercy and another chance, but that, in token of his complete triumph, he preached terrible doom to those angels who had sinned.

(c) It is argued that Christ preached *only* to those who had been righteous and that he led them out of Hades into the paradise of God. We have seen how the Jews believed that all the dead went to Hades, the shadowy land of forgetfulness. The argument is that, *before* Christ, that was indeed so; but that Christ opened the gates of heaven to all people; and, when he did so, he went to Hades and told the glad news to all the righteous men and women of all past generations and led them out to God. That is a magnificent picture. Those who hold this view often go on to say that, because of Christ, there is now no time spent in the shadows of Hades, and the way to paradise is open as soon as this world closes on us.

THE DESCENT INTO HELL (4)

1 Peter 3:18b–20, 4:6 (*contd*)

(3) There is the viewpoint that what Peter is saying is that Jesus Christ, between his death and resurrection, went to the

world of the dead and preached the gospel there. Peter says that Jesus Christ was put to death in the flesh but raised to life in the Spirit, and that it was in the Spirit that he so preached. The meaning is that Jesus lived in a human body and was under all the limitations of time and space in the days of his earthly life, and died with that body broken and bleeding upon the cross. But when he rose again, he rose with a spiritual body, in which he was rid of the necessary weaknesses of humanity and liberated from the necessary limitations of time and space. It was in this spiritual condition of perfect freedom that the preaching to the dead took place.

As it stands, this doctrine is stated in terms which are dated. It speaks of the *descent* into Hades, and the very word *descent* suggests a three-storey universe in which heaven is situated above the sky and Hades beneath the earth. But, laying aside the physical categories of this doctrine, we can find in it truths which are eternally valid and precious – three in particular.

(a) If Christ descended into Hades, then his death was no pretence. It is not to be explained in terms of a loss of consciousness on the cross, or anything like that. He really experienced death, and rose again. At its simplest, the doctrine of the descent into Hades lays down the complete identity of Christ with our human condition, even to the experience of death.

(b) If Christ descended into Hades, it means that his triumph is universal. This, in fact, is a truth which is ingrained into the New Testament. It is Paul's dream that at the name of Jesus every knee should bow, of things in heaven and things in earth and things under the earth (Philippians 2:10). In the Book of Revelation, the song of praise comes from every creature which is in heaven and on the earth and under the earth (Revelation 5:13). The one who ascended into heaven is the one who first descended into the lower parts of the earth (Ephesians 4:9–10). The total submission of the universe to Christ is woven into the thought of the New Testament.

(c) If Christ descended into Hades and preached there, there is no corner of the universe into which the message of grace has not come. There is in this passage the solution of one of the most haunting questions raised by the Christian faith – what is to happen to those who lived before Jesus Christ and to those to whom the gospel never came? There can be no salvation without repentance – but how can repentance come to those who have never been confronted with the love and holiness of God? If there is no other name by which men and women may be saved, what is to happen to those who never heard it? This is the point that the second-century Christian writer Justin Martyr fastened on to: 'The Lord, the Holy God of Israel, remembered his dead, those sleeping in the earth, and came down to them to tell them the good news of salvation.' The doctrine of the descent into Hades preserves the precious truth that no one who ever lived is left without a sight of Christ and without the offer of the salvation of God.

Many in repeating the creed have found the phrase 'He descended into hell' either meaningless or bewildering, and have quietly agreed to set it on one side and forget it. It may well be that we ought to think of this as a picture painted in terms of poetry rather than a doctrine stated in terms of theology. But it contains these three great truths – that Jesus Christ not only tasted death but drained the cup of death, that the triumph of Christ is universal and that there is no corner of the universe into which the grace of God has not reached.

CHRISTIAN BAPTISM

1 Peter 3:18–22

> For Christ also died once and for all for our sins, the
> just for the unjust, that he might bring us to God. He
> was put to death in the flesh, but he was raised to life in
> the Spirit, in which also he went and preached to the
> spirits who are in prison, the spirits who were once upon
> a time disobedient, in the time when the patience of
> God waited in the days of Noah, while the ark was being
> built, in which some few – that is, eight souls – were
> brought in safety through the water. And water now
> saves you, who were symbolically represented in Noah
> and his company, I mean the water of baptism; and
> baptism is not merely the removal of dirt from the
> body, but the pledge to God of a good conscience,
> through the resurrection of Jesus Christ, who is at the
> right hand of God, because he went to heaven, after
> angels and authorities and powers had been made subject
> to him.

PETER has been speaking about the wicked who were disobedient and corrupt in the days of Noah; they were ultimately destroyed. But, in the destruction by the flood, eight people – Noah and his wife, his sons Shem, Ham and Japheth, and their wives – were brought to safety in the ark. Immediately, the idea of being *brought to safety through the water* turns Peter's thoughts to Christian baptism, which is also a bringing to safety through the water. What Peter literally says is that baptism is an *antitype* of Noah and his people in the ark.

This word introduces us to a special way of looking at the Old Testament. There are two closely connected words. There is *tupos*, type, which means a *seal*, and there is *antitupos*, antitype, which means the *impression of the seal.* Clearly, between the seal and its impression there is the closest possible correspondence. So there are people and events and customs in the Old Testament which are types, and which find their antitypes in the New Testament. The Old Testament event or person is like the seal; the New Testament event or person is like the impression; the two answer to each other. We might put it that the Old Testament event symbolically represents and foreshadows the New Testament event. The science of finding types and antitypes in the Old and the New Testaments is very highly developed. But, to take very simple and obvious examples, the Passover lamb and the scapegoat, that bore the sins of the people, are types of Jesus; and the work of the high priest in making sacrifice for the sins of the people is a type of his saving work. Here, Peter sees the bringing of Noah and his family safely through the waters as a type of baptism.

In this passage, Peter has three great things to say about baptism. It must be remembered that at this stage of the Church's history we are still dealing with adult baptism, the baptism of people who had come straight from the worship of Greek and Roman gods into Christianity and who were taking upon themselves a new way of life.

(1) Baptism is not merely a physical cleansing; it is a spiritual cleansing of the whole heart and soul and life. Its effect must be on an individual's very soul and on that person's whole life.

(2) Peter calls baptism *the pledge of a good conscience to God* (verse 21). The word Peter uses for *pledge* is *eperōtēma.* In every business contract, there was a definite question and answer which made the contract binding. The question was: 'Do you accept the terms of this contract, and bind yourself to observe them?' And the answer, before witnesses, was:

'Yes.' Without that question and answer, the contract was not valid. The technical word for that question-and-answer clause is *eperōtēma* in Greek, *stipulatio* in Latin.

Peter is, in effect, saying that in baptism God said to those coming direct from the old religion: 'Do you accept the terms of my service? Do you accept its privileges and promises, and do you undertake its responsibilities and its demands?' And, in the act of being baptized, each individual answered: 'Yes.'

We use the word *sacrament*. *Sacrament* is derived from the Latin *sacramentum*, which means *a soldier's oath of loyalty* on entering the army. Here, we have basically the same picture. We cannot easily apply this question and answer to infant baptism, unless it is to the parents; but, as we have said, baptism in the very early Church was of adult men and women coming spontaneously from worshipping the ancestral gods into the Church. The modern parallel is entering full membership of the Church. When we enter into Church membership, God asks us: 'Do you accept the conditions of my service, with all privileges and all its responsibilities, with all its promises and all its demands?' and we answer: 'Yes.' All new members should have a clear understanding of what they are doing when they take upon themselves membership of the Church.

(3) The whole idea and effectiveness of baptism is dependent on the resurrection of Jesus Christ. It is the grace of the risen Lord which cleanses us; it is to the risen, living Lord that we pledge ourselves; it is to the risen, living Lord that we look for strength to keep the promise that we have made. Once again, where infant baptism is the practice, we must take these great ideas and apply them to the time when we enter upon full membership of the Church.

CHRISTIAN OBLIGATION

1 Peter 4:1-5

> Since, then, Christ suffered in the flesh, you too must
> arm yourselves with the same conviction, that he who
> has suffered in the flesh has ceased from sin, and as a
> result of this the aim of such a man now is to spend the
> time that remains to him of life in the flesh no longer in
> obedience to human passions, but in obedience to the
> will of God. For the time that is past is sufficient to have
> done what the Gentiles will to do, to have lived a life of
> licentiousness, lust, drunkenness, revellings, carousings
> and abominable idolatry. They think it strange when you
> do not rush to join them in the same flood of profligacy,
> and they abuse you for not doing so. They will give
> account to him who is ready to judge the living and the
> dead.

CHRISTIANS are committed to abandon the ways of the Gentiles
and to live as God would have them do.

Peter says: 'He who has suffered in the flesh has ceased
from sin.' What exactly does he mean? There are three distinct
possibilities.

(1) There is a strong line in Jewish thought that suffering
is in itself a great purifier. In the *Apocalypse of Baruch*, the
writer, speaking of the experiences of the people of Israel,
says: 'Then, therefore, were they chastened that they might
be sanctified' (13:10). In regard to the purification of human
spirits, Enoch says: 'And in proportion as the burning of their
body becomes severe, a corresponding change will take place
in their spirit for ever and ever; for before the Lord of spirits
there will be none to utter a lying word' (1 Enoch 67:9). The
terrible sufferings of the time are described in 2 Maccabees,
and the writer says: 'Now I urge those who read this book not

to be depressed by such calamities, but to recognize that these punishments were designed not to destroy but to discipline our people. In fact, it is a sign of great kindness not to let the impious alone for long, but to punish them immediately. For in the case of the other nations the Lord waits patiently to punish them until they have reached the full measure of their sins; but he does not deal in this way with us, in order that he may not take vengeance on us afterward when our sins have reached their height. Therefore he never withdraws his mercy from us. Although he disciplines us with calamities, he does not forsake his own people' (6:12–16). The idea is that suffering sanctifies and that not to be punished is the greatest punishment which God can lay upon anyone. 'Happy are those whom you discipline, O Lord', said the psalmist (Psalm 94:12). 'How happy is the one whom God reproves', said Eliphaz (Job 5:17). 'For the Lord disciplines those whom he loves, and chastises every child whom he accepts' (Hebrews 12:6).

If this is the idea, it means that those who have been disciplined by suffering have been cured of sin. That is a great thought. It enables us, as Robert Browning said in 'Rabbi Ben Ezra', 'to welcome each rebuff that turns earth's smoothness rough'. It enables us to thank God for the experiences which hurt but save the soul. But, great as this thought is, it is not strictly relevant here.

(2) Charles Bigg thinks that Peter is speaking in terms of the experience which his people had of suffering for the Christian faith. In his commentary, he puts it this way: 'He who has suffered in meekness and in fear, he who has endured all that persecution can do to him rather than join in wicked ways can be trusted to do right; temptation has manifestly no power over him.' The idea is that if someone has come through persecution and not denied the name of Christ, that person

comes out on the other side with a character so tested and a faith so strengthened that temptation can no longer have any impact.

Again there is a great thought here, the thought that every trial and every temptation is meant to make us stronger and better. Every temptation resisted makes the next easier to resist, and every temptation conquered makes us better able to overcome the next attack. But again it is doubtful if this thought is of much relevance here.

(3) The third explanation is most probably the right one. Peter has just been talking about baptism. Now the great New Testament picture of baptism is in Romans 6. In that chapter, Paul says that the experience of baptism is like being buried with Christ in death and raised with him to newness of life. We think that this is what Peter is thinking of here. He has spoken of baptism; and now he says: 'Those who in baptism have shared the sufferings and the death of Christ have risen to such newness of life with him that sin has no more dominion over them' (Romans 6:14). Again we must remember that this is the baptism of people who are voluntarily coming over from the old religion into Christianity. In that act of baptism, they are identified with Christ; they share his sufferings and even his death; and they share his risen life and power, and have, therefore, won a victory over sin.

When that has happened, they have said goodbye to their former way of life. The rule of pleasure, pride and passion is gone, and the rule of God has begun. This was by no means easy. The former associates of the new Christians would laugh at the new puritanism which had entered their lives. But Christians know very well that the judgment of God will come, when the judgments of earth will be reversed and the pleasures that are eternal will compensate a thousandfold for the short-lived pleasures which had to be abandoned in this life.

THE ULTIMATE CHANCE

1 Peter 4:6

> For this is why the gospel was preached even to the dead,
> so that, although they have already been judged in the
> flesh like men, they might live in the Spirit like God.

THIS very difficult passage ends with a very difficult verse.
Once again, we have the idea of the gospel being preached to
the dead. At least three different meanings have been attached
to *dead*. (1) It has been taken to mean those who are *dead in
sin*, not those who are physically dead. (2) It has been taken
to mean *those who died before the second coming of Christ*,
but who heard the gospel before they died and so will not
miss the glory. (3) It has been taken to mean quite simply *all
the dead*. There can be little doubt that this third meaning is
correct; Peter has just been talking about the descent of Christ
to the place of the dead, and here he comes back to the idea of
Christ preaching to the dead.

No fully satisfactory meaning has ever been found for this
verse; but we think that the best explanation is as follows.
For mortals, death is the penalty of sin. As Paul wrote: 'Just
as sin came into the world through one man, and death came
through sin, and so death spread to all because all have sinned'
(Romans 5:12). Had there been no sin, there would have been
no death, and therefore death in itself is a judgment. So, Peter
says, all people have already been judged when they die; in
spite of that, Christ descended to the world of the dead and
preached the gospel there, giving them another chance to live
in the Spirit of God.

In some ways, this is one of the most wonderful verses in
the Bible – for, if our explanation is anywhere near the truth,
it gives a breathtaking glimpse of a gospel of a second chance.

THE APPROACHING END

1 Peter 4:7a

The end of all things is near.

HERE is a note which is struck consistently all through the New Testament. It is the summons of Paul that it is time to wake out of sleep, for the night is far spent and the day is at hand (Romans 13:12). 'The Lord is near', he writes to the Philippians (Philippians 4:5). 'The coming of the Lord is near', writes James (James 5:8). John says that the days in which his people are living are the last hour (1 John 2:18). 'The time is near', says the John of the Revelation, and he hears the risen Christ testify: 'Surely I am coming soon' (Revelation 1:3, 22:20).

There are many for whom all such passages are problems – for, if they are taken literally, the New Testament writers were mistaken; almost 2,000 years have passed, and the end has not yet come. There are four ways of looking at the passages.

(1) We may hold that the New Testament writers were, in fact, mistaken. They looked for the return of Christ and the end of the world in their own day and generation; and these events did not take place. The curious thing is that the Christian Church allowed these words to stand, although it would not have been difficult to remove them quietly from the New Testament documents. It was not until late in the second century that the New Testament began to be fixed in the form in which we have it today; and yet statements such as these became unquestioned parts of it. The clear conclusion is that the people of the early Church still believed these words to be true.

(2) There is a strong line of New Testament thought which, in effect, holds that the end *has* come. The point of fulfilment to which all history moved was the coming of Jesus Christ. In him, time was invaded by eternity. In him, God entered

into the human situation. In him, the prophecies were all fulfilled. In him, the end has come. Paul speaks of himself and his people as those on whom the ends of the ages have come (1 Corinthians 10:11). Peter in his first sermon speaks of Joel's prophecy of the outpouring of the Spirit and of all that should happen in the last days, and then says that at that very time they were actually living in those last days which the prophet had foretold (Acts 2:16–21).

If we accept that, it means that in Jesus Christ the end of history has come. The battle has been won; there remain only skirmishes with the last remnants of opposition. It means that at this very moment we are living in the 'end time', in what someone has called 'the epilogue to history'. That is a very common point of view; but the trouble is that it flies in the face of the facts. Evil is as rampant as ever; the world is still far from having accepted Christ as King. It may be the 'end time', but the dawn seems as far distant as it ever was.

(3) It may be that we have to interpret *near* in the light of history's being a process of almost unimaginable length. It has been put this way. Suppose all time were to be represented by a column the height of Cleopatra's Needle with a single postage stamp on top, then the length of recorded history is represented by the thickness of the postage stamp and the unrecorded history which went before it by the height of the column. When we think of time in terms like that, *near* becomes an entirely relative word. The psalmist was literally right when he said that in God's sight 1,000 years were just like a watch in the night (Psalm 90:4). In that case, *near* can cover centuries and still be used correctly. But it is quite certain that the biblical writers did not take *near* in that sense, for they had no concept of history in those terms.

(4) The simple fact is that behind this there is one inescapable and most personal truth. *For every one of us, the*

time is near. The one thing which can be said of every one of us is that we will die. For every one of us, the Lord is at hand. We cannot tell the day and the hour when we shall go to meet him; and, therefore, all life is lived in the shadow of eternity.

'The end of all things is near', said Peter. The early Christians may have been wrong if they thought that the end of the world was round the corner, but they have left us with the warning that for every one of us personally the end is near; and that warning is as valid today as it ever was.

THE LIFE LIVED IN THE SHADOW OF ETERNITY

I Peter 4:7b–8

> Be, therefore, steady and sober in mind so that you will really be able to pray as you ought. Above all cherish for each other a love that is constant and intense, because love hides a multitude of sins.

WHEN people realize the nearness of Jesus Christ, they are bound to commit themselves to a certain kind of life. In view of that nearness, Peter makes four demands.

(1) He says that we must be steady in mind. We might render it: 'Preserve your sanity.' The verb Peter uses is *sōphronein*; connected with that verb is the noun *sōphrosunē*, which the Greeks derived from the verb *sōzein*, *to keep safe*, and the noun *phronēsis*, *the mind*. *Sōphrosunē* is the wisdom which characterizes someone who is supremely sane; and *sōphronein* means *to preserve one's sanity*. The great characteristic of sanity is that it sees things in their proper proportions; it sees what things are important and what things are not; it is not swept away by sudden and transitory enthusiasms; it is prone neither to unbalanced fanaticism nor to unconcerned indifference. It is only when we see the affairs

of earth in the light of eternity that we see them in their proper proportions; it is when God is given his proper place that everything takes its proper place.

(2) He says that we must be sober in mind. We might render it: 'Preserve your sense of self-restraint and control.' The verb Peter uses is *nēphein*, which originally meant *to be sober* as opposed to *being drunk* and then came to mean *to act soberly and sensibly*. This does not mean that Christians are to be lost in gloomy joylessness, but it does mean that their approach to life must not be frivolous and irresponsible. To take things seriously is to be aware of their real importance and always to be mindful of their consequences in time and in eternity. It is to approach life not as a huge joke, but as a serious matter for which we are answerable.

(3) He says that we must do this in order to pray as we ought. We might render it: 'Preserve your prayer life.' When people have a frivolous and irresponsible approach to life, they cannot pray as they ought. We learn to pray only when we take life so wisely and so seriously that we begin to say in all things: 'Your will be done.' The first requirement of prayer is the earnest desire to discover the will of God for ourselves.

(4) He says that we must cherish for each other a love that is constant and intense. We might render it: 'Preserve your love.' The word Peter uses to describe this love is *ektenēs*, which has two meanings, both of which we have included in the translation. It means *outstretching* in the sense of *consistent*; our love must be the love that never fails. It also means stretching out as a runner stretches out. As C. E. B. Cranfield reminds us, it describes a horse at full gallop and denotes 'the taut muscle of strenuous and sustained effort, as of an athlete'. Our love must be energetic. Here is a fundamental Christian truth. Christian love is not an easy, sentimental reaction. It demands everything an individual possesses of mental and

spiritual energy. It means loving the unlovely and the un-lovable; it means loving in spite of insult and injury; it means loving when love is not returned. The New Testament scholar Johannes Bengel translates *ektenēs* by the Latin *vehemens*, meaning *vehement*. Christian love is the love which never fails and into which every atom of our strength is directed.

In the light of eternity, Christians must preserve their sanity, preserve their self-control, preserve their prayers and preserve their love.

THE POWER OF LOVE

1 Peter 4:7b–8 (*contd*)

'LOVE', says Peter, 'hides a multitude of sins.' There are three things which this saying may mean; and it is not necessary that we should choose between them, for they are all there.

(1) It may mean that *our* love can overlook many sins. 'Love covers all offences', says the writer of the Proverbs (Proverbs 10:12). If we love a person, it is easy to forgive. It is not that love is blind, but that it loves a person just as he or she is. Love makes patience easy. It is much easier to be patient with our own children than with the children of people we don't know. If we really love our neighbours, we can accept their faults, and bear with their foolishness, and even endure their unkindness. Love indeed can cover a multitude of sins.

(2) It may mean that, if we love others, God will overlook a multitude of sins in us. In life, we meet two kinds of people. We meet those who have no faults at which the finger may be pointed; they are moral, orthodox and supremely respectable, but they are hard and austere and unable to understand why others make mistakes and fall into sin. We also meet those who have all kinds of faults, but they are kind and sympathetic

and they seldom or never condemn. It is the second kind of person to whom the heart more readily warms; and in all reverence we may say that it is so with God. He will forgive much to the person who loves others.

(3) It may mean that *God's* love covers the multitude of our sins. That is blessedly and profoundly true. It is the wonder of grace that, sinners as we are, God loves us; that is why he sent his Son.

CHRISTIAN RESPONSIBILITY

I Peter 4:9–10

> Be hospitable to one another and never grudge it. As each has received a gift from God, so let all use such gifts in the service of one another, like good stewards of the grace of God.

PETER's mind is dominated in this section by the conviction that the end of all things is near. It is of the greatest interest and significance to note that he does not use that conviction to urge people to withdraw from the world and to enter on a kind of private campaign to save their own souls; he uses it to urge them to go into the world and serve others. As Peter sees it, we will be happy if the end finds us not living a life of solitude but out in the world serving other people.

(1) First, Peter urges upon his people the duty of hospitality. Without hospitality, the early Church could not have existed. The travelling missionaries who spread the good news of the gospel had to find somewhere to stay, and there was no place for them to stay except in the homes of Christians. Such inns as did exist were impossibly expensive, impossibly filthy and notoriously immoral. Thus we find Peter lodging with Simon, a tanner (Acts 10:6); and Paul and his company were

to lodge with Mnason of Cyprus, an early disciple (Acts 21:16). Many nameless individuals in the early Church made Christian missionary work possible by opening the doors of their houses and homes.

Not only did the missionaries need hospitality; the local churches also needed it. For 200 years, there was no such thing as a church building. The church was compelled to meet in the houses of those who had bigger rooms and were prepared to lend them for the services of the congregation. Thus we read of the church which was in the house of Aquila and Priscilla (Romans 16:5; 1 Corinthians 16:19), and of the church which was in the house of Philemon (Philemon 2). Without those who were prepared to open their homes, the early Church could not have met for worship at all.

It is little wonder that again and again in the New Testament the duty of hospitality is pressed upon Christians. Christians are to extend hospitality (Romans 12:13). A bishop is to be hospitable (1 Timothy 3:2; Titus 1:8); the widows of the Church must have shown hospitality (1 Timothy 5:10). Christians must not forget to entertain strangers and must remember that some who have done so have entertained angels unawares (Hebrews 13:2). And it is always to be remembered that it was said to those on the right hand: 'I was a stranger, and you welcomed me', while the condemnation of those on the left hand was: 'I was a stranger and you did not welcome me' (Matthew 25:35, 25:43).

In the early days, the Church depended on the hospitality of its members; and to this day no greater gift can be offered than the welcome of a Christian home to the visitor to a strange place.

(2) Such gifts as anyone has must be placed ungrudgingly at the service of the community. This again is a favourite New Testament idea, which is expanded by Paul in Romans

12:3–8 and 1 Corinthians 12. The Church needs every gift
that we have. It may be a gift of speaking, of music, of the
ability to visit people. It may be a craft or skill which can be
used in the practical service of the Church. It may be a house
which we own or money which we have inherited. There is
no gift which cannot be placed at the service of Christ.

Christians have to regard themselves as stewards of God.
In the ancient world, the steward was very important. He
might be a slave, but his master's property was in his hands.
There were two main kinds of stewards – the *dispensator*, the
dispenser, who was responsible for all the domestic arrange-
ments of the household and ordered in and divided out the
household supplies; and the *vilicus*, the bailiff, who was in
charge of his master's estates and acted as landlord to his
master's tenants. The steward knew very well that none of
the things over which he had control belonged to him; they
all belonged to his master. In everything he did, he was
answerable to his master, and always it was his interests he
must serve.

Christians must live in the certain knowledge that nothing
they possess of material goods or personal qualities is their
own; they all belong to God, and they must always use what
they have in the interests of God, to whom they are always
answerable.

THE SOURCE AND OBJECT OF ALL
CHRISTIAN ENDEAVOUR

1 Peter 4:11

> If anyone speaks, let him speak as one uttering sayings
> sent from God. If anyone renders any service, let him
> do so as one whose service comes from the strength

which God supplies, so that God may be glorified in all
things through Jesus Christ to whom belong glory and
power for ever and ever. Amen.

PETER is thinking of the two great activities of the Christian
Church – preaching and practical service. The word he uses
for *sayings* is *logia*. That is a word with a kind of divine
background. The Greeks and Romans used it for the oracles
which came to them from their gods; Christians used it for
the words of Scripture and the words of Christ. So Peter is
saying: 'Whoever has the duty of preaching must preach not
as one offering personal opinions or passing on personal
prejudices, but as one with a message from God.' It was said
of one great preacher: 'First he listened to God, and then he
spoke to men.' It was said of another that from time to time
he paused 'as if listening for a voice'. There lies the secret of
preaching power.

Peter goes on to say that if Christians are engaged in
practical service they must render that service in the strength
which God supplies. It is as if he said: 'When you are engaged
in Christian service, you must not do it as if you were con-
ferring a personal favour or distributing generous gifts from
your own store, but in the consciousness that what you give
you first received from God.' Such an attitude preserves the
giver from pride and the gift from humiliation.

The aim of everything is that God should be glorified.
Preaching is done not to display the preacher but to bring men
and women face to face with God. Service is rendered not to
bring prestige to the giver but to turn people's thoughts to
God. The scholar E. G. Selwyn reminds us that the motto of
the great Benedictine Order of monks is four letters – IOGD
– which stand for the Latin words (*ut*) *in omnibus glorificetur
Deus* (*in order that in all things God may be glorified*). A

new grace and glory would enter the Church if all church people stopped doing things for themselves and did them for God.

THE INEVITABILITY OF PERSECUTION

I Peter 4:12–13

> Beloved, do not regard the fiery ordeal through which you are passing, and which has happened to you to test you, as something strange, as if some alien experience were happening to you, but rejoice in so far as you share the sufferings of Christ so that you may also rejoice with rapture when his glory shall be revealed.

IN the nature of things, persecution must have been a much more daunting experience for Gentiles than it was for Jews. The average Gentile had little experience of it; but the Jews have always been the most persecuted people upon earth. Peter was writing to Christians who were Gentiles, and he had to try to help them by showing them persecution in its true terms. It is never easy to be a Christian. The Christian life brings it own loneliness, its own unpopularity, its own problems, its own sacrifices and its own persecutions. It is, therefore, good to have certain great principles in our minds.

(1) It is Peter's view that persecution is inevitable. It is human nature to dislike and to regard with suspicion anyone who is different; Christians are bound to be different from men and women of the world. The particular impact of the Christian difference makes the matter more acute. To the world, Christians bring the standards of Jesus Christ. That is another way of saying that they are inevitably a kind of conscience to any society in which they live – and many would gladly eliminate the troublesome twinges of conscience. The

very goodness of Christianity can be an offence to a world in which goodness is regarded as a handicap.

(2) It is Peter's view that persecution is a test. It is a test in a double sense. Devotion to a principle can be measured by a person's willingness to suffer for it; therefore, any kind of persecution is a test of a person's faith. But it is equally true that it is only the real Christian who will be persecuted. The Christian who compromises with the world will not be persecuted. In a double sense, persecution is the test of the reality of a person's faith.

(3) Now we come to the uplifting things. Persecution is a sharing in the sufferings of Jesus Christ. When people have to suffer for their Christianity, they are walking the way their Master walked and sharing the cross their Master carried. This is a favourite New Testament thought. If we suffer with him, we will be glorified with him (Romans 8:17). It is Paul's desire to enter into the fellowship of the sufferings of Christ (Philippians 3:10). If we suffer with him, we shall reign with him (2 Timothy 2:12). If we remember that, anything we must suffer for the sake of Christ becomes a privilege and not a penalty.

(4) Persecution is the way to glory. The cross is the way to the crown. Jesus Christ is no one's debtor, and his joy and crown await all who, through thick and thin, remain true to him.

THE BLESSEDNESS OF SUFFERING FOR CHRIST

1 Peter 4:14–16

> If you are reproached for the name of Christ, you are blessed because the presence of the glory and the Spirit

of God rest upon you. But let none of you suffer as a
murderer, or a thief, or an evildoer or a busybody. But
if anyone suffers as a Christian, let him not be ashamed,
but let him by this name bring glory to God.

HERE, Peter says the greatest thing of all. If someone suffers
for Christ, *the presence of the glory* rests upon that person.
This is a very strange phrase. We think it can mean only one
thing. The Jews believed in what was called the *Shekinah*, the
luminous glow of the very presence of God. This idea constantly recurs in the Old Testament. 'In the morning,' said
Moses, 'you shall see the *glory* of the Lord' (Exodus 16:7).
'The *glory* of the Lord settled on Mount Sinai, and the cloud
covered it for six days' when the law was being delivered to
Moses (Exodus 24:16). In the tabernacle, God was to meet
with Israel and it was to be sanctified with his *glory* (Exodus
29:43). When the tabernacle was completed, 'then the cloud
covered the tent of meeting, and the *glory* of the Lord filled
the tabernacle' (Exodus 40:34). When the ark of the covenant
was brought into Solomon's temple, 'a cloud filled the house
of the Lord, so that the priests could not stand to minister
because of the cloud; for the *glory* of the Lord filled the house
of the Lord' (1 Kings 8:10–11). Repeatedly this idea of the
Shekinah, the luminous glory of God, occurs in the Old
Testament.

It is Peter's conviction that something of that glow of glory
rests on those who suffer for Christ. When Stephen was on
trial for his life and it was certain that he would be condemned
to death, to those who looked on him his face was like the
face of an angel (Acts 6:15).

Peter goes on to point out that it is as a Christian that a
person must suffer and not as an evildoer. The evils which he
singles out are all clear enough until we come to the last. A

Christian, Peter says, is not to suffer as an *allotriepiskopos*, which we have translated as *busybody*. The trouble is that there is no other instance of this word in Greek, and Peter may well have invented it. It can have three possible meanings, all of which would be relevant. It comes from two words, *allotrios*, *belonging to another*, and *episkopos*, *looking upon* or *looking into*. Therefore, it literally means *looking upon*, or *into*, *that which belongs to another*.

(1) To look on that which is someone else's might well be to cast covetous eyes upon it. That is how both the Latin Bible and the reformer John Calvin take this word – to mean that Christians must not *covet*.

(2) To look upon that which belongs to another might well mean to be too interested in other people's affairs and to be a meddling busybody. That is by far the most probable meaning. There are Christians who do an infinite amount of harm with misguided interference and criticism. This would mean that the Christian must never be an *interfering busybody*. That makes good sense and, we believe, the best sense.

(3) There is a third possibility. *Allotrios* means *that which belongs to someone else*; that is to say, *that which is foreign to oneself*. Along that line of thought, *allotriepiskopos* will mean *looking upon that which is foreign to oneself*. That would mean, of a Christian, entering into undertakings which do not befit the Christian life. This would mean that a Christian must never take an interest in things which are alien to the life that Christians should lead.

While all three meanings are possible, we think that the third is the right one.

It is Peter's instruction that if Christians have to suffer for Christ, they must do so in such a way that their suffering brings glory to God and to the name they bear. Their lives and conduct must be the best argument that they do not deserve the suffering which has come upon them, and their attitude to it must commend the name they bear.

ENTRUSTING ALL LIFE TO GOD

1 Peter 4:17–19

> For the time has come for judgment to begin from the household of God. And, if it begins from us, what will be the end of those who disobey the good news which comes from God? And, if the righteous man is scarcely saved, where will the impious man and the sinner appear? So, then, let those who suffer in accordance with the will of God entrust their souls to him who is a Creator on whom you can rely, and continue to do right.

As Peter saw it, it was all the more necessary for Christians to do right because judgment was about to begin.

It was to begin with the household of God. Ezekiel hears the voice of God proclaiming judgment upon his people: 'Begin at my sanctuary' (Ezekiel 9:6). Where the privilege has been greatest, there the judgment will be sternest.

If judgment is to fall upon the Church of God, what will be the fate of those who have been utterly disobedient to the invitation and command of God? Peter confirms his appeal with a quotation from Proverbs 11:31: 'If the righteous are repaid on earth, how much more the wicked and the sinner!'

Finally, Peter exhorts his people to continue to do good and, whatever happens to them, to entrust their lives to God, the Creator on whom they can rely. The word he uses for *to entrust* is *paratithesthai*, which is the technical word for *depositing money with a trusted friend*. In the ancient world, there were no banks and few really safe places in which to deposit money. So, before a man went on a journey, he often left his money in the safe-keeping of a friend. Such a trust was regarded as one of the most sacred things in life. The friend was absolutely bound by all honour and all religion to return the money intact.

Herodotus, the Greek historian (6:86), has a story about such a trust. A certain Milesian came to Sparta, for he had heard of the strict honour of the Spartans, and entrusted his money to a certain Glaucus. He said that in due time his sons would reclaim the money and would bring tokens which would establish their identity beyond doubt. The time passed and the sons came. Glaucus treacherously said that he had no recollection of any money being entrusted to him and said that he wanted four months to think about it. The Milesians departed sad and sorry. Glaucus consulted the gods as to what he ought to do, and they warned him that he must return the money. He did so, but before long he died and all his family followed him, and in the time of Herodotus there was not a single member of his family left alive because the gods were angry that he had even contemplated breaking the trust placed in him. Even to think of evading such a trust was a mortal sin.

If we entrust ourselves to God, God will not fail us. If such a trust is sacred to us, how much more is it sacred to God? This is the very word used by Jesus when he says: 'Father, into your hands I commend my spirit' (Luke 23:46). Jesus unhesitatingly entrusted his life to God, certain that God would not fail him – and so may we. The old advice is still good advice – trust in God and do the right.

THE ELDERS OF THE CHURCH

1 Peter 5:1–4

> So, then, as your fellow elder and a witness of the
> sufferings of Christ, as a sharer in the glory which is
> going to be revealed, I urge the elders who are among
> you, shepherd the flock of God which is in your charge,
> not because you are coerced into doing so, but of your
> own free will as God would have you to do, not to make
> a shameful profit out of it, but with enthusiasm, not as if
> you aimed to be petty tyrants over those allotted to your
> care, but as being under the obligation to be examples
> to the flock; and when the chief shepherd appears, you
> will receive the unfading crown of glory.

FEW passages show more clearly the importance of the
eldership in the early Church. It is to the elders that Peter
specially writes; and he, who was the chief of the apostles,
does not hesitate to call himself a fellow elder. It will be worth
our while to look at something of the background and history
of the eldership, the most ancient and the most important office
in the Church.

(1) It has a Jewish background. The Jews traced the
beginning of the eldership to the days when the children of
Israel were journeying through the wilderness to the promised
land. There came a time when Moses felt the burdens of
leadership too heavy for him to bear alone, and to help him
seventy elders were set apart and granted a share of the spirit
of God (Numbers 11:16–30). Thereafter, elders became a
permanent feature of Jewish life. We find them as the friends
of the prophets (2 Kings 6:32), as the advisers of kings
(1 Kings 20:8, 21:11) and as the colleagues of the princes in
the administration of the affairs of the nation (Ezra 10:8).
Every village and city had its elders; they met at the gate and

dispensed justice to the people (Deuteronomy 25:7). The elders were the administrators of the synagogue; they did not preach, but they saw to the good government and order of the synagogue, and they exercised discipline over its members. The elders formed a large section of the Sanhedrin, the supreme court of the Jews, and they are regularly mentioned along with the chief priests and the rulers and the scribes and the Pharisees (Matthew 16:21, 21:23, 26:3, 26:57, 27:1, 27:3; Luke 7:3; Acts 4:5, 6:12, 24:1). In the vision of the Book of Revelation, in the heavenly places there are twenty-four elders around the throne (Revelation 4:4). The elders were woven into the very structure of Judaism, both in its civil and its religious affairs.

(2) The eldership has a Greek background. Especially in Egyptian communities, we find that elders are the leaders of the community and responsible for the conduct of public affairs, much as town councillors are today. We find a woman who had suffered an assault appealing to the elders for justice. When corn is being collected as payment on the visit of a governor, we find that 'the elders of the cultivators' are the officials concerned. We find them connected with the issuing of public edicts, the leasing of land for pasture, and the collection of taxation. In Asia Minor, also, the members of councils were called elders. Even in the religious communities of the Gentile world, we find 'elder priests' who were responsible for discipline. In the Socnopaeus temple, we find the elder priests dealing with the case of a priest who is charged with allowing his hair to grow too long and with wearing woollen garments – actions which were considered unmanly and too luxurious and of which no priest should have been guilty.

We can see that, long before Christianity took it over, *elder* was a title of honour both in the Jewish and in the Graeco-Roman world.

THE CHRISTIAN ELDERSHIP

1 Peter 5:1–4 (*contd*)

WHEN we turn to the Christian Church, we find that the eldership is its basic office.

It was Paul's custom to ordain elders in every community to which he preached and in every church which he founded. On the first missionary journey, elders were ordained in every church (Acts 14:23). Titus is left in Crete to ordain elders in every city (Titus 1:5). The elders had charge of the financial administration of the Church; it is to them that Paul and Barnabas delivered the money sent to relieve the poor of Jerusalem in the time of the famine (Acts 11:30). The elders were the councillors and the administrators of the Church. We find them taking a leading part in the Council of Jerusalem, at which it was decided to fling open the doors of the Church to the Gentiles. At that Council, the elders and the apostles are spoken of together as the chief authorities of the Church (Acts 15:2, 16:4). When Paul came on his last visit to Jerusalem, it was to the elders that he reported, and they suggested the course of action he should follow (Acts 21:18–25). One of the most moving passages in the New Testament is Paul's farewell to the elders of Ephesus. We find there that the elders, as he sees them, are the overseers of the flock of God and the defenders of the faith (Acts 20:28–9). We learn from James that the elders had a healing function in the Church through prayers and anointing with oil (James 5:14). From the Pastoral Epistles, we learn that they were rulers and teachers, and by that time paid officials (1 Timothy 5:17; the phrase *double honour* is better translated as *double pay*).

When people enter the eldership, no small honour is conferred upon them, for they are entering the oldest religious

office in the world, whose history can be traced through
Christianity and Judaism for 4,000 years; and no small
responsibility falls upon them, for they have been ordained
shepherds of the flock of God and defenders of the faith.

THE PERILS AND PRIVILEGES
OF THE ELDERSHIP

1 Peter 5:1-4 (*contd*)

PETER sets down in a series of contrasts the perils and the
privileges of the eldership; and everything he says is applicable
not only to the eldership but also to all Christian service inside
and outside the Church.

The elder is to accept office, not under pressure but
willingly. This does not mean that anyone is to grasp at
office or to enter into it without self-examining thought.
All Christians will have a certain reluctance to accept
high office, because they know only too well their own
unworthiness and inadequacy. There is a sense in which
it is by compulsion that people accept office and enter
into Christian service. 'An obligation', said Paul, 'is laid
upon me, and woe betide me if I do not proclaim the
gospel' (1 Corinthians 9:16). 'The love of Christ urges us
on', he said (2 Corinthians 5:14). But, on the other hand,
there is a way of accepting office and of rendering service
as if it was a grim and unpleasant duty. It is quite possible
for someone to agree to a request in such an ungracious
way that the whole action is spoiled. Peter does not say that
people should be conceitedly or irresponsibly eager for office,
but that all Christians should be anxious to render such service
as they can, although fully aware how unworthy they are to
render it.

The elder is to accept office, not to make a shameful profit out of it, but eagerly. The word for *making a shameful profit* is the adverb *aischrokerdēs*. The noun from this is *aischrokerdeia*, and it was a characteristic which the Greeks loathed. Theophrastus, the great Greek master of the character study, has a sketch of this *aischrokerdeia*. *Meanness* – as it might be translated – is the desire for base gain. Mean people are those who never set enough food before their guests and who give themselves a double portion when they are carving the joint. They water the wine; they go to the theatre only when they can get free tickets. They never have enough money to pay the fare and always borrow from other people. When such people are selling corn, they use a measure in which the bottom is pushed up, and even then they carefully level the top. They count the half-radishes left over from dinner in case the servants eat any. Rather than give a wedding present, they will go away from home when a wedding is in the offing.

Meanness is an ugly fault. It is quite clear that there were people in the early Church who accused the preachers and missionaries of being in the job for what they could get out of it. Paul repeatedly declares that he coveted no one's property and worked with his hands to meet his own needs so that he was a burden to no one (Acts 20:33; 1 Thessalonians 2:9; 1 Corinthians 9:12; 2 Corinthians 12:14). It is certain that the payment any early office-bearer received was pitifully small, and the repeated warnings that the office-bearers must not be greedy for gain shows that there were those who coveted more (1 Timothy 3:3, 3:8; Titus 1:7, 1:11). The point that Peter is making – and it is still valid – is that no one dares accept office or render service for what can be got out of it. The desire must always be to give and not to get.

The elder is to accept office, not to be a petty tyrant, but to be the shepherd and the example of the flock. Human nature is such that, for many people, prestige and power are even more attractive than money. There are those who love authority, even if it be exercised in a narrow sphere. In *Paradise Lost*, John Milton's Satan thought it better to reign in hell than to serve in heaven. In *Measure for Measure*, Shakespeare spoke about proud man, dressed in a little brief authority, playing such fantastic tricks before high heaven as would make the angels weep. The great characteristic of shepherds is their selfless care and their sacrificial love for the sheep. Anyone who enters into office with the desire for status and superiority is looking at the task in quite the wrong way. Jesus said to his ambitious disciples: 'You know that among the Gentiles those whom they recognize as their rulers lord it over them, and their great ones are tyrants over them. But it is not so among you; but whoever wishes to become great among you must be your servant, and whoever wishes to be first among you must be slave of all' (Mark 10:42–4).

THE IDEAL OF THE ELDERSHIP

1 Peter 5:1–4 (*contd*)

ONE thing in this passage which defies translation and yet is one of the most precious and significant things in it is what we have translated as *petty tyrants over those allotted to your care*. The phrase which we have translated as *those allotted* is curious in Greek; it is *tōn klēron*, the genitive plural of *klēros*, which is a word of extraordinary interest.

(1) It begins by meaning a *die* or a *lot*. It is used in this sense in Matthew 27:35, which tells how the soldiers beneath the cross were throwing dice (*klēroi*) to see who should possess the seamless robe of Jesus.

(2) Second, it means an office gained or assigned by *lot*. It is the word used in Acts 1:26, which tells how the disciples cast lots to see who should inherit the office of Judas the traitor.

(3) It then comes to mean an inheritance allotted to someone, as used in Colossians 1:12 for the *inheritance* of the saints

(4) In classical Greek, it very often means a public allotment or estate of land. These allotments were distributed by the civic authorities to the citizens, and very often the distribution was made by drawing lots for the various pieces of land available for distribution.

Even if we were to go no further than this, it would mean that the office of the eldership and, indeed, any piece of service offered to us is never *earned* by any merit of our own but always *allotted* to us by God. It is never something that we have deserved but always something given to us by the grace of God.

But we *can* go further than this. *Klēros* means something which is allotted to a person. In Deuteronomy 9:29, we read that Israel is God's very own possession (*klēros*). That is to say, Israel is the people specially assigned to God by his own choice. Israel is the *klēros* of God; the congregation is the *klēros* of the elder. Just as Israel is allotted to God, the duties of the elders in the congregation are allotted to them. This must mean that the whole attitude of elders to their people must be the same as the attitude of God to his people.

Here we have another great thought. In verse 2, there is a phrase in the best Greek manuscripts which is not in the Authorized or the Revised Standard Versions. We have translated it as 'Shepherd the flock of God, which is in your charge, not because you are coerced into doing so, but of your own free will *as God would have you to do.*' *As God would have you to do* is in Greek *kata theon*, and that could well mean quite simply *like God*. Peter says to the elders: 'Shepherd your people *like God*.' Just as Israel is God's special allotment, the people we have to serve in the Church or anywhere else are our special allotment, and our attitude to them must be the attitude of God.

What an ideal! And what a condemnation! It is our task to show to people God's forbearance, his forgiveness, his seeking love, his service which has no end. God has allotted to us a task, and we must do it as he himself would do it. That is the supreme ideal of service in the Christian Church.

MEMORIES OF JESUS

1 Peter 5:1–4 (*contd*)

ONE of the lovely things about this passage is Peter's attitude throughout it. He begins by, as it were, taking his place beside those to whom he speaks. 'Your fellow elder', he calls himself. He does not separate himself from them but comes to share the Christian problems and the Christian experience with them. But in one thing he is different: he has memories of Jesus, and these memories colour this whole passage. Even as he speaks, they are crowding into his mind.

(1) He describes himself as a witness of the sufferings of Christ. At first sight, we might be inclined to question that statement, for we are told that, after the arrest in the garden, 'All the disciples deserted him and fled' (Matthew 26:56). But, when we think a little further, we realize that it was given to Peter to see the suffering of Jesus in a more poignant way than was given to any other human being. He followed Jesus into the courtyard of the high priest's house, and there in a time of weakness he denied his Master three times. The trial came to an end and Jesus was taken away; and there

comes what may well be the most tragic sentence in the New Testament: 'The Lord turned and looked at Peter . . . And he went out and wept bitterly' (Luke 22:61–2). In that look, Peter saw the suffering of the heart of a leader whose follower had failed him in the hour of his most bitter need. Peter was indeed a witness of the suffering that comes to Christ when people deny him, and that is why he was so eager that his people might be resolute in loyalty and faithful in service.

(2) He describes himself as a sharer in the glory which is going to be revealed. That statement has a backward and a forward look. Peter had already had a glimpse of that glory on the Mount of Transfiguration. There the three sleeping disciples had been awakened; and, as Luke puts it, 'since they had stayed awake, they saw his glory' (Luke 9:32). Peter had seen the glory. But he also knew that there was glory to come, for Jesus had promised his disciples a share in the glory when the Son of Man should come to sit on his glorious throne (Matthew 19:28). Peter remembered both the experience and the promise of glory.

(3) There can surely be no doubt that, when Peter speaks of shepherding the flock of God, he is remembering the task that Jesus had given to him when he had told him to feed his sheep (John 21:15–17). The reward of love was the appointment as a shepherd; and Peter is remembering it.

(4) When Peter speaks of Jesus as the chief shepherd, many memories must be in his mind. Jesus had likened himself to the shepherd who searched at the peril of his life for the sheep which was lost (Matthew 18:12–14; Luke 15:4–7). He had sent out his disciples to gather in the lost sheep of the house of Israel (Matthew 10:6). He was moved with pity for the crowds, for they were as sheep without a shepherd (Matthew 9:36; Mark 6:34). Above all, Jesus had likened himself to the

good shepherd who was ready to lay down his life for the
sheep (John 10:1–18). The picture of Jesus as the shepherd
was a precious one, and the privilege of being a shepherd of
the flock of Christ was for Peter the greatest privilege that a
servant of Christ could enjoy.

THE GARMENT OF HUMILITY

1 Peter 5:5

> In the same way, you younger people must be submissive
> to those who are older. In your relationships with one
> another you must clothe yourselves with the garment of
> humility, because God opposes the proud but gives grace
> to the humble.

PETER returns to the thought that the denial of self must be
the mark of the Christian. He clinches his argument with
a quotation from the Old Testament: 'Toward the scorners
he [God] is scornful, but to the humble he shows favour'
(Proverbs 3:34).

Here again, it may well be that the memories of Jesus are
in Peter's heart and are colouring all his thought and language.
He tells his people that they must *clothe themselves* with the
garment of humility. The word he uses for *to clothe oneself* is
very unusual; it is *egkombousthai*, which is derived from
kombos, and describes anything tied on with a knot. Connected
with it is *egkombōma*, a garment tied on with a knot. It was
commonly used for protective clothing; it was used for a pair
of sleeves drawn over the sleeves of a robe and tied behind
the neck. And it was used for a slave's apron. There was a
time when Jesus had put upon himself just such an apron. At
the Last Supper, John says of him that he tied a towel around
himself, and took water and began to wash his disciples' feet

(John 13:4–5). Jesus put on the apron of humility, and so must his followers.

It so happens that *egkombousthai* is used of another kind of garment. It is also used of putting on a long, stole-like garment which was the sign of honour and prestige.

To complete the picture, we must put both images together. Jesus once put on the slave's apron and undertook the humblest of all duties, washing his disciples' feet; so we must in all things put on the apron of humility in the service of Christ and of other people; but that very apron of humility will become the garment of honour for us, for it is the one who is the servant of all who is greatest in the kingdom of heaven.

THE LAWS OF THE CHRISTIAN LIFE (1)

I Peter 5:6–11

So, then, humble yourselves under the mighty hand of God that in his good time he may exalt you.

Cast all your anxiety upon him because he cares for you.

Be sober; be watchful. Your adversary the devil prowls around like a roaring lion, seeking someone to devour. Stand up to him, staunch in the faith, knowing how to pay the same tax of suffering as your brethren in the world.

And after you have experienced suffering for a little while, the God of every grace, who called you to his eternal glory in Christ, will himself restore, establish, strengthen, settle you.

To him be dominion for ever and ever. Amen.

HERE, Peter speaks in imperatives: he gives orders laying down certain laws for the Christian life.

(1) There is the law of humility before God. Christians must humble themselves under his mighty hand. The phrase *the mighty hand of God* is common in the Old Testament, and it is most often used in connection with the deliverance which God performed for his people when he brought them out of Egypt. 'With a strong hand,' said Moses, 'the Lord brought you out of Egypt' (Exodus 13:9). 'You have only begun to show your servant your greatness and your might' (Deuteronomy 3:24). God brought his people forth out of Egypt with a mighty hand (Deuteronomy 9:26). The idea is that God's mighty hand is on the destiny of his people, if they will humbly and faithfully accept his guidance. After all the varied experiences of life, Joseph could say to the brothers who had once sought to eliminate him: 'Even though you intended to do harm to me, God intended it for good' (Genesis 50:20). Christians never resent the experiences of life and never rebel against them, because they know that the mighty hand of God is in control of their lives and that he has a destiny for them.

(2) There is the law of Christian serenity in God. Christians must cast all their anxiety upon God. 'Cast your burden on the Lord', said the psalmist (Psalm 55:22). 'Do not worry about tomorrow', said Jesus (Matthew 6:34). The reason we can do this with confidence is that we can be certain that God cares for us. As Paul had it, we can be certain that he who gave us his only Son will with him give us all things (Romans 8:32). We can be certain that, since God cares for us, life is out not to break us but to make us; and, with that assurance, we can accept any experience which comes to us, knowing that in everything God works for good with those who love him (Romans 8:28).

(3) There is the law of Christian effort and of Christian vigilance. We must be sober and watchful. The fact that we

cast everything upon God does not give us the right to sit back and to do nothing. The advice of the Lord Protector of England, Oliver Cromwell, to his troops was: 'Trust in God, and keep your powder dry.' Peter knew how hard this vigilance was, for he remembered how in Gethsemane he and his fellow disciples had slept when they should have been watching with Christ (Matthew 26:38–46). Christians are men and women who trust but at the same time put all their effort and all their vigilance into the business of living for Christ.

(4) There is the law of Christian resistance. The devil is always out to see whom he can ruin. Again, Peter must have been remembering how the devil had overcome him and he had denied his Lord. Our faith must be like a solid wall against which the attacks of the devil exhaust themselves in vain. The devil is like any bully, and retreats when he is bravely resisted in the strength of Jesus Christ.

THE LAWS OF THE CHRISTIAN LIFE (2)

1 Peter 5:6–11 (contd)

(5) Finally, Peter speaks of the law of Christian suffering. He says that, after Christians have gone through suffering, God will restore, establish, strengthen and settle them. Every one of the words which Peter uses has behind it a vivid picture. Each tells us something about what suffering is designed by God to do for us.

(a) Through suffering, God will *restore* us. The word for *restore* is difficult in this case to translate. It is *kartarizein*, the word commonly used for setting a fracture, the word used in Mark 1:19 for mending nets. It means to supply that which is missing, to mend that which is broken. So suffering, if accepted in humility and trust and love, can repair weaknesses of character and add the greatness which has not yet been achieved. It is said that the composer Sir Edward Elgar once listened to a young girl singing a solo from one of his own works. She had a voice of exceptional purity and clarity and range, and an almost perfect technique. When she had finished, Sir Edward said softly: 'She will be really great when something happens to break her heart.' The writer J. M. Barrie tells how his mother lost her favourite son, and then says: 'That is where my mother got her soft eyes, and that is why other mothers ran to her when they had lost a child.' Suffering had done something for her that an easy way could never have done. Suffering is meant by God to add an intensity to life.

(b) Through suffering, God will *establish* us. The word is *stērixein*, which means to make as solid as granite. Suffering of body and sorrow of heart do one of two things to us. They either make us collapse or they leave us with a solidity of character which we could never have gained anywhere else. If we meet them with continuing trust in Christ, we emerge like hardened steel that has been toughened in the fire.

(c) Through suffering, God will *strengthen* us. The Greek is *sthenoun*, which means *to fill with strength*. Here is the same sense again. A life with no effort and no discipline almost inevitably becomes a flabby life. We never really know what our faith means to us until it has been tried in the furnace of affliction. There is something doubly precious about a faith which has come victoriously through pain and sorrow and disappointment. The wind will extinguish a weak flame, but it will fan a strong flame into a still greater blaze. So it is with faith.

(d) Through suffering, God will *settle* us. The Greek is *themelioun*, which means *to lay the foundations*. When we have to meet sorrow and suffering, we are driven down to the

very bedrock of faith. It is then that we discover the things
which cannot be shaken. It is in time of trial that we discover
the great truths on which real life is founded.

Suffering is very far from doing these precious things for
everyone. It may well drive some people to bitterness and
despair, and may well take away such faith as they have. But,
if it is accepted in the trusting certainty that a father's hand
will never cause his child a needless tear, then out of suffering
come things which the easy way may never bring.

A FAITHFUL COLLEAGUE TO THE APOSTLES

I Peter 5:12

> I have written this brief letter to you through Silvanus,
> the faithful brother, as I reckon him to be, to encourage
> you and to testify that this is the true grace of God. Stand
> fast in it.

PETER bears witness that what he has written is indeed the
grace of God, and he bids his people, through all their
difficulties, to stand fast in it.

He says that he has written *through Silvanus*. The Greek
phrase (*dia Silouanou*) means that Silvanus was his agent in
writing. Silvanus is the full form of the name Silas, and he is
almost certainly to be identified with the Silvanus of Paul's
letters and the Silas of Acts. When we gather up the references
to Silas or Silvanus, we find that he was one of the pillars of
the early Church.

Along with Judas Barsabas, Silvanus was sent to Antioch
with the epoch-making decision of the Council of Jerusalem
that the doors of the Church were to be opened to the Gentiles;
and in the account of that mission Silvanus and Judas are
called leading men among the Christian community (Acts

15:22, 15:27). Not only did he simply bear the message, he commended it in powerful words, for Silvanus was also a prophet (Acts 15:32). During the first missionary journey, Mark left Paul and Barnabas and returned home from Pamphylia (Acts 13:13); in preparing for the second missionary journey, Paul refused to have Mark with him again; the result was that Barnabas took Mark as his companion and Paul took Silvanus (Acts 15:37–40). From that time forward, Silvanus was for a long period Paul's right-hand man. He was with Paul in Philippi, where he was arrested and imprisoned with him (Acts 16:19, 16:25, 16:29). He rejoined Paul in Corinth and preached the gospel there with him (Acts 18:5; 2 Corinthians 1:19). So closely was he associated with Paul that in both the letters to the Thessalonians he is joined with Paul and Timothy as the senders of the letters (1 Thessalonians 1:1; 2 Thessalonians 1:1). It is clear that Silvanus was a most notable man in the early Church.

As we saw in the introduction, it is most probable that Silvanus was far more than merely the scribe who wrote this letter for Peter and the bearer who delivered it. One of the difficulties of 1 Peter is the excellence of the Greek. It is Greek with such a classical tinge that it seems impossible that Peter the Galilaean fisherman could have written it for himself. Now, Silvanus was not only a man of standing in the Church; he was also a Roman citizen (Acts 16:37), and he would be much better educated than Peter was. Most probably, he had a large part in the composition of this letter. We are told that in China, when a missionary wanted to send a message to his people, he often wrote it in the best Chinese he could achieve, and then gave it to a Chinese Christian to correct and put into proper form; or he might even just tell the Chinese Christian what he wanted to say, leaving him to put it into literary form for his approval. That is most likely what Peter did. Either he gave his letter to Silvanus to polish into excellent Greek or else he told Silvanus what he had in mind and left him to say it, adding the last three verses as his personal greeting.

Silvanus was one of those people the Church can never do without. He was content to take second place and to serve almost in the background as long as God's work was done. It was enough for him that he was Paul's assistant, even if Paul always overshadowed him. It was enough for him to be Peter's penman, even if it meant only a bare mention of his name at the end of the letter. For all that, it is no small thing to go down in history as the faithful colleague on whom both Peter and Paul depended. The Church always has need of people like Silvanus, and many who cannot be Peters or Pauls can still assist the Peters and Pauls to do their work.

GREETINGS

1 Peter 5:13

> She who is at Babylon, and who has been chosen as you have been chosen, greets you, and so does Mark my son.

ALTHOUGH it sounds so simple, this is a troublesome verse. It presents us with certain questions to which it is difficult to find a solution.

(1) From whom are these greetings sent? The Authorized Version has 'the church that is at Babylon elected together with you, saluteth you'. But *the church that is* is in italics, which means that there is no equivalent in the Greek, which simply says *the one elected together with you at Babylon* – and the phrase is feminine. There are two possibilities.

(a) It is quite possible that the Authorized Version is correct. That is the way James Moffatt takes it when he

translates it as 'your sister church in Babylon'. The phrase
could well be explained as being based on the fact that the
Church is the bride of Christ and may be spoken of in this
way. On the whole, the most common view is that it is a church
which is meant.

(b) But it does have to be remembered that there is actually
no word for *church* in the Greek, and this feminine phrase
might equally well refer to some well-known Christian lady.
If it does, by far the best suggestion is that the reference is to
Peter's wife. We know that she did actually accompany him
on his preaching journeys (1 Corinthians 9:5). Clement of
Alexandria (*Stromateis*, 7:11:63) tells us that she died a martyr,
executed in Peter's own sight, while he encouraged her by
saying: 'Remember the Lord.' She was clearly a well-known
figure in the early Church.

We would not wish to speak dogmatically on this question.
It is perhaps more likely that the reference is to a church, but
it is not impossible that Peter is associating his wife and fellow
evangelist in the greetings which he sends.

(2) From where was this letter written? The greetings are
sent from *Babylon*. There are three possibilities.

(a) There was a Babylon in Egypt, near Cairo. It had been
founded by Babylonian refugees from Assyria and was called
by the name of their ancestral city. But, by this time, it was
almost exclusively a great military camp; and in any event
the name of Peter is never connected with Egypt. This Babylon
may be disregarded.

(b) There was the Babylon in the east to which the Jews
had been taken in captivity. Many had never come back, and
it was a centre of Jewish scholarship. The great commentary
on the Jewish law is called the Babylonian Talmud. So
important were the Jews of Babylon that the Jewish historian
Josephus had issued a special edition of his histories for them.

There is no doubt that there was a large and important colony of Jews there; and it would have been quite natural for Peter, the apostle of the Jews, to preach and to work there. But we do not find the name of Peter ever connected with Babylon, and there is no trace of him having ever been there. Even such great Reformation scholars as Calvin and Erasmus have taken Babylon to be this great eastern city; but, on the whole, we think the probabilities are against it.

(c) Rome was regularly called Babylon, both by the Jews and by the Christians. That is undoubtedly the case in the Book of Revelation, where Babylon is the great whore, drunk with the blood of the saints and the martyrs (Revelation 17–18). The godlessness, lust and luxury of ancient Babylon were, so to speak, reincarnated in Rome. Peter is definitely connected in tradition with Rome; and the likelihood is that it was from there that the letter was written.

(3) Who is the Mark, whom Peter calls his son, and from whom he sends greetings? If we take the elect lady to be Peter's wife, Mark might quite well be literally Peter's son. But it is much more likely that he is the Mark who wrote the gospel. Tradition has always closely connected Peter with Mark, and has handed down the story that he was intimately involved with Mark's gospel. Papias, who lived towards the end of the second century and was a great collector of early traditions, describes Mark's gospel in this way: 'Mark, who was Peter's interpreter, wrote down accurately, though not in order, all that he recollected of what Christ had said or done. For he was not a hearer of the Lord, or a follower of his; he followed Peter, as I have said, at a later date, and Peter adapted his instructions to practical needs, without any attempt to give the Lord's words systematically. So that Mark was not wrong in writing down some things in this way from memory, for his one concern was neither to omit nor to falsify anything

that he had heard.' According to Papias, Mark's gospel is nothing other than the preaching material of Peter. In similar vein, Irenaeus, the second-century Bishop of Lyons, says that, after the deaths of Peter and Paul at Rome, 'Mark, the disciple and interpreter of Peter, also handed down to us in writing what had been preached by Peter.' It is the consistent story of tradition that Mark, the evangelist, was indeed a son to Peter; and all the likelihood is that these greetings are from him.

So, we may gather up the possibilities. 'She who is at Babylon, and who has been chosen, as you have been chosen' may either be the church or the wife of Peter, herself a martyr. Babylon may be the Babylon of the east but is more likely to be the great and wicked city of Rome. Mark might possibly be the actual son of Peter about whom we know nothing else, but is more likely to be Mark, the writer of the gospel, who was like a son to Peter.

AT PEACE WITH ONE ANOTHER

1 Peter 5:14

> Greet each other with a kiss of love. Peace be to you all
> that are in Christ.

THE most interesting thing here is the instruction to give each other the kiss of love. This was for centuries an integral and precious part of Christian fellowship and worship; and its history, and gradual elimination, is of the greatest interest.

With the Jews, it was the custom for a disciple to kiss his Rabbi on the cheek and to lay his hands upon his shoulder. That is what Judas did to Jesus (Mark 14:44). The kiss was the greeting of welcome and respect, and we can see how much Jesus valued it, for he was grieved when it was not given to him (Luke 7:45). Paul's letters frequently end with the bidding to salute each other with a holy kiss (Romans 16:16; 1 Corinthians 16:20; 2 Corinthians 13:12; 1 Thessalonians 5:26).

In the early Church, the kiss became an essential part of Christian worship. 'What prayer is complete', asks Tertullian, 'from which the holy kiss is divorced? What kind of sacrifice is that from which men depart without the peace?' (*Dex Oratione*, 18). The kiss, we see here, was called *the peace*. It was specially a part of the communion service. St Augustine says that, when Christians were about to receive communion, 'they demonstrated their inward peace by the outward kiss' (*De Amicitia*, 6). It was usually given after the catechumens, those who were still being instructed in the faith, had been dismissed, when only members of the church were present, and after the prayer before the elements were brought in. Justin Martyr says: 'When we have ceased from prayer, we salute one another with a kiss. There is then brought to the president bread and a cup of wine' (1:65). The kiss was preceded by the prayer 'for the gift of peace and of unfeigned love, undefiled by hypocrisy or deceit', and it was the sign that 'our souls are mingled together, and have banished all remembrance of wrongs' (Cyril of Jerusalem, *Catechetical Lectures*, 25:5:3). The kiss was the sign that all injuries were forgotten, all wrongs forgiven, and that those who sat at the Lord's table were indeed one in the Lord.

This was a lovely custom, and yet it is clear that it was sadly open to abuse. It is equally clear from the warnings so often given that abuses did creep in. Athenagoras insists that the kiss must be given with the greatest care, for 'if there be mixed with it the least defilement of thought, it excludes us from eternal life' (*Legatio Christianis*, 32). Origen insists that the kiss of peace must be 'holy, chaste and sincere', not like the kiss of Judas (*Commentaria in Epistolam B. Pauli ad*

Romanos, 10:33). Clement of Alexandria condemns the shameless use of the kiss, which ought to be mystic, for with the kiss 'certain persons make the churches resound, and thereby occasion foul suspicions and evil reports' (*Paedagogus*, 3:11). Tertullian speaks of the natural reluctance of the non-Christian husband to think that his wife should be greeted in this way in the Christian Church (*Ad Uxorem*, 2:4).

In the church of the west, these inevitable problems gradually brought the end of this lovely custom. By the time of the *Apostolic Constitutions* in the fourth century, the kiss is confined to those of the same sex – the clergy are to salute the bishop, the men the men and the women the women. In this form, the kiss of peace lasted in the church of the west until the thirteenth century. Sometimes substitutes were introduced. In some places, a little wooden or metal tablet, with a picture of the crucifixion on it, was used. It was kissed first by the priest, and then passed to the congregation, who each kissed it and handed it on to the person next to them, in token of their mutual love for Christ and in Christ. In the oriental churches, the custom still continues; it is not extinct in the Greek church; the Armenian church substituted a courteous bow.

We may note certain other uses of the kiss in the early Church. At baptism, the person baptized was kissed, first by the baptizer and then by the whole congregation, as a sign of welcome into the household and family of Christ. A newly ordained bishop was given 'the kiss in the Lord'. The marriage ceremony was sealed by a kiss, a natural action taken over from non-Christian practices. Those who were dying first kissed the cross and were then kissed by all present. The dead were kissed before burial.

To us, the kiss of peace may seem very far away. It came from the day when the Church was a real family and fellowship, when Christians really did know and love one another. It is a tragedy that the modern Church, often with vast congregations who do not know each other and do not even want to know each other, could not use the kiss of peace except as a formality. It was a lovely custom which was bound to cease when the reality of fellowship was lost within the Church.

'Peace to all of you that are in Christ', says Peter; and so he leaves his people to the peace of God, which is greater than all the troubles and distresses the world can bring.

INTRODUCTION TO THE
SECOND LETTER OF PETER

The Neglected Book and its Contents

Second Peter is one of the neglected books of the New Testament. Very few people will claim to have read it, still less to have studied it in detail. The New Testament scholar E. F. Scott says: 'it is far inferior in every respect to 1 Peter', and goes on: 'it is the least valuable of the New Testament writings'. It was only with the greatest difficulty that 2 Peter gained entry into the New Testament, and for many years the Christian Church seemed to be unaware of its existence. But, before we approach its history, let us look at its contents.

The Threat of the Lawless Life

Second Peter was written to combat the beliefs and activities of a group of people who were a threat to the Church. It begins by insisting that Christians are people who have escaped from the corruption of the world (1:4) and must always remember that they have been purged of their past sins (1:9). There is laid upon them the duty of moral goodness, which culminates in the great Christian virtue of love (1:5–8).

Let us set out the characteristics of those whom 2 Peter rebukes. They twist Scripture to make it suit their own purpose (1:20, 3:16). They bring the Christian faith into disrepute (2:2). They are greedy and seek personal gain, and they exploit others (2:3, 2:14–15). They are doomed and will share the fate of the sinning angels (2:4), the world before the Flood (2:5), the citizens of Sodom and Gomorrah (2:6) and the false prophet Balaam (2:15). They are irrational and sensual creatures, ruled by their animal instincts (2:12) and dominated by their lusts (2:10, 2:18). Their eyes are full of adultery (2:14). They are presumptuous, self-willed and arrogant (2:10, 2:18). They spend even the daylight hours in abandoned and luxurious revelry (2:13). They speak of liberty; but what they call liberty is unrestrained licence, and they themselves are the slaves of their own lusts (2:19). Not only are they deluded, they also delude others and lead them astray (2:14, 2:18). They are worse than those who never knew the right, because they knew what goodness is and have lapsed into evil, like a dog returning to its vomit and a sow returning to the mud after it has been washed (2:20–2).

It is clear that Peter is describing antinomians, those who used God's grace as a justification for sinning. In all probability they were Gnostics, who said that only spirit was good and that matter was essentially evil and that, therefore, what we did with the body was not important and that we could follow physical appetites to excess and it made no difference. They lived the most immoral lives and encouraged others to do so, and they justified their actions by distorting grace and interpreting Scripture to suit themselves.

The Denial of the Second Coming

Further, these evil people denied the second coming (3:3–4). They argued that this was a stable world in which things remained unalterably the same, and that God was so slow to act that it was possible to assume that the second coming was never going to happen at all. The answer of 2 Peter is that this is not a stable world; that it has, in fact, been destroyed by water in the Flood and that it will be destroyed by fire in the final conflagration (3:5-7). What they regard as unnecessary delay is in fact God withholding his hand in patience to give men and women another chance to repent (3:8-9). But the day of destruction is coming (3:10). A new heaven and a new earth are on the way; therefore, goodness is an absolute necessity if people are to be saved in the day of judgment (3:11-14). With this Paul agrees, however difficult his letters may be to understand, and however false teachers deliberately misinterpret them (3:15-16). The duty of Christians is to stand fast, firmly founded in the faith, and to grow in grace and in the knowledge of Jesus Christ (3:17-18).

The Doubts of the Early Church

Such are the contents of the letter. For a long time, it was regarded with doubt and with something very like misgiving. There is no trace of it until after AD 200. It is not included in the Muratorian Canon of AD 170, which was the first official list of New Testament books. It did not exist in the Old Latin Version of the Scriptures, nor in the New Testament of the early Syrian church.

The famous scholars of Alexandria either did not know it or were doubtful about it. Clement of Alexandria, who wrote outlines of the books of Scripture, does not appear to have included 2 Peter. The third-century biblical scholar Origen says that Peter left behind one epistle which is generally acknowledged; 'perhaps also a second, for it is a disputed question'. The blind theologian Didymus, writing in the fourth century, commented on it, but concluded his work by saying: 'It must not be forgotten that this letter is spurious; it may be read in public; but it is not part of the canon of Scripture.'

Eusebius, the great scholar of Caesarea, who made a careful investigation of the Christian literature of his day, comes to the conclusion: 'Of Peter, one Epistle, which is called his former Epistle, is acknowledged by all; of this the ancient presbyters have made frequent use in their writings as indisputably genuine; but that which is circulated as his second Epistle we have received to be not canonical although, since it appeared to be useful to many, it has been diligently read with the other Scriptures.'

It was not until well into the fourth century that 2 Peter came to rest in the canon of the New Testament.

The Objections

Scholars of the past and of modern times are close to unanimity in their judgment that Peter is not the author of 2 Peter. Even the reformer John Calvin regarded it as impossible that Peter could have spoken of Paul as 2 Peter speaks of him (3:15–16), although he was willing to believe that someone else wrote the letter at Peter's request. What, then, are the arguments against Peter's authorship?

(1) There is the extreme slowness, and even reluctance, of the early Church to accept it. If it had been truly Peter's, there can be little doubt that the Church would have welcomed and honoured it from the beginning. But the reality of the situation was very different. For the first two centuries, there is no certain instance of the letter being quoted; it is regarded with doubt and suspicion for more than another century; and only late in the fourth century is it accepted.

(2) The contents make it difficult to believe that it is Peter's. There is no mention of the passion, the resurrection and the ascension of Jesus Christ; no mention of the Church as the true Israel; no mention of that faith which is a combination of undefeatable hope and trust; no mention of the Holy Spirit, of prayer, of baptism; and no passionate desire to call men and women to the supreme example of Jesus Christ. If one took away these great truths from 1 Peter, there

would be little or nothing left – and yet none of them occurs in 2 Peter.

(3) It is wholly different in character and style from 1 Peter. This was realized in the fourth century by the biblical scholar Jerome, who wrote: 'Simon Peter wrote two Epistles which are called Catholic, of which the authenticity of the second is denied by many because of the difference of the style from the first.' The Greek style of this letter is very difficult. F. B. Clogg calls it ambitious, artificial and often obscure, and remarks that it is the only book in the New Testament which is improved by translation. F. H. Chase, Bishop of Ely in the early part of the twentieth century, writes: 'The Epistle does produce the impression of being a somewhat artificial piece of rhetoric. It shows throughout signs of self-conscious effort. The author appears to be ambitious of writing in a style which is beyond his literary power.' He concludes that it is hard to reconcile the literary character of this letter with the supposition that Peter wrote it. James Moffatt says: '2 Peter is more periodic and ambitious than 1 Peter, but its linguistic and its stylistic efforts only reveal by their cumbrous obscurity a decided inferiority of conception, which marks it off from 1 Peter.'

It might be claimed, as Jerome did indeed claim, that, while Peter used Silvanus for 1 Peter, he used someone else to assist in writing down 2 Peter and that this explains the change in style. But, in his commentary on 2 Peter, J. B. Mayor compares the two letters. He quotes some of the great passages of 1 Peter and then says: 'I think that none who read these words can help feeling that, not even in Paul, not even in John, is there to be found a more beautiful or a more living description of the secret of primitive Christianity, of the force that overcame the world, than in the perfect quaternion of faith and hope and love and joy, which pervades this short epistle [i.e. 1 Peter]. No one could make the same assertion with regard to 2 Peter: thoughtful and interesting as it is, it lacks that intense sympathy, that flame of love, which marks 1 Peter . . . No change of circumstances can account for the change of tone of which we are conscious in passing from one epistle to the other.' It is the conclusion of that great and conservative scholar that no explanation, other than difference of authorship, can explain not so much the difference in style as the difference in atmosphere between 1 and 2 Peter. It is true that from the purely linguistic point of view there are 369 words which occur in 1 Peter which do not occur in 2 Peter, and there are 230 words which occur in 2 Peter and not in 1 Peter. But there is more than a difference in style. Writers can change their style and their vocabulary to suit a particular audience and occasion. But the difference between the two letters in atmosphere and attitude is so wide that it is hardly possible that the same person could have written both.

(4) Certain things within 2 Peter point strongly to a late date. So much time has passed that people have begun to abandon hope of the second coming altogether (3:4). The apostles are spoken of as figures of the past (3:2). The fathers, that is the founders of the Christian faith, are now figures of the almost dim and distant past; there have been generations between this letter and the beginnings of the Christian faith (3:4).

There are references which require the passing of the years to explain them. The reference to Peter's approaching death looks very like a reference to Jesus' prophecy in John 21:18–19; and the Fourth Gospel was not written until about AD 100. The statement that Peter is going to leave something which will continue his teaching after he has gone looks very like a reference to Mark's gospel (1:12–14).

Above all, there is the reference to the letters of Paul (3:15–16). From this, it is quite certain that Paul's letters are known and used throughout all the Church; they are public property, and furthermore they are regarded as Scripture and on a level with 'the other Scriptures' (3:16). It was not until at least AD 90 that these letters were collected and published, and it would take many years for them to acquire the position of sacred Scripture. It is practically impossible that anyone should write like this until mid-way through the second century AD.

All the evidence converges to prove that 2 Peter is a late book. It is not until the third century that it is quoted. The great scholars of the early Church did not regard it as Peter's, although they did not question its usefulness. The letter has references which require the passing of the years to explain them. The great interest of 2 Peter lies in the very fact that it was the last book in the New Testament to be written and the last to gain entry into the New Testament.

In Peter's Name

How, then, did it become attached to the name of Peter? The answer is that it was *deliberately* attached. This may seem to us a strange thing to do, but in the ancient world this was common practice. Plato's letters were written not by Plato but by a disciple in the master's name. The Jews repeatedly used this method of writing. Between the Old and the New Testament, books were written under the names of Solomon, Isaiah, Moses, Baruch, Ezra, Enoch and many others. And, in New Testament times, there is a whole literature around the name of Peter – the Gospel of Peter, the Preaching of Peter, the Apocalypse of Peter.

One significant fact makes this method of writing even more intelligible. The heretics used it. They issued misleading and damaging books under the names of the great apostles, claiming that they were the secret teaching of the great founders of the Church handed down by word of mouth to them. Faced with this, the Church retaliated in kind and issued books in which Christians set down for their own generation the things they were quite sure that the apostles would have said had they been facing this new situation. There is nothing either unusual or discreditable in a book being issued under the name of Peter although Peter did not write it. The writer, in humility, was putting the message which the Holy Spirit had given him into the mouth of Peter because he felt that his own name was unworthy to appear upon the book.

We will not find 2 Peter easy to read; but it is a book of major importance because it was written to people who were undermining the Christian ethic and the Christian doctrine and who had to be stopped before the Christian faith was wrecked by their distortion of the truth.

2 PETER

THE MAN WHO OPENED DOORS

2 Peter 1:1

> Simeon Peter, a servant and apostle of Jesus Christ,
> writes this letter to those to whom there has been allotted
> a faith equal in honour and privilege with our own,
> through the impartial justice of our God and Saviour
> Jesus Christ.

THE letter opens with a very subtle and beautiful allusion for
those who have eyes to see it and knowledge enough of the
New Testament to grasp it. Peter writes to 'those to whom
there has been allotted a faith equal in honour and privilege
with our own' – and he calls himself *Simeon Peter*. Who were
these people? There can really be only one answer to that.
They must once have been Gentiles as distinct from the Jews
who were uniquely the chosen people of God. Those who at
one time were not a people are now the chosen people of God
(1 Peter 2:10); those who were once aliens and strangers to
the commonwealth of Israel, and who were once far off, have
been brought near (Ephesians 2:11–13).

Peter puts this very vividly, using a word which would at
once strike an answering chord in the minds of those who
heard it. Their faith is *equal in honour and privilege*. The

335

Greek is *isotimos*; *isos* means *equal*, and *time* means *honour*. This word was particularly used in connection with foreigners who were given equal citizenship in a city with the native inhabitants. The Jewish historian Josephus, for instance, says that in Antioch the Jews were made *isotimoi, equal in honour and privilege*, with the Macedonians and the Greeks who lived there. So Peter addresses his letter to those who had once been despised Gentiles but who had been given equal rights of citizenship with the Jews and even with the apostles themselves in the kingdom of God.

Two things have to be noted about this great privilege which had been extended to the Gentiles. (1) It had been *allotted* to them. That is to say, they had not earned it; it had fallen to them through no merit of their own, as some prize falls to an individual by lot. In other words, their new citizenship was completely through grace. (2) It came to them through the impartial justice of their God and Saviour Jesus Christ. It came to them because with God there is no 'most favoured nation' clause; his grace and favour go out impartially to every nation upon earth.

What has this to do with the name *Simeon*, by which Peter is called here? In the New Testament, he is most often called Peter; he is fairly often called Simon, which was indeed his original name before Jesus gave him the name of Cephas or Peter (John 1:41–2); but only once in the rest of the New Testament is he called *Simeon*. It is in the story of the Council of Jerusalem in Acts 15, which decided that the door of the Church should be opened wide to the Gentiles. There, James says: 'Simeon has related how God first visited the Gentiles, to take out of them a people for his name' (Acts 15:14). In this letter, which begins with greetings to the Gentiles who have been granted by the grace of God privileges of equal citizenship in the kingdom with the Jews and with the apostles,

Peter is called by the name of *Simeon*; and the only other
time he is called by that name is when he is the principal
instrument whereby that privilege is granted.

Simeon has in it the memory that Peter is the man who
opened doors. He opened the doors to Cornelius, the Gentile
centurion (Acts 10); his great authority was cast on the side
of the open door at the Council of Jerusalem (Acts 15).

THE GLORIOUS SERVITUDE

2 Peter 1:1 *(contd)*

PETER calls himself the *servant* of Jesus Christ. The word is
doulos, which really means *slave*. Strange as it may seem,
here is a title, apparently one of humiliation, which the greatest
figures took as a title of highest honour. Moses, the great
leader and law-giver, was the *doulos* of God (Deuteronomy
34:5; Psalm 105:26; Malachi 4:4). Joshua, the great commander, was the *doulos* of God (Joshua 24:29). David, the
greatest of the kings, was the *doulos* of God (2 Samuel 3:18;
Psalm 78:70). In the New Testament, Paul is the *doulos* of
Jesus Christ (Romans 1:1; Philippians 1:1; Titus 1:1), a title
which James (James 1:1) and Jude (Jude 1) both proudly claim.
In the Old Testament, the prophets are the *douloi* of God
(Amos 3:7; Isaiah 20:3). And, in the New Testament, the
Christian is frequently referred to as Christ's *doulos* (Acts
2:18; 1 Corinthians 7:22; Ephesians 6:6; Colossians 4:12;
2 Timothy 2:24). There is deep meaning here.

(1) To call the Christian the *doulos* of God means that he
or she is absolutely possessed by God. In the ancient world, a
master possessed his slaves in the same sense as he possessed
his tools. Servants can change their master; but slaves cannot.
The Christian belongs to God absolutely.

(2) To call the Christian the *doulos* of God means that he or she is unreservedly at the disposal of God. In the ancient world, the master could do what he liked with his slaves; he even had the power of life and death over them. Christians have no rights of their own, for all their rights are surrendered to God.

(3) To call the Christian the *doulos* of God means that he or she owes an unquestioning obedience to God. A master's command was a slave's only law in ancient times. In any situation, Christians have only one question to ask: 'Lord, what will *you* have me do?' The command of God is *their* only law.

(4) To call the Christian the *doulos* of God means that he or she must be constantly in the service of God. In the ancient world, the slaves had literally no time of their own, no holidays, no leisure. All their time belonged to their master. Christians cannot, either deliberately or unconsciously, compartmentalize life into the time and activities which belong to God, and the time and activities in which they do what they like. Christians, by definition, are people every moment of whose time is spent in the service of God.

We note one further point. Peter speaks of the impartial justice of *our God and Saviour Jesus Christ*. The Authorized Version translates this as 'the righteousness of God and our Saviour Jesus Christ', as if this referred to two persons, God and Jesus; but, as James Moffatt's translation and the Revised Standard Version both show, in the Greek there is only one person involved and the phrase is correctly rendered *our God and Saviour Jesus Christ*. Its great interest is that it does what the New Testament very seldom does. It calls Jesus God. The only real parallel to this is the adoring cry of Thomas: 'My Lord and my God!' (John 20:28). This is not a matter to argue about; it is not even a matter of theology; for Peter and Thomas

to call Jesus God was not a matter of theology but an outpouring of adoration. It was simply that they felt that human
terms could not contain this person they knew as Lord.

THE ALL-IMPORTANT KNOWLEDGE

2 Peter 1:2

> May grace and peace be multiplied to you by the
> knowledge of God, and of Jesus, our Lord,

PETER puts this in an unusual way. Grace and peace are to
come from *knowledge*, the knowledge of God and of Jesus
Christ, our Lord. Is he turning Christian experience into
something dependent on knowledge? Or is there some
other meaning here? First, let us look at the word which he
uses for knowledge (*epignōsis*). It can be interpreted in two
ways.

(a) It can mean *increasing knowledge*. *Gnōsis*, the normal
Greek word for *knowledge*, is here preceded by the preposition
epi which means *towards*, *in the direction of*. *Epignōsis* then
could be interpreted as knowledge which is always moving
further in the direction of that which it seeks to know. Grace
and peace are multiplied to Christians as they come to know
Jesus Christ better and better. It has been expressed in this
way: 'The more Christians realize the meaning of Jesus Christ,
the more they realize the meaning of grace and the experience
of peace.'

(b) *Epignōsis* has a second meaning. Often in Greek it
means *full knowledge*. For instance, Plutarch, the Greek
historian, uses it of the scientific knowledge of music as
opposed to the knowledge of the mere amateur. So it may be
that the implication here is that knowledge of Jesus Christ is
what we might call 'the master science of life'. The other

sciences may bring new skill, new knowledge, new abilities; but the master science, the knowledge of Jesus Christ, alone brings the grace which men and women need and the peace for which their hearts crave.

There is still more. Peter has a way of using words which were commonly on the lips of the non-Christians of his day and giving to them a new meaning. Knowledge was a much-used word in the thought of the ancient religions in the days when this letter was written. To take but one example, the Greeks defined *sophia*, *wisdom*, as knowledge of things both human and divine. The Greek seekers after God sought that knowledge in two main ways.

(1) They sought it by philosophic speculation. They sought to reach God by the sheer power of human thought. There are obvious problems there. For one thing, God is infinite; the human mind is finite, and the finite can never grasp the infinite. In the Book of Job, Zophar had asked: 'Can you [by searching] find out the deep things of God?' (Job 11:7). If God is ever to be known, he must be known not because human reasoning discovers him but because he chooses to reveal himself. For another thing, if religion is based on philosophic speculation, at its highest it can be the preserve of only the few, for it is not given to everyone to be a philosopher. Whatever Peter meant by *knowledge*, he did not mean that.

(2) They sought it by mystical experience of the divine, until they could say: 'I am thou, and thou art I.' This was the way of the mystery religions. They were all passion plays, the dramatically acted story of some god who suffered and died and rose again. The initiate was carefully prepared by instruction in the inner meaning of the story, by long fasting and sexual abstinence, and by the deliberate building up of psychological tension. The play was then played out with a magnificent liturgy, sensuous music, carefully calculated

lighting and the burning of incense. The aim was that, as the initiate watched, he should so enter into this experience that he became actually one with the suffering, dying, rising and eternally triumphant God. Again there are difficulties here. For one thing, not everyone is capable of mystical experience. For another thing, any such experience is bound to be of the moment; it may leave an effect, but it cannot be a continual experience. Mystical experience is the privilege of the few.

(3) If this knowledge of Jesus Christ does not come by philosophic speculation or by mystical experience, what is it and how does it come? In the New Testament, knowledge is characteristically *personal* knowledge. Paul does not say: 'I know *what* I have believed'; he says, as the Authorized Version has it: 'I know *whom* I have believed' (2 Timothy 1:12). Christian knowledge of Christ is personal acquaintance with him; it is knowing him as a person and entering day by day into a more intimate relationship with him.

When Peter speaks of grace and peace coming through the knowledge of God and of Jesus Christ, he is not intellectualizing religion; he is saying that Christianity means an ever-deepening personal relationship with Jesus Christ.

THE GREATNESS OF
JESUS CHRIST FOR US

2 Peter 1:3-7

> Since his divine power has bestowed upon us all things
> that are necessary for true life and true religion, through
> the knowledge of him who called us to his own glory
> and excellence, and since through these gifts there
> have been bestowed upon us precious and very great
> promises, that through them we might escape the

world's corruption caused by lust and become sharers
in the divine nature – since all this is so, bend all your
energy to the task of equipping your faith with courage,
your courage with knowledge, your knowledge with
self-control, your self-control with steadfastness, your
steadfastness with piety, your piety with brotherly
affection, your brotherly affection with Christian love.

In verses 3 and 4, there is a tremendous and comprehensive
picture of Jesus Christ.

(1) He is the *Christ of power*. In him, there is the divine
power which cannot be ultimately defeated or frustrated. In
this world, one of the tragedies of life is that love is so
often frustrated because it cannot give what it wants to
give, cannot do what it wants to do and must so often stand
helpless while the loved one meets disaster. But Christ's love
is always backed by his power and is, therefore, a victorious
love.

(2) He is the *Christ of generosity*. He bestows on us all
things necessary for true life and true religion. The word Peter
uses for religion is *eusebeia*, the usual meaning of which is
practical religion. Peter is saying that Jesus Christ tells us
what life is and then enables us to live it as it ought to be
lived. He gives us a religion which is not withdrawal from
life but triumphant involvement in it.

(3) He is the *Christ of the precious and great promises*.
That does not so much mean that he brings us the great and
precious promises as that in him these promises come true.
Paul put the same thing in a different way when he said
that all the promises of God are Yes and Amen in Christ
(2 Corinthians 1:20). That is to say, Christ says: 'Yes. So let
it be' to these promises; he confirms and guarantees them. It
has been expressed in this way: once we know Jesus Christ,
every time we meet a promise in Scripture which begins with

the word 'Whoever', we can immediately say to ourselves: 'That means me.'

(4) He is the *Christ by whom we escape the world's corruption*. Peter had to meet the antinomians, the people who used the grace of God as an excuse for sin. They declared that grace was wide enough to cover every sin; therefore sin does not matter any more, as the grace of Christ will win forgiveness for anything. For people to speak like that is simply to show that they *want* to sin. But Jesus Christ is the person who can help us overcome the fascination of the world's lust and cleanse us by his presence and his power. As long as we live in this world, sin will never completely lose its fascination for us; but in the presence of Christ we have our defence against that fascination.

(5) He is the *Christ who makes us sharers in the divine nature*. Here again, Peter is using an expression which was well known in the world outside the Church, where the major thinkers spoke much about sharing in the divine nature. But there was this difference – they believed that human beings had a share in the divine nature by virtue of being human. All that people had to do was to live in accordance with the divine nature already in them. The trouble about that is that life flatly contradicts it. On every side we see bitterness, hatred, lust, crime; on every side we see moral failure, helplessness and frustration. Christianity says that men and women are *capable of becoming* sharers in the divine nature. It realistically faces the actuality of human existence but at the same time sets no limit to the potentiality. 'I came', said Jesus, 'that they may have life, and have it abundantly' (John 10:10). As one of the great early fathers said, 'He became what we are to make us what he is.' We have it in us to share the nature of God – but only in Jesus Christ can that potentiality be brought to fruition.

EQUIPMENT FOR THE WAY

2 Peter 1:3-7 (*contd*)

PETER says that we must make every effort *to equip* ourselves with a series of fine qualities. The word he uses for *to equip* is *epichorēgein*, which he uses again in verse 11 when he speaks of us being *richly gifted* with the right of entry into the eternal kingdom.

This is one of the many Greek words that have a pictorial background. The verb *epichorēgein* comes from the noun *chorēgos*, which literally means *the leader of a chorus*. Perhaps the greatest gift that Greece, and especially Athens, gave to the world was the plays and dramatic works of men like Aeschylus, Sophocles and Euripides, which are still among its most cherished possessions. All these plays needed large choruses and were, therefore, very expensive to produce. In the great days of Athens, there were public-spirited citizens who voluntarily took on the duty, at their own expense, of collecting, maintaining, training and equipping such choruses. It was at the major religious festivals that these plays were produced. For instance, at the city Dionysia, three tragedies, five comedies and five wild and riotous choruses were produced. Men had to be found to provide the choruses for them all, a duty which could cost as much as 3,000 drachmae. The men who undertook these duties out of their own pocket and out of love for their city were called *chorēgoi*, and *chorēgein* was the verb used for undertaking such a duty. The word has a certain lavishness in it. It never means to equip in any miserly way; it means lavishly to pour out everything that is necessary for a fine performance. The word *epichorēgein* went out into a larger world, and it grew to mean not only to equip a chorus but to be responsible for any kind of equipment. It can mean to equip an army with all necessary provisions; it can mean to equip the soul with all the necessary virtues for life. But behind it there is always this idea of a lavish generosity in the action.

So Peter urges his people to equip their lives with every virtue, and that must not be simply equipping to a necessary minimum, but lavishly and with generosity. The very word is an encouragement to be content with nothing less than the loveliest and the most splendid life.

But there is something else behind this. In verses 5 and 6, Peter continues by saying that we must, as the Revised Standard Version has it, *add* virtue to virtue, until the whole culminates in Christian love. Behind this is a Stoic idea. The Stoics insisted that in life there must continuously be what they called *prokopē*, *moral progress*. *Prokopē* can be used for *the advance of an army towards its objective*. In the Christian life, there must be steady moral advance. James Moffatt quotes a saying that 'the Christian life must not be an initial spasm followed by a chronic inertia'. There is a tendency for it to be just that – a moment of enthusiasm, when the wonder of Christianity is realized, and then a failure to work out the Christian life in continuous progress.

That brings us to still another basic idea here. Peter bids his people to *bend every energy*, to make every effort, to do this. That is to say, in the Christian life, the supreme human effort must co-operate with the grace of God. As Paul has it: 'Work out your own salvation with fear and trembling; for it is God who is at work in you, enabling you both to will and to work for his good pleasure' (Philippians 2:12–13). It is true that everything comes from faith; but a faith which does not lead to new life is not faith at all, as Paul would heartily have agreed. Faith is not only commitment to the promises of Christ; it is also commitment to his demands.

Charles Bigg points out that Aristotle, in the *Nicomachean Ethics*, says that there are three theories of the source of happiness. (1) It is something which can come by training, by learning and by the formation of good habits. (2) It is a matter of divine allotment; the gift of God. (3) It is all a matter of chance.

The truth is that, as Christians see it, happiness depends *both* on God's gift and on our effort. We do not earn salvation, but at the same time we have to bend every energy towards the Christian objective of a lovely life. Johannes Bengel, the eighteenth-century New Testament scholar, in commenting on this passage, asks us to compare the parable of the ten virgins, five of whom were wise and five of whom were foolish. He writes: 'The flame is that which is imparted to us by God and from God without our own labour; but the oil is that which a man must pour into life by his own study and his own faithful effort, so that the flame may be fed and increased.'

Faith does not exempt us from works; the generosity of God does not absolve us from effort. Life is at its noblest and its best when our effort co-operates with God's grace to produce the necessary loveliness.

THE LADDER OF VIRTUES (1)

2 Peter 1:3–7 (*contd*)

LET us then look at the list of virtues which have to be added to one another. It is worth noting that in the ancient world such lists were common. It was a world in which books were not nearly so cheap and so readily available as they are today. Instruction, therefore, for the most part had to be carried in the pupil's head, and easily memorized lists were one of the most common ways of fixing in the mind what had to be learned. One ingenious way of teaching children the names of the virtues was by means of a game played with counters which could be won or lost, each of which bore the name of one of the virtues. Lists of virtues were common in the early Christian writings. Paul gives us the fruit of the Spirit – love, joy, peace, patience, kindness, goodness, faithfulness, gentleness and self-control (Galatians 5:22–3). In the Pastoral Epistles, the man of God is told to follow after righteousness, godliness, faith, love, steadfastness and gentleness (1 Timothy 6:11). In the Shepherd of Hermas (*Visions*, 3:8:1–7), faith, self-control, simplicity, innocence and reverence, understanding and love are daughters of one another. In the Epistle of Barnabas (2), fear and endurance are the helpers of faith; patience and self-control are our allies; and when these are present it is possible to develop and possess wisdom, prudence, understanding and knowledge. Let us look one by one at the stages in the list which this letter gives us.

(1) It begins with *faith* (*pistis*); everything goes back to that. For Peter, faith is the conviction that what Jesus Christ says is true and that we can commit ourselves to his promises and launch ourselves on his demands. It is the unquestioning certainty that the way to happiness and peace and strength on earth and in heaven is to accept him at his word.

(2) To faith must be added what the Revised Standard Version calls *virtue* and we have called *courage*. The word is *aretē*; it is very rare in the New Testament, but it is the supreme Greek word for virtue in every sense of the term. It means *excellence*. There are two ways in which it may be understood. (a) *Aretē* is what we might call *operative* or *efficient excellence*. To take two examples of its usage from widely differing spheres – it can be used of land which is fertile;

and it can be used of the mighty deeds of the gods. *Aretē* is that virtue which makes someone a good citizen and friend; it is that virtue which makes someone an expert in the technique of living a good life. (b) *Aretē* often means *courage*. The Greek historian and philosopher Plutarch says that God is a hope of *aretē*, not an excuse for cowardice. In 2 Maccabees, we read of how Eleazar died rather than be false to the laws of God and his ancestors; and the story ends by saying that in his death he left an example of noble courage (*aretē*) and a memorial of virtue, not only to the young, but also to the nation (2 Maccabees 6:31).

In this passage, it is not necessary to choose between these two meanings; they are both there. Faith must lead not to the retreat and seclusion of the cloister and the hermit's cell, but to a life effective in the service of God and other people; and it must produce the courage always to show whose life it is and whom it serves.

(3) To courage must he added *knowledge*. The word is *gnōsis*. In ethical Greek language, there are two words which have a similar meaning with a very significant difference. *Sophia* is wisdom, in the sense of 'knowledge of things both human and divine, and of their causes'. It is knowledge of first causes and of deep and ultimate things. *Gnōsis* is *practical knowledge*; it is the ability to apply to particular situations the ultimate knowledge which *sophia* gives. *Gnōsis* is that knowledge which enables people to decide to take the right course and to act honourably and efficiently in the day-to-day circumstances of life. So, to faith must be added courage and effectiveness; to courage and effectiveness must be added the practical wisdom to deal with life.

THE LADDER OF VIRTUES (2)

2 Peter 1:3–7 (contd)

(4) To this practical knowledge must be added *self-control*. The word is *egkrateia*, and it means literally *the ability to take a grip of oneself*. This is a virtue of which the great Greeks spoke and wrote and thought much. In regard to human passions, Aristotle distinguishes four states in life. There is *sōphrosunē*, in which passion has been put entirely under the control of reason; we might call it *perfect self-discipline*. There is *akolasia*, which is the precise opposite; it is the state in which reason is entirely suppressed by passion; we might call it *unrestrained lust*. In between these two states, there is *akrasia*, in which reason fights but passion prevails; we might call it *lack of self-restraint*. There is *egkrateia*, in which reason fights against passion and prevails; we call it *self-control*.

Egkrateia is one of the great Christian virtues; and the place it holds is an example of the realism of the Christian ethic. That ethic does not contemplate a situation in which a person is stripped of all passion; it envisages a situation in which passions remain, but are under perfect control and so become servants, not tyrants.

(5) To this self-control must be added *steadfastness*. The word is *hupomonē*. The fourth-century Church father John Chrysostom called *hupomonē* 'The Queen of the Virtues'. In the Authorized Version, it is usually translated as *patience*; but *patience* is too passive a word. *Hupomonē* always has a background of courage. Cicero defines *patientia*, its Latin equivalent, as 'the voluntary and daily suffering of hard and difficult things, for the sake of honour and usefulness'. Didymus of Alexandria, writing in the third century on the attitude of Job, says: 'It is not that the righteous man must be

349

without feeling, although he must patiently bear the things which afflict him; but it is true virtue when a man deeply feels the things he toils against, but nevertheless despises sorrows for the sake of God.'

Hupomonē does not simply accept and endure; it always has a sense of looking forward. It is said of Jesus, by the writer to the Hebrews, that for the joy that was set before him he *endured* the cross, despising the shame (Hebrews 12:2). That is *hupomonē*, Christian steadfastness. It is the courageous acceptance of everything that life can do to us and the transforming of even the worst event into another step on the upward way.

(6) To this steadfastness must be added *piety*. The word is *eusebeia* and is quite untranslatable into an English equivalent. Even *piety* is inadequate, carrying as it does a suggestion sometimes of something not altogether attractive. The great characteristic of *eusebeia* is that it looks in two directions. Those who have *eusebeia* always worship God correctly and give him his due, but also they always serve others correctly and give them their due. The person who is *eusebēs* (the corresponding adjective) is in a right relationship both with God and with other people. *Eusebeia* is piety but in its most practical aspect.

We may best see the meaning of this word by looking at the man whom the Greeks held to be its finest example. That man was Socrates, whom his disciple Xenophon describes as follows: 'He was so pious and devoutly religious that he would take no step apart from the will of heaven; so just and upright that he never did even a trifling injury to any living soul; so self-controlled, so temperate, that he never at any time chose the sweeter instead of the better; so sensible, so wise, and so prudent that in distinguishing the better from the worse he never erred' (*Memorabilia*, 1:5:8–11).

In Latin, the word is *pietas*; and the classical scholar Warde Fowler describes the Roman idea of the man who possesses that quality: 'He is superior to the enticements of individual passion and of selfish ease; [*pietas* is] a sense of duty which never left a man, of duty first to the gods, then to father and to family, to son and to daughter, to his people and to his nation.'

Eusebeia is the nearest Greek word for *religion*; and, when we begin to define it, we see the intensely practical character of the Christian religion. When people become Christians, they acknowledge a double duty, to God and to their neighbours.

(7) To this piety must be added *brotherly affection*. The word is *philadelphia*, which literally means *love of the brethren*. The point is this – there is a kind of religious devotion which separates individuals from one another. The claims of other people become an intrusion on our prayers, our study of God's word and our meditation. The ordinary demands of human relationships become a nuisance. Epictetus, the great Stoic philosopher, never married. Half-jokingly, he said that he was doing far more for the world by being a philosopher without any ties than if he had produced 'two or three dirty-nosed children'. 'How can he who has to teach mankind run to get something in which to heat the water to give the baby his bath?' What Peter is saying is that there is something wrong with the religion which finds the claims of personal relationships a nuisance.

(8) The ladder of Christian virtue must end in Christian love. Not even mutual affection is enough; Christians must end with a love which is as wide as that love of God which causes his sun to rise on the just and on the unjust, and sends his rain on the evil and on the good. Christians must show to the world the love which God has shown to them.

ON THE WAY

2 Peter 1:8–11

> For, if these things exist and increase within you, they
> will make you not ineffective and not unfruitful in your
> progress towards the knowledge of our Lord Jesus
> Christ. For whoever does not possess these things is
> blind, short-sighted, and has lapsed into forgetfulness
> that the sins of his old way of life have been cleansed
> away. So, brothers, be the more eager to confirm your
> calling and your choice. For, if you do practise these
> virtues, you will never slip; for you will be richly gifted
> with the right of entry into the eternal kingdom of our
> Lord Jesus Christ.

PETER strongly urges his people to keep climbing up this ladder
of virtues which he has set before them. The more we know
of any subject, the more we are able to know. It is always true
that 'to those who have more will be given'. Progress is the
way to more progress. James Moffatt says of ourselves and
Jesus Christ: 'We learn him as we live with him and for him.'
As the hymn attributed to the twelfth-century saint Bernard
of Clairvaux, 'O Jesus, King most wonderful', has it:

> May every heart confess thy name.
>   And ever thee adore,
> And, seeking thee, itself inflame
>   To seek thee more and more.

To keep climbing up the ladder of the virtues is to come nearer
and nearer to knowing Jesus Christ; and the further we climb,
the further we are able to climb.

On the other hand, if we refuse to make the effort of the
upward climb, certain things happen. (1) We grow blind; we
are left without the guiding light that the knowledge of Jesus

Christ brings. As Peter sees it, to walk without Christ is to walk in the dark and not to be able to see the way. (2) We become what Peter calls *muōpazōn*. This word can have either of two meanings. It can mean *short-sighted*. It is easy to become short-sighted in life, to see things only as they appear at the moment and to be unable to take the long view of things, to have our eyes so fixed upon earth that we never think of the things beyond. It can also mean *blinking, shutting the eyes*. Again, it is easy in life to shut our eyes to what we do not wish to see, and to walk, as it were, in blinkers. To walk without Christ is to be in danger of taking the short-sighted or the blinkered view of life.

Further, to fail to climb the ladder of virtue is to forget that the sins of the old way of life have been cleansed away. Peter is thinking of baptism. At that time, baptism was adult baptism; it was a deliberate act of decision to leave the old way and to enter the new. Those who, after baptism, do not begin the upward climb have forgotten, or never realized, the meaning of the experience through which they have passed. For many of us, the parallel to baptism in this sense is entry into the membership of the Christian Church. To make our commitment and then to remain exactly the same is to fail to understand what church membership means, for our entry into it should be the beginning of a climb upon the upward way.

In view of all this, Peter urges his people to make every effort to confirm their calling by God. Here is a most significant demand. In one way, all is from God; it is God's call which gives us entry into the fellowship of his people; without his grace and his mercy, we could do nothing and could expect nothing. But that does not absolve us from every possible effort.

Let us take an analogy, which, although not perfect, may help us to understand. Suppose someone offers financial assistance and the chance of a university education to a young student. The benefactor is giving that person something which could never have been achieved without help; but the student cannot make use of that privilege without being prepared to work, and the harder he or she works the greater the effect of the privilege offered will be. The gracious free offer and the personal hard work have to combine before the privilege becomes fully effective.

It is the same with us and God. God has called us in his free mercy and his unmerited grace, but at the same time we have to make every possible effort to toil upwards and onwards on the way.

If we follow this upward way, Peter says, we shall in the end be richly rewarded with the right of entry into his eternal kingdom, and we shall not slip upon the way. By this, Peter does not mean that we will never sin. The picture in his mind is of a column of soldiers marching, and he means that we will never fall out from that column and be left behind. If we set out upon this upward and onward way, the effort will be great, but God's help will also be great; and, in spite of all the toil, he will enable us to keep going until we reach our journey's end.

THE PASTOR'S CARE

2 Peter 1:12–15

> It is for this reason that I intend constantly to remind you of these things, although you already know them, and although you are already firmly established in the truth which you possess. I think it is right, so long as I am in this tent, to rouse you by reminding you, for I know that the time to put off my tent is coming soon, as

indeed our Lord Jesus Christ has told me. Yes, and I will make it my endeavour to see to it that after my departure you will constantly remember these things.

HERE speaks the pastor's care. In this passage, Peter shows us two things about preaching and teaching. First, preaching is very often reminding people of what they already know. It is bringing back to the memory that truth which has been forgotten, or at which people refuse to look, or whose meaning they have not fully appreciated. Second, Peter is going to go on to uncompromising rebuke and warning; but he begins with something very like a compliment. He says that his people already possess the truth and are firmly established in it. A preacher, a teacher or a parent will always achieve more by encouragement than by scolding. We do more to reform people and to keep them safe by trusting them than by the use of harsh words. Peter was wise enough to know that the first essential to make people listen is to show that we believe in them.

Peter looks ahead to his early death. He talks of his body as his tent, as Paul does (2 Corinthians 5:4). This was a favourite picture with the early Christian writers. The Epistle to Diognetus says: 'The immortal soul dwells in a mortal tent.' The picture comes from the journeyings of the patriarchs in the Old Testament. They had no permanent residence, but lived in tents because they were on the way to the promised land. Christians know that life in this world is not a permanent residence but a journey towards the world beyond. We get the same idea in verse 15. There, Peter speaks of his approaching death as his *exodos*, his departure. *Exodos* is, of course, the word which is used for the departure of the children of Israel from Egypt, and their setting out to the promised land. Peter sees death not as the end but as the going out into the promised land of God.

Peter says that Jesus Christ has told him that for him the end will soon be coming. This may be a reference to the prophecy in John 21:18–19, when Jesus foretells that there will come a day when Peter also will be stretched out upon a cross. That time is about to come.

Peter says that he will take steps to see that what he has got to say to them will be held in their memory even when he is gone from this earth. That may well be a reference to the gospel according to St Mark. The consistent tradition is that it is the preaching material of Peter. Irenaeus, the second-century Bishop of Lyons, says that, after the deaths of Peter and Paul, Mark, who had been his disciple and interpreter, handed on in writing the things which it had been Peter's custom to preach.

Papias, who lived towards the end of the second century and collected many traditions about the early days of the Church, hands down the same tradition about Mark's gospel: 'Mark, who was Peter's interpreter, wrote down accurately, though not in order, all that he recollected of what Christ had said or done. For he was not a hearer of the Lord, or a follower of his; he followed Peter, as I have said, at a later date, and Peter adapted his instructions to practical needs, without any attempt to give the Lord's words systematically. So that Mark was not wrong in writing down some things in this way from memory, for his one concern was neither to omit nor to falsify anything that he had heard.' It may well be that the reference here means that Peter's teaching continued to be available to his people in Mark's gospel after his death.

In any event, the pastor's aim was to bring to his people God's truth while he was still alive and to take steps to keep it in their memories after he was dead. He wrote to preserve not his own name but the name of Jesus Christ.

THE MESSAGE AND THE RIGHT TO GIVE IT

2 Peter 1:16–18

> For it was not cleverly invented fables that we followed
> when we made known to you the power and the coming
> of our Lord Jesus Christ; it was because we were made
> eyewitnesses of his majesty. This happened to us on that
> occasion when he received honour and glory from God
> the Father, when this voice was borne to him by the
> majestic glory – 'This is my Son, the Beloved, in whom
> I am well pleased.' It was this voice that we heard, borne
> from heaven, when we were with him in the sacred
> mountain.

PETER comes to the message which it was his great aim to
bring to his people, concerning 'the power and the coming of
our Lord Jesus Christ'. As we shall see quite clearly as we go
on, the great aim of this letter is to bring people back to
certainty with regard to the second coming of Jesus Christ.
The heretics whom Peter is attacking no longer believed in it;
it was so long delayed that people had begun to think it would
never happen at all.

Such, then, was Peter's message. Having stated it, he goes
on to speak of his right to state it – and he does something
which is, at least at first sight, surprising. His right to speak is
that he was with Jesus on the Mount of Transfiguration and
that there he saw the glory and the honour which were given
to him and heard the voice of God speak to him. That is to
say, Peter uses the transfiguration story not as a foretaste of
the resurrection of Jesus, as it is commonly viewed, but as
a foretaste of the triumphant glory of the second coming.
The transfiguration story is told in Matthew 17:1–8, Mark
9:2–8 and Luke 9:28–36. Was Peter right in seeing in it a

foretaste of the second coming rather than a prefiguring of the resurrection?

There is one particularly significant thing about the transfiguration story. In all three gospels, it immediately follows the prophecy of Jesus that said that there were some standing there who would not pass from the world until they had seen the Son of Man coming in his kingdom (Matthew 16:28; Mark 9:1; Luke 9:27). That would certainly seem to indicate that the transfiguration and the second coming were in some way linked together.

Whatever we may say, this much is certain: that Peter's great aim in this letter is to bring his people back to a living belief in the second coming of Christ, and he bases his right to do so on what he saw on the Mount of Transfiguration.

In verse 16, there is a very interesting word. Peter says: 'We were made *eyewitnesses* of his majesty.' The word he uses for *eyewitness* is *epoptēs*. In the Greek usage of Peter's day, this was a technical word. We have already spoken about the mystery religions. Their practices took the form of passion plays, in which the story of a god who lived, suffered, died and rose again was played out. It was only after a long course of instruction and preparation that the worshipper was finally allowed to be present at the passion play, and to be offered the experience of becoming one with the dying and rising God. When he reached this stage, he was an initiate, and the technical word to describe him was *epoptēs*; he was a privileged eyewitness of the experiences of God. So Peter says that Christians are eyewitnesses of the sufferings of Christ. With the eye of faith, they see the cross; in the experience of faith, they die with Christ to sin and rise to righteousness. Their faith has made them one with Jesus Christ in his death and in his risen life and power.

THE WORDS OF THE PROPHETS

2 Peter 1:19–21

> So this makes the word of the prophets still more certain
> for us; and you will do well to pay attention to it, as it
> shines like a lamp in a dingy place, until the day dawns
> and the Morning Star rises within your hearts. For
> you must first and foremost realize that no prophecy in
> Scripture permits of private interpretation; for no
> prophecy was ever borne to us by the will of man, but
> men spoke from God, when they were carried away by
> the Holy Spirit.

THIS is a particularly difficult passage, because in both halves
of it the Greek can mean quite different things. We look at
these different possibilities, and in each case we take the less
probable first.

(1) The first sentence could mean: 'In prophecy we have
an even surer guarantee, that is, of the second coming.' If
Peter did say this, he means that the words of the prophets
are an even surer guarantee of the reality of the second
coming than his own experience on the Mount of Transfiguration.

However unlikely it may seem, it is by no means impossible
that he did say just that. When he was writing, there was a
tremendous interest in the words of prophecy whose fulfilment
in Christianity was seen to prove its truth. In the days of the
early Church, we find case after case of people converted by
reading the Old Testament books and seeing their prophecies
fulfilled in Jesus. It would be quite in line with that to declare
that the strongest argument for the second coming is that the
prophets foretold it.

(2) But we think that the second possible translation is to
be preferred: 'What we saw on the Mount of Transfiguration

makes it even more certain that what is foretold in the prophets about the second coming must be true.'

However we take it, the meaning is that the glory of Jesus on the mountain top and the visions of the prophets combine to make it certain that the second coming is a living reality which everyone must expect and for which everyone must prepare.

There is also a double possibility about the second part of this passage. 'No prophecy of the Scripture', as the Revised Standard Version has it, 'is a matter of one's own inter-pretation.'

(1) Many of the early scholars took this to mean: 'When any of the prophets interpreted any situation in history or told how history was going to unfold itself, they were not expressing a private opinion of their own; they were passing on a revelation which God had given to them.' This is a perfectly possible meaning. In the Old Testament, the mark of false prophets was that they were speaking *themselves*, as it were, *privately*, and not saying what God had told them to say. Jeremiah condemns the false prophets: 'They speak visions of their own minds, not from the mouth of the Lord' (Jeremiah 23:16). Ezekiel says: 'Alas for the senseless prophets who follow their own spirit, and have seen nothing' (Ezekiel 13:3). The third-century Christian writer Hippolytus describes the way in which the words of the true prophets came: 'They did not speak of their own power, nor did they proclaim what they themselves wished, but first they were given right wisdom by the word, and were then instructed by visions.'

On this view, the passage means that, when the prophets spoke, it was no private opinion they were giving; it was a revelation from God, and therefore their words must be carefully heeded.

(2) The second way to take this passage is as referring to *our* interpretation of the prophets. A situation was confronting Peter in which the heretics and the evildoers were interpreting the prophets to suit themselves. On this view, which we support, Peter is saying: 'You cannot go to Scripture and interpret it in whatever way suits you.'

This is of supreme practical importance. Peter is saying that we never have the right to interpret Scripture, to use our own word, *privately*. How then must it be interpreted?

To answer that question, we must ask another. How did the prophets receive their message? They received it from the Spirit. It was sometimes even said that the Spirit of God used the prophets as a writer uses a pen or as a musician uses a musical instrument. In any event, the Spirit gave the prophets their message. The obvious conclusion is that it is only through the help of that same Spirit that the prophetic message can be understood.

As Paul had already said, spiritual things are spiritually discerned (1 Corinthians 2:14–15). As the Jews viewed the Holy Spirit, he has two functions – he brings God's truth to men and women *and* he enables them to understand that truth when it is brought. So, Scripture is not to be interpreted by private cleverness or private prejudice; it is to be interpreted by the help of the Holy Spirit, by whom it was first given.

In practice, that means two things.

(a) Throughout all the ages, the Spirit has been working in devoted scholars who, under the guidance of God, have opened the Scriptures to others. If, then, we wish to interpret Scripture, we must never arrogantly insist that our own interpretation must be correct; we must humbly go to the works of the scholars to learn what they have to teach us because of what the Spirit taught them.

(b) There is more than that. The one place in which the Spirit especially resides and is operative is the Church, and therefore Scripture must be interpreted in the light of the teaching, the belief and the tradition of the Church. God is our Father in the faith, but the Church is our mother in the faith. If we find that our interpretation of Scripture is at variance with the teaching of the Church, we must humbly examine ourselves and ask whether our guide has not been our private wishes rather than the Holy Spirit.

It is Peter's insistence that Scripture does not consist of any individual's private opinions but is the revelation of God to men and women through his Spirit, and that therefore its interpretation must depend on anyone's private opinions but must always be guided by that same Spirit who is still especially operative within the Church.

FALSE PROPHETS

2 Peter 2:1

> There were times when false prophets arose among the people, even as among you too there will be false teachers, men who will insidiously introduce destructive heresies and deny the Lord who bought them; and by so doing they will bring swift destruction on themselves.

THAT there should arise false prophets within the Church was something only to be expected, for in every generation false prophets had been responsible for leading God's people astray and for bringing disaster on the nation. It is worth while looking at the false prophets in the Old Testament story, for their characteristics were recurring in the time of Peter and still appear today.

(1) The false prophets were more interested in gaining popularity than in telling the truth. Their policy was to tell people what they wanted to hear. The false prophets said: '"Peace, peace", when there is no peace' (Jeremiah 6:14). They saw visions of peace when the Lord God was saying that there was no peace (Ezekiel 13:16). In the days of Jehosaphat, Zedekiah, the false prophet, donned his horns of iron and said that Israel would push the Syrians out of the way as he pushed with these horns; Micaiah, the true prophet, foretold disaster if Jehosaphat went to war. Of course, Zedekiah was popular and his message was accepted; but Jehosaphat went to war with the Syrians and perished tragically (1 Kings 22). In the days of Jeremiah, Hananiah prophesied the swift end of the power of Babylon, while Jeremiah prophesied the servitude of the nation to it; and again the prophet who told people what they wished to hear was the popular one (Jeremiah 28). Diogenes, the great Cynic philosopher, spoke of the false teachers of his day whose method was to follow wherever the applause of the crowd led. One of the first characteristics of false prophets is that they tell people what they want to hear and not the truth they need to hear.

(2) The false prophets were interested in personal gain. As Micah said, 'Its priests teach for a price, its prophets give oracles for money' (Micah 3:11). They teach for sordid gain (Titus 1:11), and they identify godliness and gain, making their religion a money-making thing (1 Timothy 6:5). We can see these exploiters at work in the early Church. In the *Didache*, *The Teaching of the Twelve Apostles*, which is what might be called the first service order book, it is laid down that a prophet who asks for money or for a table to be spread in front of him is a false prophet. 'Traffickers in Christ', the *Didache* calls such people (*Didache*, 11). False prophets are

covetous individuals who regard people as easily deceived and to be exploited for their own ends.

(3) The false prophets were immoral in their personal life. Isaiah writes: 'The priest and the prophet reel with strong drink, they are confused with wine' (Isaiah 28:7). Jeremiah says: 'In the prophets of Jerusalem I have seen a more shocking thing: they commit adultery and walk in lies; they strengthen the hands of evildoers . . . [They] lead my people astray by their lies and their recklessness' (Jeremiah 23:14, 23:32). The false prophets are a temptation to evil rather than an attraction to good.

(4) The false prophets were above all people who led others further away from God instead of closer to him. The prophet who invites the people: 'Let us go after other gods' must be mercilessly destroyed (Deuteronomy 13:1–5, 18:20). The false prophets take people in the wrong direction.

These were the characteristics of the false prophets in the days of ancient Israel and in Peter's time, and they are their characteristics still.

THE SINS OF THE FALSE PROPHETS AND THEIR END

2 Peter 2:1 (*contd*)

In this verse, Peter has certain things to say about these false prophets and their actions.

(1) They subtly and cunningly introduce destructive heresies. The Greek for *heresy* is *hairesis*. It comes from the verb *haireisthai*, which means *to choose*, and originally it was a perfectly honourable word. It simply meant a line of belief and action which someone had chosen for him- or herself. In the New Testament, we read of the *hairesis* of the Sadducees,

the Pharisees and the Nazarenes (Acts 5:17, 15:5, 24:5). It was perfectly possible to speak of the *hairesis* of Plato and to mean nothing more than those who were Platonist in their thought. It was perfectly possible to speak of a group of doctors who practised a certain method of treatment as a *hairesis*. But, very soon in the Christian Church, *hairesis* changed its tone. In Paul's thought, heresies and schisms go together as things to be condemned (1 Corinthians 11:18–19); *haireseis* (the plural form of the word) are part of the works of the flesh; anyone who is a heretic is to be warned and even given a second chance, and then rejected (Titus 3:10).

Why the change? The point is that, before the coming of Jesus, who is the way, the truth and the life, there was no such thing as definite, God-given truth. People were presented with a number of alternatives, any one of which they were perfectly free to choose to believe. But, with the coming of Jesus, God's truth came to the world, and people had either to accept or to reject it. A heretic then became someone who believed what *he or she* wished to believe instead of accepting the truth of God, which all ought to believe.

What was happening in the case of Peter's people was that certain self-styled prophets were by subtle means persuading people to believe the things they wished to be true rather than the things which God had revealed to be true. They did not set themselves up as opponents of Christianity – far from it. They set themselves up as the finest fruits of Christian thinking; and so it was gradually and subtly that people were being lured away from God's truth to other people's private opinions, which is what heresy is.

(2) These heretics *denied the Lord, who had bought them*. This idea of Christ buying men and women for himself is one which runs through the whole New Testament. It comes from his own word that he had come to give his life a ransom for

many (Mark 10:45). The idea was that men and women were slaves to sin and that, at the cost of his life, Jesus purchased them for himself and therefore for freedom. 'You were bought with a price', says Paul (1 Corinthians 7:23). 'Christ redeemed us [bought us out] from the curse of the law' (Galatians 3:13). In the new song in the Book of Revelation, the hosts of heaven tell how Jesus Christ bought them with his blood out of every tribe and language and people and nation (Revelation 5:9). This clearly means two things. It means that Christians by right of purchase belong absolutely to Christ, and it means that a life which cost so much cannot be squandered on sin or on cheap things.

The heretics in Peter's letter were *denying* the Lord, who bought them. That could mean that they were saying that they did not know Christ, and it could mean that they were denying his authority. But it is not as simple as that; one might say that it is not as honest as that. We have seen that these people claimed to be Christians; what is more, they claimed to be the wisest and the most advanced of Christians. Let us take a human analogy. Suppose a man says that he loves his wife and yet is consistently unfaithful to her. By his acts of infidelity he denies, gives the lie to, his words of love. Suppose a woman protests eternal friendship to someone, and yet is consistently disloyal to that friend. Her actions deny, give the lie to, her protestations of friendship. What these evil people, who were troubling Peter's community, were doing was to say that they loved and served Christ, while the things they taught and did were a complete denial of him.

(3) The end of these evil people was destruction. They were subtly introducing destructive heresies, but these heresies would in the end destroy them. There is no more certain way to ultimate condemnation than to teach another person to sin.

THE WORK OF FALSEHOOD

2 Peter 2:2–3

> And many will follow the way of their blatant immor-
> alities, and through them the true way will be brought
> into disrepute. In their evil ambition, they will exploit
> you with cunningly forged arguments. Their sentence
> was settled long ago, and now it is not inactive, and
> their destruction is not asleep.

IN this short passage, we see four things about the false
teachers and their teaching.

(1) We see the *cause* of false teaching. It is *evil ambition*.
The word is *pleonexia*; *pleon* means *more*, and *exia* comes
from the verb *echein*, which means *to have*. *Pleonexia* is *the
desire to possess more*; but it acquires a certain flavour. It is
by no means always a sin to desire to possess more; there are
many cases in which that is a perfectly honourable desire, as
in the case of virtue, or knowledge, or skill. But *pleonexia*
comes to mean the desire to possess that which we have
no right to desire, still less to take. So it can mean covetous
desire for money and for other people's goods; lustful desire
for someone's person; unholy ambition for prestige and power.
False teaching comes from the desire to put its own ideas in
the place of the truth of Jesus Christ; the false teacher is guilty
of nothing less than of falsely assuming the place of Christ.

(2) We see the *method* of false teaching. It is the use of
cunningly prepared arguments. Falsehood is easily resisted
when it is presented as falsehood; it is when it is disguised as
truth that it becomes menacing. There is only one true test.
Any teacher's teaching must be tested by the words and
presence of Jesus Christ himself.

(3) We see the *effect* of the false teaching. It was twofold.
It encouraged people to take the way of blatant immorality.

The word is *aselgeia*, which describes the attitude of the person who is lost to shame and cares for the judgment of neither other people nor God. We must remember what was behind this false teaching. It was distorting the grace of God into a justification for sin. The false teachers were telling people that grace was inexhaustible and that, therefore, they were free to sin as they liked, for grace would forgive.

This false teaching had a second effect. It brought Christianity into disrepute. In the early days, just as now, every Christian was a good or bad advertisement for Christianity and the Christian Church. It is Paul's accusation to the Jews that through them the name of God has been brought into disrepute (Romans 2:24). In the Pastoral Epistles, the younger women are urged to behave with such modesty and chastity that the Church will never be brought into disrepute (Titus 2:5). Any teaching which produces a person who puts others off Christianity instead of attracting them to it is false teaching and is the work of those who are enemies of Christ.

(4) We see the *ultimate end* of false teaching – and that is destruction. Sentence was passed on the false prophets long ago; the Old Testament pronounced their doom (Deuteronomy 13:1–5). It might look as if that sentence of destruction was no longer effective or was slumbering; but it was still valid, and the day would come when the false teachers would pay the terrible price of their falsehood. Those who lead others astray will never escape their own judgment.

THE FATE OF THE WICKED
AND THE RESCUE OF THE RIGHTEOUS

2 Peter 2:4–11

> If God did not spare even angels who had sinned, but
> condemned them to the lowest hell and committed them

to the pits of darkness, where they remain kept for
judgment; if he did not spare the ancient world, but
preserved in safety Noah, the preacher of righteousness, with seven others, when he despatched the flood
on a world of impious men; if he reduced the cities
of Sodom and Gomorrah to ashes, when he sentenced
them to destruction and so gave an example of what
would happen to those who would one day act with
impiety, but rescued righteous Lot, who was distressed
by the blatantly immoral conduct of lawless men,
for, to such a man, righteous in his looking and in his
hearing, it was torture for his righteous soul to live his
daily life amid such people and amid such lawless
deeds – if all this is so, you can be sure that the Lord
knows how to rescue truly religious men from trial
and how to preserve the unrighteous under punishment, until the day of judgment comes, especially
those whose lives are dominated by the polluting lusts
of the flesh and who despise the celestial powers.
Audacious, self-willed men they are; they do not shrink
from speaking evil of the angelic glories, whereas angels
who are greater in strength and power do not bring an
accusation of evil against them in the presence of the
Lord.

HERE is a passage which for us combines undoubted power
and equally undoubted obscurity. The white heat of its
rhetorical intensity glows through it to this day; but it moves
in allusions which would be familiar and terrifyingly effective
to those who heard it for the first time, but which have become
unfamiliar to us today. It cites three notorious examples of
sin and its destruction; and in two of the cases it shows how,
when sin was obliterated, righteousness was rescued and
preserved by the mercy and the grace of God. Let us look at
these examples one by one.

1. THE SIN OF THE ANGELS

Before we retell the story which lies behind this in Jewish legend, there are two separate words at which we must look.

Peter says that God condemned the sinning angels to the lowest depths of hell. Literally, the Greek says that God condemned the angels to *Tartarus* (*tartaroun*). Tartarus was not a Hebrew concept; it was Greek. In Greek mythology, Tartarus was the lowest hell; it was as far beneath Hades as the heaven is high above the earth. In particular, it was the place into which the Titans, who had rebelled against Zeus, the Father of gods and human beings, had been cast.

The second word speaks of the *pits* of darkness. Here there is a doubt. There are two Greek words, both rather uncommon, which are confused in this passage. One is *siros* or *seiros*, which originally meant a great earthenware jar for the storing of grain. Then it came to mean the great underground pits in which grain was stored and which served as granaries. *Siros* has come into English via Provençal in the form of *silo*, which still describes the towers in which grain is stored. Still later, the word went on to mean a pit in which a wolf or other wild animal was trapped. If we think that this is the word which Peter uses (and according to the best manuscripts it is), it will mean that the wicked angels were cast into great subterranean pits and kept there in darkness and in punishment. This fits well with the idea of a Tartarus beneath the lowest depths of Hades.

But there is a very similar word *seira*, which means a *chain*. This is the word which the Authorized Version translates when it speaks of *chains of darkness* (verse 4). The Greek manuscripts of 2 Peter vary between *seiroi*, pits, and *seirai*, chains. But the better manuscripts have *seiroi*, and *pits of darkness* makes better sense than *chains of darkness*; so we may take *seiros* as right, and assume that here the Authorized Version is in error.

The story of the fall of the angels is one which rooted itself deeply in Hebrew thought and which underwent much development as the years went on. The original story is in Genesis 6:1–5. There, the angels are called *the sons of God*, as they commonly are in the Old Testament. In Job, heavenly beings or *sons of God* come to present themselves before the Lord, and Satan comes among them (Job 1:6; cf. 2:1, 38:7). Similarly, the psalmist speaks of heavenly beings or the sons of gods (Psalm 89:6). These angels came to earth and seduced mortal women. The result of this lustful union was the race of giants, and through them wickedness came upon the earth. Clearly, this is an old story belonging to the childhood of the race.

This story was much developed in the Book of Enoch, and it is from it that Peter is drawing his allusions, for in his day that was a well-known book. In Enoch, the angels are called the Watchers. Their leader in rebellion was Semjaza or Azazel. At his instigation, they descended to Mount Hermon in the days of Jared, the father of Enoch. They took mortal wives and instructed them in magic and in arts that gave them power. They produced the race of the giants, and the giants produced the *nephillim*, the giants who inhabited the land of Canaan and of whom the people were afraid (Numbers 13:33).

These giants became cannibals and were guilty of every kind of lust and crime, and especially of insolent arrogance to God and human beings. The apocryphal literature has many references to them and their pride. Wisdom (14:6) tells how the proud giants perished. Ecclesiasticus (16:7) tells how the ancient giants fell away in the strength of their foolishness. They had no wisdom, and they perished in their folly (Baruch 3:26–8). The Jewish historian Josephus says that they were arrogant and contemptuous of all that was good, and trusted in their own strength (*Antiquities*, 1:3:1). Job says that God charged his angels with folly (Job 4:18).

This old story makes a strange and fleeting appearance in the letters of Paul. In 1 Corinthians 11:10, Paul says that women must have their hair covered in the Church *because of the angels*. Behind that strange saying lies the old belief that it was the loveliness of the long hair of the women of past times which moved the angels to desire; and Paul wants to be sure that the angels are not tempted again.

In the end, people complained of the sorrow and misery brought into the world by these giants through the sin of the angels. The result was that God sent out his archangels. Raphael bound Azazel hand and foot and shut him up in darkness; Gabriel slew the giants; and the Watchers, the sinning angels, were shut up in the abysses of darkness under the mountains for seventy generations and then confined forever in everlasting fire. This is the story which is in Peter's mind, and which his readers knew well. The angels had sinned and God had sent his destruction, and they were shut up forever in the pits of darkness and the depths of hell. That is what happens to rebellious sin.

The story does not stop there, and it reappears in another of its forms in this passage of 2 Peter. In verse 10, Peter speaks of those who live lives dominated by depraved lust and who despise the *celestial powers*. The word is *kuriotēs*, which is the name of one of the ranks of angels. They speak evil of the *angelic glories*. The word is *doxai*, which is also a word for one of the ranks of angels. They slander the angels and bring them into disrepute.

Here is where the second turn of the story comes in. Obviously, this story of the angels is very primitive; and, as time went on, it became rather an awkward and embarrassing story because it suggested that angels were capable of lust. So, in later Jewish and Christian thought, two strands developed. First, it was denied that the story involved angels at all. The sons of God were said to be good men who were the descendants of Seth, and the daughters of men were said to be evil women who were the daughters of Cain and corrupted the good men. There is no scriptural evidence for this distinction and this way of escape. Second, the whole story was allegorized. It was claimed, for instance by the Jewish writer Philo, that it was never meant to be taken literally and that it described the fall of the human soul under the attack of the seductions of lustful pleasures. St Augustine declared that no one could take this story literally and talk of the angels like that. In the fifth century, Cyril of Alexandria said that it could not be taken literally, for did not Jesus say that in the afterlife we would be like angels and there would be no marrying or giving in marriage (Matthew 22:30)? John Chrysostom said that, if the story was taken literally, it was nothing short of blasphemy. And Cyril went on to say that the story was nothing other than an incentive to sin, if it was taken as literally true.

It is clear that people began to see that this was indeed a dangerous story. Here, we get our clue as to what Peter means when he speaks of those who despise the celestial powers and bring the angelic glories into disrepute by speaking slanderously of them. Those whom Peter was opposing were turning their religion into an excuse for blatant immorality. Cyril of Alexandria makes it clear that in his day the story could be used as an incentive to sin. Most probably, what was happening was that the wicked heretics of Peter's time were citing the example of the angels as a justification for their own sin. They were saying: 'If angels came from heaven and took mortal women, why should not we?' They were making the conduct of the angels an excuse for their own sin.

We have to go still further with this passage. In verse 11, it finishes very obscurely. It says that angels who are greater in strength and in power do not bring a slanderous charge against them in the presence of God. Once again, Peter is using allusions that would be clear enough to the people of his day but which are obscure to us. His reference may be to either of two stories.

(1) He may be referring to the story to which Jude refers in Jude 9, that the archangel Michael was entrusted with burying the body of Moses. Satan claimed the body on the grounds that all matter belonged to him and that Moses had once murdered an Egyptian. Michael did not bring any charge against Satan; all he said was: 'The Lord rebuke you.' The point is that even an angel as great as Michael would not bring an evil charge against an angel as dark as Satan. He left the matter to God. If Michael refrained from slandering an evil angel, how can anyone bring slanderous charges against the angels of God?

(2) He may be referring to a further development of the Enoch story. Enoch tells that, when the conduct of the giants on earth became intolerable, people made their complaint to the archangels Michael, Uriel, Gabriel and Raphael. The archangels took this complaint to God, but they did not accuse the evil angels who were responsible for it all; they simply took the story to God for him to deal with (1 Enoch 9).

As far as we can see today, the situation behind Peter's allusions is that the wicked who were the slaves of lust claimed that the angels were their examples and their justification, and so slandered them; Peter reminds them that not even archangels dared slander other angels and demands how any mortal can dare to do so.

This is a strange and difficult passage; but the meaning is clear. Even angels, when they sinned, were punished. How much more shall we be punished? Angels could not rebel against God and escape the consequences. How shall we escape? And we need not seek to put the blame on others, not even on angels; nothing but our own rebelliousness is responsible for our sin

2. THE FLOOD AND THE RESCUE OF NOAH

The second illustration of the destruction of wickedness which Peter chooses may be said to lead on from the first. The sin introduced into the world by the sinning angels led to that intolerable sin which ended in the destruction by the deluge (Genesis 6:5). In the midst of this destruction, God did not forget those who had clung to him. Noah was saved together with seven others – his wife, his sons Shem, Ham and Japhet, and their wives. In Jewish tradition, Noah acquired a very special place. He was regarded not only as the one man who had been saved but also as the preacher who had done his best to turn people from the evil of their ways. Josephus says: 'Many angels of God lay with women and begat sons, who were violent and who despised all good, on account of their reliance on their own strength . . . But Noah, displeased and distressed at their behaviour, tried to induce them to alter their dispositions and conduct for the better' (*Antiquities*, 1:3:1).

Attention in this passage is concentrated not so much on the people who were destroyed as on the man who was saved. Noah is offered as the type of man who, amid the destruction of the wicked, receives the salvation of God. He had two outstanding qualities.

(1) In the midst of a sinning generation, he remained faithful to God. Later, Paul was to urge his people not to be conformed to the world but to be transformed from it (Romans 12:2). It may well be said that often the most dangerous sin of all is conformity. To be the same as others is always easy;

to be different is always difficult. But, from the days of Noah until now, whoever would be the servant of God must be prepared to be different from the world.

(2) The later legends pick out another characteristic of Noah. He was the preacher of righteousness. The word for preacher used here is *kērux*, which literally means *a herald*. Epictetus called the philosopher the *kērux* of the gods. The preacher is the one who brings to others an announcement from God. Here is something of very considerable significance. Good people are concerned not only with the saving of their own souls but just as much with the saving of the souls of others. They do not, in order to preserve their own purity, live apart from others. They are concerned to bring God's message to others. We ought never to keep to ourselves the grace which we have received. It is always our duty to bring light to those who sit in darkness, guidance to the wanderer and warning to those who are going astray.

3. THE DESTRUCTION OF SODOM AND GOMORRAH AND THE RESCUE OF LOT

The third example is the destruction of Sodom and Gomorrah and the rescue of Lot.

The terrible and dramatic story is told in Genesis 18–19. It begins with Abraham's plea that God should not destroy the righteous with the guilty and his request that, if even ten who are righteous are found in these cities, they may be spared (Genesis 18:16–33). Then follows one of the grimmest tales in the Old Testament.

The angelic visitors came to Lot, and he persuaded them to stay with him; but his house was surrounded by the men of Sodom demanding that these strangers might be brought out for them to use for their unnatural lust (Genesis 19:1–11). By that terrible deed – at one and the same time the abuse of hospitality, the insulting of angels and the raging of unnatural lust – the doom of the cities was sealed. As the destruction of heaven came upon them, Lot and his family were saved, except his wife, who lingered and looked back and turned into a pillar of salt (Genesis 19:12–26). 'So it was that, when God destroyed the cities of the Plain, God remembered Abraham, and sent Lot out of the midst of the overthrow, when he overthrew the cities in which Lot had settled' (Genesis 19:29). Here again is the story of the destruction of sin and the rescue of righteousness. As in Noah, we see in Lot the characteristics of the righteous person.

(1) Lot lived in the midst of evil, and the very sight of it was a constant distress to him. James Moffatt reminds us of the saying of the nineteenth-century churchman Cardinal John Henry Newman: 'Our great security against sin lies in being shocked at it.' Here is something very significant. It often happens that, when evils first emerge, people are shocked by them; but, as time goes on, they cease to be shocked and accept them as a matter of course. There are many things which ought to shock us. In our own generation, there are the problems of prostitution and promiscuity, drunkenness and drugs, gambling, the breakdown of marriages, violence, vandalism and crime, death upon the roads, still-existing slum conditions and many others. In many cases, the tragedy is that these things have ceased to shock and are accepted in a matter-of-fact style as part of the normal order of things. For the good of the world and of our own souls, we must keep alive the sensitivity that is shocked by sin.

(2) Lot lived in the midst of evil, and yet he escaped its contamination. Surrounded by the sin of Sodom, he remained true to God. If we only remember it, in the grace of God we have an antiseptic which will preserve us from the infection

of sin. There is no need to be slaves of the environment in which we happen to find ourselves.

(3) When the worst came to the worst, Lot was willing to make a clean break with his environment. He was prepared, however much he did not want to do so, to leave it forever. It was because his wife was not prepared to make the clean break that she perished. There is a strange verse in the Old Testament story. It says that, when Lot lingered, the angelic messengers took hold of his hand (Genesis 19:16). There are times when the influence of heaven tries to force us out of some evil situation. It may come to any one of us to have to make the choice between security and a new start; and there are times when people can save their souls only by breaking clean away from their present situation and beginning all over again. It was in doing just this that Lot found his salvation, and it was in failing to do just this that his wife lost hers.

THE PICTURE OF THOSE WHO ARE EVIL

2 Peter 2:4–11 (contd)

VERSES 9–11 give us a picture of those who are evil. Peter, with a few swift, vivid strokes of the pen, paints the outstanding characteristics of those who may properly be described as bad.

(1) They are people who are *desire-dominated*. Their lives are dominated by the lusts of the flesh. Such people are guilty of two sins.

(a) We all have two sides to our nature. We have a physical side; we have instincts, passions and impulses which we share with the animal creation. These instincts are good – *if they are kept in their proper place*. They are even necessary for the preservation of individual life and the continuation of the race. The word *temperament* literally means a *mixture*. The picture behind it is that human nature consists of a large variety of ingredients all mixed together. It is clear that the effectiveness of any mixture depends on each ingredient being there in its proper proportion. Wherever there is either excess or defect, the mixture is not what it ought to be. Human beings have a physical nature and also a spiritual nature; and true humanity depends on a correct mixture of the two. The person dominated by desire has allowed the animal nature to take over a place it should not have, and has allowed the ingredients to get out of proportion, so that the recipe for being human has gone wrong.

(b) There is a reason for this loss of proportion – *selfishness*. The root evil of the life dominated by lust is that it proceeds on the assumption that nothing matters but the gratification of its own desires and the expression of its own feelings. It has ceased to have any respect or care for others. Selfishness and desire go hand in hand.

Bad people are those who have allowed one side of their nature a far greater place than it ought to have and who have done so because they are essentially selfish.

(2) They are *audacious people*. The Greek is *tolmētēs*, from the verb *tolman, to dare.* There are two kinds of daring. There is the daring which is a fine thing, the mark of true courage. There is the daring which is an evil thing, the shameless performance of things which are an affront to decency and right. As Shakespeare's Macbeth had it: 'I dare do all becomes a man. Who dares do more is none.' The bad person is someone who has the audacity knowingly to defy the will of God.

(3) They are *self-willed people*. *Self-willed* is not really an adequate translation. The Greek is *authadēs*, derived from *autos, self*, and *hadōn, pleasing*, and used of those who had no idea of anything other than pleasing themselves. In it, there

is always the element of obstinacy. If someone is *authadēs*, no logic, nor common sense, nor appeal, nor sense of decency will keep that person from doing what he or she wants to do. As R. C. Trench, the nineteenth-century Archbishop of Dublin, says: 'Thus obstinately maintaining his own opinion, or asserting his own rights, he is reckless of the rights, opinions and interests of others.' Those who are described as *authadēs* are stubbornly and arrogantly and even brutally determined on their own way. The bad person is someone who has no regard for either human appeal or divine guidance.

(4) They are people *who are contemptuous of the angels*. We have already seen how this goes back to allusions in Hebrew tradition which are obscure to us. But it has a wider meaning. Bad people insist on living in one world. To them, the spiritual world does not exist, and they never hear the voices from beyond. They are bound by this world – worldly. They have forgotten that there is a heaven and are blind and deaf when the sights and sounds of heaven break through to them.

DELUDING SELF AND DELUDING OTHERS

2 Peter 2:12–14

> But these, like brute beasts, knowing no law but their instincts, born only for capture and corruption, speak evil of the things about which they know nothing; they will be destroyed with their own corruption, and, like a man who is cheated, they will even lose the reward at which their iniquity aimed. They regard daylight debauchery as pleasure. They are spots and blots, revelling in their dissipations, carousing in their cliques among you. They have eyes full of adultery, eyes which can never gaze their fill on sin. They entrap souls which

are not firmly founded in the faith. They have a heart
which is trained in unbridled ambition for the things
they have no right to have. They are accursed.

PETER launches out into a long passage of magnificent bitter
accusation. Through it glows the fiery heat of burning moral
indignation.

The evil people are like irrational animals, slaves of their
lower instincts. But an animal is born only for capture and
death, says Peter; it has no other destiny. Even so, there is
something self-destroying in fleshly pleasure. To make such
pleasure the be-all and the end-all of life is a suicidal policy,
and in the end even the pleasure is lost. The point Peter is
making is this, and it is eternally valid. If people dedicate
themselves to these fleshly pleasures, in the end they so ruin
themselves in physical health and in spiritual and mental
character that these pleasures become no longer pleasurable.
In the end, gluttons destroy their appetite, drunkards their
health, those who live for physical pleasure their bodies, and
the self-indulgent their character and peace of mind.

These people regard daylight debauchery, dissolute revel-
ling and unrestrained bingeing as pleasure. They are blots on
the Christian fellowship; they are like the blemishes on an
animal which make it unfit to be offered to God. Once again,
we must note that what Peter is saying is not only religious
truth but also sound common sense. The pleasures of the body
are demonstrably subject to the law of diminishing returns.
In themselves, they lose their thrill, so that as time goes on it
takes more and more of them to satisfy. The luxury must
become increasingly luxurious; the wine must flow more
freely; everything must be done to make the thrill sharper
and more intense. Further, people become less and less able
to enjoy these pleasures. They have given themselves to a
life that has no future and to pleasure which ends in pain.

So Peter goes on. In verse 14, he uses an extraordinary phrase which, strictly, will not translate into English at all. We have translated it as 'They have eyes full of adultery.' The Greek literally is: 'They have eyes which are full of an adulteress.' Most probably, the meaning is that they see a possible adulteress in every woman, wondering how she can be persuaded to gratify their lusts. 'The hand and the eye', said the Jewish teachers, 'are the brokers of sin.' As Jesus said, such people look in order to lust (Matthew 5:28). They have come to such a stage that they cannot look at anyone in a way that is free from lust.

As Peter speaks of this, there is a terrible deliberateness about it. They have *hearts trained in unbridled ambition for the things they have no right to have*. We have taken a whole phrase to translate the one word *pleonexia*, which means the desire to have more of the things which no one has any right even to desire, let alone have. The picture is a terrible one. The word used for *trained* is used for an athlete exercising for the games. These people have actually trained their minds to concentrate on nothing but the forbidden desire. They have deliberately fought with conscience until they have destroyed it; they have deliberately struggled with their finer feelings until they have strangled them.

There remains in this passage one further charge. It would be bad if these people deceived only themselves; it is worse that they deceive others. They entrap souls not firmly founded in the faith. The word used for *to entrap* is *deleazein*, which means *to catch with a bait*. People become really bad when they set out to make others as bad as themselves. The hymn has it:

All the mischief we have wrought,
All forbidden things we've sought.
All the sin to others taught:
    Forgive, O Lord, for Jesus' sake.

We must all bear the responsibility for our own sins, but to add to that the responsibility for the sins of others is to carry an intolerable burden.

ON THE WRONG ROAD

2 Peter 2:15–16

> They have left the straight road and have gone a-wandering, and have followed the road of Balaam, the son of Beor, who loved the profit which unrighteousness brings and who was convicted of his lawlessness. A dumb ass spoke with a man's voice and checked the prophet's folly.

PETER likens the evil people of his time to the prophet Balaam. In the popular Jewish tradition, Balaam had come to stand as the type of all false prophets. His story is told in Numbers 22–4. Balak, King of Moab, was alarmed at the steady and apparently irresistible advance of the Israelites. In an attempt to check it, he sent for Balaam to come and curse the Israelites for him, offering him great rewards. To the end of the day, Balaam refused to curse the Israelites, but he longed for the rich rewards which Balak was offering. At Balak's renewed request, Balaam played with fire enough to agree to meet him. On the way, his donkey stopped, because it saw the angel of the Lord standing in its path, and rebuked Balaam.

It is true that Balaam did not give in to Balak's bribes; but, if ever a man wanted to accept a bribe, that man was Balaam. In Numbers 25, there follows another story. It tells how the Israelites were seduced into the worship of Baal and into lustful alliances with Moabite women. Jewish belief was that Balaam was responsible for leading the children of Israel astray; and, when the Israelites entered into possession of the land, 'they also killed Balaam son of Beor with the sword' (Numbers 31:8). In view of all this, Balaam became increasingly the supreme example of the false prophet. He had two characteristics which were repeated in the evil people of Peter's day.

(1) Balaam was *covetous*. As the Numbers story unfolds, we can see his fingers itching to get at the gold of Balak. True, he did not take it; but the desire was there. The evil people of Peter's day were covetous, out for what they could get and ready to exploit their membership of the Church for gain.

(2) Balaam *taught Israel to sin*. He led the people out of the straight and into the crooked way. He persuaded them to forget their promises to God. The evil people of Peter's day were seducing Christians from the Christian way and causing them to break the pledges of loyalty they had given to Jesus Christ.

Anyone who loves gain and who lures others to evil stands eternally condemned.

THE PERILS OF RELAPSE

2 Peter 2:17–22

> These people are waterless springs, mists driven by a squall of wind; and the gloom of darkness is reserved for them. With talk at once arrogant and futile, they ensnare by appeals to shameless, sensual passions those who are only just escaping from the company of those who live in error, promising them freedom, while they themselves are the slaves of moral corruption; for a man is in a state of slavery to that which has reduced him to helplessness.

If they have escaped the pollution of the world by the knowledge of the Lord and Saviour Jesus Christ, and if they allow themselves again to become involved in these things and to be reduced to moral helplessness by them, the last state is for them worse than the first. It would be better for them not to have known the way of righteousness than to have known it and then to turn back from the holy commandment which was handed down to them. In them the truth of the proverb is plain to see: 'A dog returns to his own vomit' and 'The sow which has been washed returns to rolling in the mud.'

Peter is still rolling out his tremendous denunciation of those who are evil.

They flatter only to deceive. They are like wells with no water and like mists blown past by a squall of wind. Think of travellers in the desert being told that ahead lies a spring where they can quench their thirst, and then arriving at that spring to find it dried up and useless. Think of the farmers praying for rain for their parched crops and then seeing the cloud that promised rain blown uselessly by. As Charles Bigg has it in his commentary: 'A teacher without knowledge is like a well without water.' These men are like the shepherds in John Milton's *Lycidas* whose 'hungry sheep look up, and are not fed'. They promise a gospel and in the end have nothing to offer thirsty souls.

Their teaching is a combination of arrogance and futility. Christian freedom always involves danger. Paul tells his people that they have indeed been called to liberty but that they must not use it as an opportunity for self-indulgence (Galatians 5:13). Peter tells his people that indeed they are free but they must not use their freedom as an excuse for maliciousness (1 Peter 2:16). These false teachers offered freedom, but it was freedom to sin as much as anyone liked.

They appealed not to the best but to the worst in human nature. Peter is quite clear that they did this because they were slaves to their own lusts. Seneca said: 'To be enslaved to oneself is the heaviest of all servitudes.' Persius, the Roman satirist, spoke to the corrupt and immoral citizens of his day of 'the masters that grow up within that sickly breast of yours'. These false teachers were offering liberty when they themselves were slaves, and the liberty they were offering was the liberty to become slaves of lust. Their message was *arrogant* because it was the contradiction of the message of Christ; it was *futile* because those who followed it would find that they had become slaves. Here again in the background is the fundamental heresy which makes grace a justification for sin instead of a power and a summons to an honourable and generous life.

If they have once known the real way of Christ and have relapsed into this, their case is even worse. They are like the person in the parable whose last state was worse than his first (Matthew 12:45; Luke 11:26). If people have never known the right way, they cannot be condemned for not following it. But, if they have known it and then deliberately taken the other way, they sin against the light; and it would have been better for them if they had never known the truth, for their knowledge of the truth has become their condemnation. We should never forget the responsibility which knowledge brings.

Peter ends with contempt. These evil people are like dogs who return to their vomit (Proverbs 26:11) or like a sow which has been scrubbed and then goes back to rolling in the mud. They have seen Christ but are so morally degraded by their own choice that they prefer to wallow in the depths of sin rather than to climb the heights of virtue. It is a dreadful warning that people can create a situation where ultimately the tentacles of sin are inextricably wound around them, and virtue for them has lost its beauty.

THE PRINCIPLES OF PREACHING

2 Peter 3:1-2

> Beloved, this is now the second letter that I have written to you, and my object in both of them is to rouse by reminder your pure mind to remember the words spoken by the prophets in former times, and the commandment of the Lord and Saviour which was brought to you by your apostles.

IN this passage, we see clearly set out the principles of preaching which Peter observed.

(1) He believed in the value of *repetition*. He knows that it is necessary for a thing to be said over and over again if it is to penetrate the mind. When Paul was writing to the Philippians, he said that to repeat the same thing over and over again was not troublesome to him, and for them it was the only safe way (Philippians 3:1). It is by continued repetition that the rudiments of knowledge are settled in the minds of children. There is something of significance here. It may well be that often we are too keen to embrace novelty, too eager to say new things, when what is needed is a repetition of the eternal truths which people so quickly forget and whose significance they so often refuse to see. There are certain foods of which we do not get tired; necessary for our daily sustenance, they are set before us every day. We speak about our *daily bread.* And there are certain great Christian truths which have to be repeated again and again and which must never be pushed into the background in the desire for novelty.

(2) He believed in *the need for reminder*. Again and again, the New Testament makes it clear that preaching and teaching are so often the means not of introducing new truth but of reminding the people of what they already know. Moffatt quotes a saying of the famed man of letters Dr Johnson: 'It is not sufficiently considered that men more frequently require to be reminded than informed.' The Greeks spoke of 'time which wipes all things out', as if the human mind were a slate and time a sponge which passes across it erasing what has been written on it. We are so often in the position of men and women whose need is not so much to be taught as to be reminded of what we already know.

(3) He believed in *the value of a compliment*. It is his intention to rouse *their pure mind*. The word he uses for *pure* is *eilikrinēs*, which has two possible meanings. It may mean that which is sifted until there is no chaff or impure material left; or it may mean that which is so flawless that it may be held up to the light of the sun. Plato uses this same phrase – *eilikrinēs dianoia* – in the sense of *pure reason*, reason which is unaffected by the seductive influence of the senses. By using this phrase, Peter appeals to his people as having minds uncontaminated by heresy. It is as if he said to them: 'You really are fine people – if you would only remember it.' The approach adopted by preachers should be not that their hearers are wretched creatures who deserve to be damned but rather that they are splendid creatures who must be saved. They are not so much like rubbish fit to be burned as like jewels to be rescued from the mud into which they have fallen. Donald Hankey, one of the great figures of the First World War, tells of 'the beloved captain' whose men would follow him anywhere. He looked at them and they looked at him, and they were filled with the determination to be what he believed them to be. We always get further with

people when we believe in them than when we despise them.

(4) He believed in *the unity of Scripture*. As he saw it, there was a pattern in Scripture, and the Bible was a book centred in Christ. The Old Testament foretells Christ; the gospels tell of Jesus the Christ; and the apostles bring the message of that Christ to men and women,

THE DENIAL OF THE SECOND COMING

2 Peter 3:3–4

> To begin with, you are well aware that in the last days there will come mockers with their mocking, guiding their steps by the law of their own lusts and saying: 'What has happened to the promise of his coming? For, since the day when our fathers fell asleep, everything remains the same as it was from the foundation of the world.'

THE characteristic of the heretics which worried Peter most of all was their denial of the second coming of Jesus. Literally, their question was: 'Where is the promise of his coming?' That was a form of Hebrew expression which implied that the thing asked about did not exist at all. 'Where is the God of justice?' asked the evil men of Malachi's day (Malachi 2:17). 'Where is your God?' was the question asked of the psalmist (Psalm 42:3, 79:10). 'Where is the word of the Lord?' his enemies asked Jeremiah (Jeremiah 17:15). In every case, the implication of the question is that the thing or the person asked about does not exist. The heretics of Peter's day were denying that Jesus Christ would ever come again. It will be best here at the beginning to summarize their argument and Peter's answer to it.

The argument of Peter's opponents was twofold (verse 4). 'What has happened', they demanded, 'to the promise of the second coming?' Their first argument was that the promise had been so long delayed that it was safe to take it that it would never be fulfilled. Their second assertion was that their ancestors had died and the world was going on precisely as it always did. Their argument was that this was by its very nature a stable universe, and convulsive upheavals like the second coming did not happen in such a universe.

Peter's response is also twofold. He deals with the second argument first (verses 5–7). His argument is that, in fact, this is not a stable universe, that once it was destroyed by water in the time of the Flood and that a second destruction, this time by fire, is on the way.

The second part of his reply is in verses 8 and 9. His opponents speak of a delay so long that they can safely assume that the second coming is not going to happen at all. Peter's is a double answer. (1) We must see time as God sees it. With him, a day is as 1,000 years, and 1,000 years as a day. (2) In any event, God's apparent slowness to act is not the result of indifference. It is, in fact, mercy. He holds back in order to give the sinful world another chance to repent and find salvation.

Peter goes on to his conclusion (verse 10). The second coming is on the way, and it will come with a sudden terror and destruction which will dissolve the universe in melting heat.

Finally comes his practical demand which follows from all this. If we are living in a universe on which Jesus Christ is going to descend and which is hastening towards the destruction of the wicked, surely that means that we must live in holiness so that we may be spared when the terrible day does come. The second coming is used as a tremendous motive for putting right our lives so that we may all prepare ourselves to meet our God.

Such, then, is the general scheme of this chapter; and now we look at it section by section.

DESTRUCTION BY FLOOD

2 Peter 3:5–6

> What they wilfully fail to see is that long ago the heavens were created and the earth was composed out of water and through water; and through these waters the ancient world perished, when it was overwhelmed in a deluge of water.

PETER's first argument is that the world is not eternally stable. The point he is making is that the ancient world was destroyed by water, just as the present world is going to be destroyed by fire. The detail of this passage is, however, difficult.

He says that the earth was composed out of water and through water. According to the Genesis story, in the beginning there was a kind of watery chaos. 'The [Spirit of God moved] over the face of the waters . . . God said, Let there be a dome in the midst of the waters, and let it separate the waters from the waters' (Genesis 1:2, 1:6). Out of this watery chaos, the world was formed. Further, it is through water that the world is sustained, because life is sustained by the rain which comes down from the skies. What Peter means is that the world was created out of water and is sustained by water; and it was through this same element that the ancient world was destroyed.

To clarify this passage further, we have to note that the flood legend developed. As so often in 2 Peter and Jude, the picture behind this comes not directly from the Old Testament but from the Book of Enoch. In 1 Enoch 83:3–5, Enoch has a vision: 'I saw in a vision how the heaven collapsed and fell to the earth, and, where it fell to the earth, I saw how the earth was swallowed up in a great abyss.' In the later stories, the flood involved not only the obliteration of sinners but the total destruction of heaven and earth. So the warning which Peter is giving may be put like this: 'You say that as things are, so they always have been and so they always will be. You build your hopes on the idea that this is an unchanging universe. You are wrong, for the ancient world was formed out of water and was sustained by water, and it perished in the flood.'

We may say that this is only an old legend more than half-buried in the antiquities of the past. But we cannot say that a passage like this has no significance for us. When we strip away the old Jewish legend and its later development, we are still left with this permanent truth that those who will read history with open eyes can see within it the moral law at work and God's dealings with humanity. James Froude, the great nineteenth-century historian, said that history is a voice sounding across the centuries that in the end it is always ill with the wicked and well with the good. When Oliver Cromwell, the Lord Protector of England, was arranging his son Richard's education, he said: 'I would have him know a little history.' In fact, the lesson of history is that there is a moral order in the universe and that we defy it at our peril.

DESTRUCTION BY FIRE

2 Peter 3:7

> But by the same word the present heavens and earth are treasured up for fire, reserved for the day of judgment and the destruction of impious men.

It is Peter's conviction that, as the ancient world was destroyed by water, the present world will be destroyed by fire. He says that that is stated 'by the same word'. What he means is that the Old Testament tells of the flood in the past and warns of the destruction by fire in the future. There are many passages in the prophets which he would take quite literally and which must have been in his mind. Joel foresaw a time when God would show blood, fire and pillars of smoke (Joel 2:30). The psalmist has a picture in which, when God comes, a devouring fire shall precede him (Psalm 50:3). Isaiah speaks of a flame of devouring fire (Isaiah 29:6, 30:30). The Lord will come with fire; by fire and by his sword will the Lord execute judgment on all flesh (Isaiah 66:15–16). Nahum has it that the hills melt and the earth is burned at his presence; his fury is poured out like fire (Nahum 1:5–6). In the picture of Malachi, the day of the Lord shall burn as an oven (Malachi 4:1). If the old pictures are taken literally, Peter has plenty of material for his prophecy.

The Stoics also had a doctrine of the destruction of the world by fire; but it was a grim teaching. They held that the universe completed a cycle; that it was consumed in flames; and that everything then started all over again, exactly as it was. They had the strange idea that at the end of the cycle the planets were in exactly the same position as when the world began. 'This produces the conflagration and destruction of everything which exists', says the Stoic philosopher Chrysippus. He goes on: 'Then again the universe is restored anew in a precisely similar arrangement as before . . . Socrates and Plato and each individual man will live again, with the same friends and fellow citizens. They will go through the same experiences and the same activities. Every city and village and field will be restored, just as it was. And this restoration of the universe takes place, not once, but over and over again – indeed to all eternity without end . . . For there will never be any new thing other than that which has been before, but everything is repeated down to the minutest detail.' History as an eternal treadmill, the unceasing recurrence of our sins, sorrows and mistakes – that is one of the grimmest views of history that the human mind has ever produced.

It must always be remembered that, as the Jewish prophets saw it, and as Peter saw it, this world will be destroyed with the conflagration of God, but the result will not be obliteration and the grim repetition of what has been before; the result will be a new heaven and a new earth. For the biblical view of the world, there is something beyond destruction; there is the new creation of God. The worst that the prophet can conceive is not the death agony of the old world so much as the birth-pangs of the new.

THE MERCY OF GOD'S DELAY

2 Peter 3:8–9

> Beloved, you must not shut your eyes to this one fact that with the Lord one day is as 1,000 years and 1,000 years as one day. It is not that God is dilatory in fulfilling his promise, as some people reckon dilatoriness; but it is that for your sakes he patiently withholds his hand, because he does not wish any to perish, but wishes all to take the way to repentance.

In this passage, there are three great truths which can nourish the mind and bring rest to the heart.

(1) Time is not the same to God as it is to us. As the psalmist had it: 'For a thousand years in your sight are like yesterday when it is past, or like a watch in the night' (Psalm 90:4). When we think of the world's hundreds of thousands

of years of existence, it is easy to feel dwarfed into insignificance; when we think of the slowness of human progress, it is easy to become discouraged into pessimism. There is comfort in the thought of a God who has all eternity to work in. It is only against the background of eternity that things appear in their true proportions and assume their real value.

(2) We can also see from this passage that time is always to be regarded as an opportunity. As Peter saw it, the years God gave the world were a further opportunity for men and women to repent and turn to him. Every day which comes to us is a gift of mercy. It is an opportunity to develop ourselves, to render some service to our neighbours, to take one step nearer to God.

(3) Finally, there is another echo of a truth which so often lies in the background of New Testament thought. God, says Peter, does not want anyone to perish. God, says Paul, has shut them all up together in unbelief, that he might have mercy on all (Romans 11:32). Timothy, in a tremendous phrase, speaks of God who desires everyone to be saved (1 Timothy 2:4). Ezekiel hears God ask: 'Have I any pleasure in the death of the wicked . . . and not rather that they should turn from their ways and live?' (Ezekiel 18:23).

Time after time, we see in Scripture the glint of the larger hope. We are not forbidden to believe that somehow and at some time the God who loves the world will bring the whole world to himself.

THE DREADFUL DAY

2 Peter 3:10

> But when it does come, the day of the Lord will come
> as a thief and in it the heavens will pass away with a

crackling roar; the stars will blaze and melt; and the
earth and all its works will disappear.

It is always the case that we have to speak and think in the
terms which we know. That is what Peter is doing here. He is
speaking of the New Testament teaching of the second coming
of Jesus Christ, but he is describing it in terms of the Old
Testament teaching of the day of the Lord.

The day of the Lord is a concept which runs all through
the prophetic books of the Old Testament. The Jews saw
time in terms of two ages – *this present age*, which is wholly
bad and beyond remedy, and *the age to come*, which is the
golden age of God. How was the one to turn into the other?
The change could not come about by human effort or by a
process of development, for the world was on the way to
destruction. As the Jews saw it, there was only one way in
which the change could happen; it must be by the direct
intervention of God. They called the time of that intervention
the day of the Lord. It was to come without warning. It was to
be a time when the universe was shaken to its foundations. It
was to be a time when the judgment and obliteration of sinners
would come to pass, and therefore it would be a time of terror.
'See, the day of the Lord comes, cruel, with wrath and fierce
anger, to make the earth a desolation, and to destroy its sinners
from it' (Isaiah 13:9). 'For the day of the Lord is coming, it is
near – a day of darkness and gloom, a day of clouds and thick
darkness' (Joel 2:1–2). 'That day will be a day of wrath, a
day of distress and anguish, a day of ruin and devastation, a
day of darkness and gloom, a day of clouds and thick darkness'
(Zephaniah 1:15). 'The sun shall be turned to darkness and
the moon to blood, before the great and terrible day of the
Lord comes' (Joel 2:31). 'For the stars of the heaven and their
constellations will not give their light; the sun will be dark at

its rising, and the moon will not shed its light . . . Therefore I will make the heavens tremble, and the earth will be shaken out of its place, at the wrath of the Lord of hosts on the day of his fierce anger' (Isaiah 13:10–13).

What Peter and many of the New Testament writers did was to identify the Old Testament pictures of the day of the Lord with the New Testament belief about the second coming of Jesus Christ. Peter's picture here of the second coming of Jesus is drawn in terms of the Old Testament picture of the day of the Lord.

He uses one very vivid phrase. He says that the heavens will pass away with a crackling roar (*roizēdon*). That word is used for the whirring of a bird's wings in the air, for the sound a spear makes as it hurtles through the air, for the crackling of the flames of a forest fire.

We need not take these pictures absolutely literally. It is enough to note that Peter sees the second coming as a time of terror for those who are the enemies of Christ.

One thing has to be remembered. The whole concept of the second coming is full of difficulties. But this is certain – there comes a day when God breaks into every life, for there comes a day when we must die; and for that day we must be prepared. We may say what we will about the coming of Christ as a future event; we may feel it is a doctrine we have to lay aside; but we cannot escape from the certainty of the entry of God into our own experience.

THE MORAL DYNAMIC

2 Peter 3:11-14

> Since these things are going to be dissolved like that,
> what kind of people ought you to be, living a life of

> constant holiness and true piety, you who are eagerly
> awaiting and doing your best to hasten on the day of the
> Lord, by whose action the heavens will burn and be dis-
> solved and the stars blaze and melt! For it is new heavens
> and a new earth, as he promised, for which we wait, in
> which righteousness has its home. So, then, beloved, since
> these are the things for which you eagerly wait, be eager
> to be found by him at peace, without spot and blemish.

THE one thing in which Peter is supremely interested is the moral dynamic of the second coming. If these things are going to happen and the world is hastening to judgment, obviously people must live lives of piety and of holiness. If there are to be a new heaven and a new earth, and if that heaven and earth are to be the home of righteousness, obviously people must seek with all their minds and hearts and souls and strength to be fit to dwell in that new world. To Peter, as James Moffatt puts it, 'it was impossible to give up the hope of the advent without ethical deterioration'. Peter was right. If there is nothing in the nature of a second coming, nothing in the nature of a goal to which the whole creation moves, then life is going nowhere. That, in fact, was the position held by the Gentile world. If there is no goal, either for the world or for the individual life, other than extinction, certain attitudes to life become almost inevitable. These attitudes emerge in epitaphs from the Greek and Roman world.

(1) If there is nothing to come, people may well decide to make what they can of the pleasures of this world. So we come on an epitaph like this: 'I was nothing: I am nothing. So thou who art still alive, eat, drink, and be merry.'

(2) If there is nothing to live for, people may well be utterly indifferent. Nothing matters much if the end of everything is extinction, in which there will be no consciousness of that extinction. So we come on such an epitaph as this: 'Once I

had an existence; now I have none. I am not aware of it. It does not concern me.'

(3) If there is nothing to live for but extinction, and the world is going nowhere, there can enter into life a kind of lostness. Human beings cease to be in any sense pilgrims, for there is nowhere to which they can make pilgrimage. They must simply drift in a kind of lostness, coming from nowhere and on the way to nowhere. So we come on an epigram like that of Callimachus. 'Charidas, what is below?' 'Deep darkness.' 'But what of the paths upward?' 'All a lie.' 'And Pluto?' (the god of the underworld). 'Mere talk.' 'Then we're lost.' Even the Gentiles found a certain almost intolerable quality in life without a goal.

When we have stripped the teaching about the second coming of all its temporary and local imagery, the tremendous truth it preserves is that life is going somewhere – and without that conviction there is nothing to live for.

HASTENING THE DAY

2 Peter 3:11–14 (*contd*)

THERE is in this passage yet another great concept Peter speaks of Christians as not only eagerly awaiting the coming of Christ but as actually hastening it on. The New Testament tells us certain ways in which this may be done.

(1) It may be done by *prayer*. Jesus taught us to pray: 'Your kingdom come' (Matthew 6:10). The earnest prayer of the Christian heart hastens the coming of the King. If in no other way, it does so in this – that those who pray open their own hearts for the entry of the King.

(2) It may be done by *preaching*. Matthew tells us that Jesus said: 'And this good news of the kingdom will be

proclaimed throughout the world, as a testimony to all the
nations; and then the end will come' (Matthew 24:14).
Everyone must be given the chance to know and to love Jesus
Christ before the end of creation is reached. The missionary
activity of the Church is the hastening of the coming of the
King.

(3) It may be done by *penitence* and *obedience*. Of all
things, this would be nearest to Peter's mind and heart.
The Rabbis had two sayings: 'It is the sins of the people which
prevent the coming of the Messiah. If the Jews would
genuinely repent for one day, the Messiah would come.' The
other form of the saying means the same: 'If Israel would
perfectly keep the law for one day, the Messiah would come.'
In true penitence and in real obedience, men and women open
their own hearts to the coming of the King and bring nearer
that coming throughout the world. We do well to remember
that our coldness of heart and our disobedience delay the
coming of the King.

DISTORTERS OF SCRIPTURE

2 Peter 3:15–16

> Regard the Lord's willingness to wait as an opportunity
> of salvation, as indeed our beloved brother Paul has
> written to us, in the wisdom which has been given to
> him, and as he says in all his letters, when he touches on
> these subjects, letters which contain some things which
> are difficult to understand, things which those who lack
> knowledge and a firm foundation in the faith twist, as
> they do the rest of the Scriptures, to their own destruction.

PETER here cites Paul as teaching the same things as he himself
teaches. It may be that he is citing Paul as agreeing that a

pious and a holy life is necessary in view of the approaching second coming of the Lord. More likely, he is citing Paul as agreeing that the fact that God holds back is to be regarded not as indifference on God's part but as an opportunity to repent and to accept Jesus Christ. Paul speaks of those who despise the riches of God's goodness and forbearance and patience, forgetting that his kindness is designed to lead people to repentance (Romans 2:4). More than once, Paul stresses the forbearance and the patience of God (Romans 3:25, 9:22). Both Peter and Paul were agreed that the fact that God withholds his final action is never to be used as an excuse for sinning but always as a means of repentance and an opportunity for amendment.

With its reference to Paul and its tinge of criticism of him, this is one of the most intriguing passages in the New Testament. It was this passage which made the reformer John Calvin certain that Peter did not himself write 2 Peter because, he says, Peter would never have spoken about Paul like this. What do we learn from it?

(1) We learn that Paul's letters by this time were known and used throughout the Church. They are spoken of in such a way as to make it clear that they have been collected and published, and that they are generally available and widely read. We are fairly certain that it was about the year AD 90 that Paul's letters were collected and published in Ephesus. This means that 2 Peter cannot have been written before that and, therefore, cannot be the work of Peter, who was martyred in the middle sixties of the century.

(2) It tells us that Paul's letters have come to be regarded as Scripture. The misguided heretics twist them as they do the other Scriptures. This again goes to prove that 2 Peter must come from a time well on in the history of the early Church, for it would take many generations for the

letters of Paul to rank alongside the Scriptures of the Old Testament.

(3) It is a little difficult to determine just what the attitude to Paul is in this passage. He is writing 'in the wisdom which has been given to him'. Charles Bigg says neatly that this phrase can be equally a commendation or a caution! The truth is that Paul suffered the fate of all outstanding people. He had his critics. He suffered the fate of all who fearlessly face the truth and state it. Some regarded him as great but dangerous.

(4) There are things in Paul's letters which are hard to understand and which ignorant people twist to their own downfall. The word used for *hard to understand* is *dusnoētos*, which is used of the utterance of an oracle. The utterances of Greek oracles were always ambiguous. There is the classic example of the king about to go to war who consulted the oracle at Delphi and was given the answer: 'If you go to war, you will destroy a great nation.' He took this as a prophecy that he would destroy his enemies; but it happened that he suffered such a devastating defeat that by going to war he destroyed his own country. This was typical of the dangerous ambiguity of the ancient oracles. It is that very word which Peter uses of the writings of Paul. They have things in them which are as difficult to interpret as the ambiguous utterance of an oracle.

Not only, Peter says, are there things in Paul's writings that are hard to understand; there are things which people may twist to their own destruction. Three things come immediately to mind. Paul's doctrine of *grace* was twisted into an excuse and even a reason for sin (Romans 6). Paul's doctrine of Christian *freedom* was twisted into an excuse for un-Christian licence (Galatians 5:13). Paul's doctrine of *faith* was twisted into an argument that Christian action was unimportant, as we see in James (James 2:14–26).

The writer G. K. Chesterton once said that orthodoxy was like walking along a narrow ridge; one step to either side was a step to disaster. Jesus is God and man; God is love and holiness; Christianity is grace and morality; Christians live in this world and in the world of eternity. Overemphasize either side of these great two-sided truths, and immediately destructive heresy emerges. One of the most tragic things in life is when people twist Christian truth and Holy Scripture into an excuse and even a reason for doing what they want to do instead of taking them as guides for doing what God wants them to do.

A FIRM FOUNDATION
AND A CONTINUAL GROWTH

2 Peter 3:17–18

> As far as you are concerned, beloved, you have been forewarned. You must, therefore, be on your guard not to be carried away by the error of lawless men and so to fall from your own foundation; rather, you must see to it that you grow in grace and in understanding of our Lord and Saviour Jesus Christ.
> To him be glory both now and to the day of eternity.

IN conclusion, Peter tells us certain things about the Christian life.

(1) Christians are people who are forewarned. That is to say, they cannot plead ignorance. They know the right way and its rewards; they know the wrong way and its disasters. They have no right to expect an easy way, for they have been told that Christianity means a cross, and they have been warned that there will always be those who are ready to attack and to distort the faith. To be forewarned is to be

forearmed; but to be forewarned is also a grave respon-sibility, for anyone who knows what is right and does wrong is under a double condemnation.

(2) Christians are people with a basis for life. They ought to be rooted and founded in the faith. There are certain things of which they are absolutely certain. The theatre critic James Agate once declared that his mind was not a bed to be made and remade, but that on certain things it was finally made up. There is a certain inflexibility in the Christian life; there is a certain basis of belief which never changes. Christians will never cease to believe that 'Jesus Christ is Lord' (Philippians 2:11), and they will never cease to be aware that there is laid on them the duty of making their lives fit that belief.

(3) Christians are people with a developing life. The inflexibility of the Christian life is not the rigidity of death. Christians must experience the wonder of grace daily, and each day they must grow in the gifts which grace can bring. They must enter more and more deeply into the wonder which is in Jesus Christ as each day passes. It is only on a firm foundation that a great building can tower into the air, and it is only because it has a deep root that a great tree can reach out to the sky with its branches. The Christian life is both a life with a firm foundation and at the same time a life which continues to grow outward and upward.

And so the letter finishes by giving glory to Christ, both now and to the end of time.